AF766499

A PHILOSOPHY OF INTELLECTUAL PROPERTY

In memory of Joe

A PHILOSOPHY OF INTELLECTUAL PROPERTY

PETER DRAHOS
Faculty of Law
The Australian National University

Routledge
Taylor & Francis Group
LONDON AND NEW YORK

First published 1996 by Ashgate Publishing

2 Park Square, Milton Park, Abingdon, Oxon OX14 4RN
711 Third Avenue, New York, NY 10017, USA

Routledge is an imprint of the Taylor & Francis Group, an informa business

First issued in paperback 2016

British Library Cataloguing in Publication Data
Drahos, Peter
A philosophy of intellectual property. – (Applied legal philosophy)
1. Intellectual property 2. Law – Philosophy
I. Title
342.6'48

Library of Congress Cataloging-in-Publication Data
Drahos, Peter 1955–
A philosophy of intellectual property / Peter Drahos.
p. cm. – (Applied legal philosophy)
Includes bibliographical references and index.
ISBN 978-1-85521-240-4
1. Intellectual property. I. Title. II. Series
K1401.D73 1996
346.04'8—dc20
[342.648] 96–24900
CIP

ISBN 978-1-85521-240-4 (hbk)
ISBN 978-1-138-25470-1 (pbk)

Contents

Series Preface

The objective of the Dartmouth Series in Applied Legal Philosophy is to publish work which adopts a theoretical approach to the study of particular areas or aspects of law or deals with general theories of law in a way which focusses on issues of practical moral and political concern in specific legal contexts.

In recent years there has been an encouraging tendency for legal philosophers to utilize detailed knowledge of the substance and practicalities of law and a noteworthy development in the theoretical sophistication of much legal research. The series seeks to encourage these trends and to make available studies in law which are both genuinely philosophical in approach and at the same time based on appropriate legal knowledge and directed towards issues in the criticism and reform of actual laws and legal systems.

The series will include studies of all the main areas of law, presented in a manner which relates to the concerns of specialist legal academics and practitioners. Each book makes an original contribution to an area of legal study while being comprehensible to those engaged in a wide variety of disciplines. Their legal content is principally Anglo-American, but a wide-ranging comparative approach is encouraged and authors are drawn from a variety of jurisdictions.

TOM D. CAMPBELL
Series Editor
The Faculty of Law
The Australian National University

Preface and Acknowledgements

Property theory, for the most part, uses for its examples physical objects. Land, hunting on land, fisheries and the turfs which servants have cut are amongst the favourites. Intellectual property law deals with abstract objects. Abstract objects are not like physical objects. They do not, for instance, have obvious boundaries. For this reason at least intellectual property rights are worth a separate philosophical investigation.

This book develops one line of investigation using the tools of analytical philosophy. It is interdisciplinary minded in its approach. It draws on history, economics and sociology in the arguments it develops. For the purpose of illustration and example it uses the intellectual property law of Australia and England and, to a lesser extent, US intellectual property law. It is not and could not hope to be a survey of intellectual property law in these jurisdictions. Many excellent legal texts would have to be combined to do that job. The book should be of interest to intellectual property teachers, social and political theorists with an interest in property and intellectual property lawyers. The arguments are presented in a way which makes them accessible to the non-specialist.

Books are usually written with the support of a broader community. In my case I have been fortunate to have a community in which people have been generous in sharing their ideas and arguments. The people I would like to thank include Chris Arup, Stephen Bottomley, William van Caenegem, Mark Goldi, Bob Goodin, Kevin Gray, Nicholas Gruen, Neil Gunningham, Knud Haakonssen, Geoff Harcourt, Ross Harrison, Richard Joseph, Ian McEwin, Peter Menzies, Bob Moles, Stephen Parker, Bob Rowthorn, Bob Summers and Richard Tuck.

There are some people who deserve a special mention for the help they have given me. Dennis Pearce has been a valuable discussant of the principles of intellectual property law. Philip Pettit has encouraged the pursuit of the project and provided suggestions. Don Lamberton has contributed enormously to my understanding of the literature in the economics of information. With John Braithwaite I am conducting a study of, amongst other things, the internationalization of intellectual property standards in the global economy. It is a project funded by the US National Science Foundation, the American Bar Foundation and the Australian Research Council. The philosophical direction of this book has been significantly shaped by work that Braithwaite and I have carried out in our study of international business regulation and the many discussions I have had with him concerning our findings. There can be few better exponents of the inductive style of theory building than John Braithwaite. From him I have learnt much. I owe him a great debt. I owe a similar debt to Tom Campbell. His interests in applied legal philosophy have helped to encourage mine. In many different ways he has helped to bring this project to fruition. I was fortunate enough to spend 1994 as a Research Fellow at the Research School of Social Sciences, Australian National University. There can be few better interdisciplinary research environments than the Research School. I take this opportunity to thank Geoffrey Brennan, Director of the School, Paul Finn, Head of the Law Program (as he then was) at the School and the scholars I came into contact with while I was there. I also take this opportunity to thank Julie Ayling, my wife. She has been patient. In the role of the intelligent lay reader she has helped to add clarity to the present work. Nick Seddon did not want to be thanked, for reasons too long to go into. But he performed a great service. He read all the draft chapters of the book and suggested many valuable changes. I do not thank him but merely acknowledge his contribution. I claim paternity of all remaining errors.

Peter Drahos,
Law Faculty, Australian
National University

1 Introduction

A lot has been written about the theory of property. Property has been and remains one of the bedrock subjects of social science theorizing. In its rights form (the idea that property is a bundle of rights[1]) property continues to be a key target for philosophical analysis. While the literature on property is vast, relatively little of it has explicitly dealt with intellectual property. It may be that the assumption has been that any general theory of property illuminates all property forms, including intellectual property. Perhaps this assumption is correct and perhaps not. Like other property rights, intellectual property rights are relations between individuals. Unlike real property law, intellectual property law posits rights in abstract objects. An algorithm and the formulae for penicillin and its derivatives are examples of abstract objects. Many people need, use and depend on such objects. Many of the relationships of interdependence that characterize social life and work in modern 'on-line' societies are linked to such objects. A property form that allows private hands to capture important abstract objects creates, amongst other things, many person-dependent relationships in a society. It swells the growth of private power. The negative liberty of individuals, the right not to be interfered with, faces greater dangers. There is a lot at stake when property extends its reach to abstract objects. For these reasons at least it seems worth asking whether we can accommodate intellectual property within one or more of the existing general accounts of property or whether we should develop a distinctive theory of intellectual property.

This book represents the beginnings of an answer to this question. It takes the writings of three important thinkers on property, Locke, Hegel and Marx, and concludes, not surprisingly, that these writings help us to understand a great deal about the phenomenon of intellectual property. No comprehensive theory of intellectual property is proposed here. Instead the final chapter argues that a philosophical attitude of instrumentalism should be our guide in constructing interdisciplinary approaches and theories of intellectual property. Amongst other things, this means that in the case of intellectual property the language of privilege should replace the existing language of property rights. Privilege-bearing duties, the final chapter argues, should form the core of intellectual property theory.

Some Distinctions

Theorizing within the liberal tradition about property has usually taken the form of theorizing about property rights. This treatment of property as a species of rights has, predictably, resulted in a considerable cross-pollination between general rights theory and property theory. It has led to questions like: are all rights property rights?[2] There are some distinctions which inquiries within rights based property theory typically use to demarcate their scope and subject matter. The classifying distinctions are those between the ontological, linguistic, analytical (or conceptual) and normative. We need quickly to say something about where the present work stands in relation to these distinctions. But first a word about the distinctions themselves.

Ontological analyses focus on the question of whether rights exist and, if so, in what way. The debate over the existence of natural rights or natural rights of property is an example of an ontological issue. Linguistic approaches try to settle the meaning of property or right by reference to the meanings and distinctions to be found in ordinary language use.[3] It is hard to distinguish between linguistic and analytical approaches in a short space.[4] Very roughly, we might say that analytical approaches do not confine themselves to ordinary language as a resource but propose and construct, under the restraints of reason and established deductive techniques, various stipulative distinctions and models of the concepts under scrutiny. Analytical approaches tend to focus on the logical qualities of concepts like property and right. They strive through the process of definition and conceptual analysis for a better model, or structural and relational understanding of a concept. Working analytically, philosophers ask questions such as who can have rights and under what conditions? They draw distinctions between, for example, what it is to have a right and what rights we ought to recognize. An example of a very influential analytical approach in the rights and property area is Hohfeld's model of rights as a set of jural correlatives, contradictories and contradictories of correlatives that is, between interdefinable concepts such as right, duty, privilege and no-right.[5] (We will discuss the scheme and its implications for intellectual property in Chapter 7.) Finally, normative approaches in property and rights theory bring into play values in one way or another so as to reach ought conclusions of some kind. They concern themselves with either prescription or justification. Rules of conduct are proposed or defended.

Much of normative property theory has examined the justifiability of the right of private property.[6] The preoccupation with this particular enterprise is not just modern. Like most philosophical questions, it has a history. The continuing interest in private property stems from an inquiry that mattered to those working in the natural law tradition. It consisted of the search for the origin and foundation of the right of property.

For natural law theorists, an investigation into the origins of property could have threatened the legitimacy of all established individual property holdings. That such a revolutionary conclusion might have been possible came from taking the existence of God and the contents of the Bible seriously. Blackstone in his *Commentaries* nicely captures the nature of the problem. He points out that, strictly speaking, 'there is no foundation in nature or in natural law, why a set of words upon parchment should convey the dominion of land'.[7] In the Christian God-centred universe this problem was especially worrying because there was no doubt that God had given the earth to its inhabitants in common. How then could one justify the 'sole and despotic dominion' which individual proprietors in the world had come to exercise over its contents?[8] Actually, Blackstone does not use the word 'justify'. Rather, he assumes that private ownership, which is widespread and widely accepted by the general populace, is something that requires explanation. Private property is a phenomenon that law, operating as a rational science, must explain.

The importance of this explanatory mode of analysis in the natural law theories of property can be seen in Grotius' discussion of property. For Grotius, one of the causes of war is injury to those things which belong to us.[9] This leads him to investigate the conditions under which something can be said to belong to somebody, which in turn leads him to state that 'it will be necessary to know the origin of proprietorship'.[10] The knowledge which Grotius has in mind is historical knowledge. Drawing on 'sacred history', poets and philosophers, he proceeds to give a description of the way private ownership evolved out of the world which God had given to men in common.[11] This historical investigation establishes certain fundamental principles. These are used by Grotius to generate specific prescriptive conclusions (rights to the sea, the rights of refugees and so on). At least in Grotius the natural law theory of property has both explanatory and justificatory aims.

Over time, the emphasis on providing an explanation from factual axioms for the origin of the right of private property has, within the context of first order ethical theorizing, faded. The interest in providing a justification for the right of private property – in offering an account of the legitimacy of acquiring property – has remained strong. The task of explaining the origin of property rights seems to have become the province of the empirical sciences such as psychology, sociology and economics.[12]

With this brief sketch of some of property theory's fundamental distinctions in place, we can now set out the way in which this book develops its analysis of intellectual property. The analytical parts of the present work rest on some assumptions. Two crucial ones need to be specified at the outset. First, analytical property theory takes property in its rights form as the object of conceptual analysis. The object of clarification is the right of property (sometimes used interchangeably with the right of ownership). Following Hohfeld, we shall not treat rights as a base term, but as a generic term which can be decomposed into a series of more fundamental categories. Rights, including property rights, have a logical architecture. This logical architecture takes the form of a deontic logic.[13] There is more than one deontic logic to choose from in specifying an architecture for property rights.[14] Within property theory, Hohfeld's system is usually chosen to do the job.[15] This fashion is followed here.

The view that property is a thing is nowadays seen as quaint and false, or at least not helpful. Property is thought to be a rights relation between one person and another (that is, a single-place relation) or between one person and many others (a many-place relation).[16] Property is a contest for the control of objects that people need or want and sometimes upon which their very survival, either individually or as a group, depends. As Honoré reminds us, 'the idiom which directly couples the owner with the thing owned is far from pointless; where the right to exclude others exists, there is indeed (legally) a very special relation between the holder of the right and the thing'.[17]

Without further argument, our second assumption is that property rights entail relations between two people *and* between a person and an object. In the case of intellectual property law, the objects in question are abstract objects. As it happens, abstract objects do not exist, or so we claim. Abstract objects in intellectual property law take the form of a convenient legal fiction. The argument for this is to be found in Chapters 2 and 7. The psychological operation of this fiction is probably best explained in terms of a theory of performative utterances, but this is not a matter we pursue here.[18]

Many texts on intellectual property law begin by saying something about the definition of intellectual property.[19] Definitions can proceed by extension or intension. An extensional definition of intellectual property would list certain traditional core areas of intellectual property: copyright, patents, trademarks, designs, protection against unfair competition and the protection of trade secrets. (A brief explanatory note of these areas is contained in the last section of this introduction.) Over time new subject areas have appeared on this list. Protection for integrated circuits and plant varieties are two examples.[20] Intensional definitions of intellectual property are harder to formulate.[21] We shall say that intellectual property rights are rule-governed privileges that regulate the ownership and exploitation of abstract objects in many fields of human activity. This definition is more a conceptual conclusion. It rests on a particular theoretical view of intellectual property that is presented in the following chapters.

The normative conclusion to which the argument in this book leads is that intellectual property rights are liberty-intruding privileges of a special kind. It is argued that they promote factionalism and dangerous levels of private power. From the point of view of distributive justice, their scope should be limited. The way to think about such rights is through the lenses of a naturalistic empiricism. The arguments for these claims are to be found in Chapters 6, 7, 8 and 9. There is in this book no attempt to search for a new justification for private property. As Epstein observes, the 'desirability of private property has been endlessly debated across the disciplines'.[22] There is no shortage of coherent philosophical proposals in favour of private property. There may be, as Becker has recently suggested, too many.[23] Perhaps, as Becker hints, we should be more concerned with the empirically determinable consequences of private property in various areas of social life than with multiplying the available number of moral justifications for private property. There are strong reasons for supporting private property rights, but we should do so in a contingent, consequentially minded way. If it turns out that intellectual property rights, a species of private property rights, stimulate patterns of organization and practices that threaten negative liberty there is a case for severely limiting the scope of these rights, or eliminating some of them altogether. This book provides reasons for thinking that intellectual property rights pose this threat. Ultimately, however, this is not a matter that can be decided on the basis of *a priori* justifications of private property. The approach we have in mind is guided by a philosophically defensible view of the role of property in social life and democratic culture. Our suggestion in this regard comes in the form of an instrumentalism that subscribes to a principle of humanism.

Economic Theory

Intellectual property rights are intimately related to markets. They play a crucial role in constituting markets in information. Economic theory is too important a resource to ignore in a philosophical treatment of intellectual property. It is also too big a resource to cover in one work. Economics is a discipline which is rich in approaches. There is nothing narrow about its scope. For instance, the new economic history exemplified by the work of Douglass North is a stern critic of neoclassical approaches.[24] Information economics seems to play the role of the dangerous supplement to the neoclassical paradigm.[25] Institutional economics recognizes that power is a more complex notion than just market power.[26] Public choice theory has proved to be a fruitful venture, at least in the eyes of its exponents, into political theory.[27] The Chicago School continues to generate important and provocative theses about the nature of law.[28] There is also an important body of empirical work, much of which happens to be on the patent system.[29]

There is a lot therefore for the non-economic theorist of property to draw on. Given that this book is about the philosophy of intellectual property rather than its economics, it has been necessary to be selective.

Given the overtly economic character of much intellectual property legislation, one possibility worth investigating is that economic theory of one kind or another provides a justification for the enactment of intellectual property rights. Of course, these rights are very different from each other in terms of legal detail and character. A patent monopoly gives the owner rights against the independent discoverer of the same invention, while copyright offers rights against copying but does not prohibit the independent creation of the same work. Despite important differences like these, intellectual property rights share a fundamental character – they are rights in abstract objects. This similarity allows the economist and the philosopher to ask the same question, what are the justifications for creating property rights in abstract objects?

The economist coming to this question starts with some fundamental intuitions or, if you like, a metaphysic of human nature. People respond positively to incentives and rewards. If there is to be individual profit in the creation of these objects then they have to be locked up in some way, at least temporarily. This leads the economist to consider the possibility that property rights might be the best way in which to ensure that individuals devote sufficient resources to the creation of abstract objects. Here we have in outline an economic argument that provides a reason for the creation of intellectual property rights. We examine it in Chapter 6.

Economists, like social and political theorists, are interested in power. Very often they are most concerned with market power: in a nutshell, the capacity to price above marginal cost. Within institutional economics, power seems to be more broadly conceived of as something that shapes and creates markets rather than just something that is delivered through the pricing mechanism. In Chapter 7 we draw on the work of one classical institutional theorist, Veblen, in order to develop an analysis of the links between intellectual property and power.

Economists are also interested in logical relations, formal properties and deductive truths. The justificatory economic argument for intellectual property which we have just sketched is an example of a deductive or analytical argument. One can go further and construct formal models of intellectual property protection which explain how these rights promote overall welfare gains.[30] While formalization can deliver interesting analytical truths, statistical quantification and/or empirical work are required to confirm truths about the world. There is a hard-edged empirical side to economics by which the normative output of its formal theorizing must live or die. It is possible to develop an *a priori* economic argument for having intellectual property rights. But that is not an end of the matter. Economic judgement on intellectual property rights ultimately has to be based on the outcome of a cost–benefit calculation. Take a simple example. Imagine, which is the case in many jurisdictions, that design law does not extend to the protection of spare parts for motor vehicles.[31] An economist hired by the motor vehicle manufacturer's association develops a model which shows that there would be a net gain to design innovation if design protection were extended to spare parts. The same economist now tests some of the assumptions of the model. He finds that certain key ones are wrong. In particular, he finds that what motivates manufacturers to continue to invest in design is market pressures rather than the given level of design protection. Furthermore, the actual level of design investment represents a small part of car manufacturers' costs, less than one per cent, in fact. This means that the cost effect which free-riders generate in terms of a loss in design activity is very small. It turns out that there are no real efficiency gains to be had from extending design protection.[32] The motor vehicle manufacturers leave disappointed, muttering something about getting a lawyer to do a 'proper job'.

There are many other illustrations of this cost–benefit approach in intellectual property. The debate over the optimal length of the patent term is one.[33] Probably, the greatest service that economics can perform in the area of intellectual property is to track empirically the consequences of various intellectual property arrangements. The instrumentalism we propose in the final chapter relies heavily on such an economic contribution. Without the cost–benefit approach intellectual property would remain an opaque institution. Amongst other things, we would not know who the real winners and losers are when states, legislatures and judges shift the boundaries of abstract objects and draw new enclosure lines in the intellectual commons.

Overview of the Chapters

We begin with a very compressed treatment of the history of abstract objects in intellectual property law. The purpose is to show how English law came to invent the category of the abstract object or, in lawyer's language, incorporeal rights. The source of this invention is Roman law. Chapter 2 also deals with those justifications for intellectual property that are to be found in common law judicial discussions. The common law had to deal with the question of justification for copyright and patents because, especially in their pre-statutory form, they cut across a fundamental principle of the common law: the right of subjects to trade or, more accurately, the right to enter the marketplace of trades. The conceptual apparatus for dealing with this problem was provided by the natural law tradition. It was within this tradition that contrasting justificatory approaches were worked out.

One member of that tradition was John Locke. The first half of Chapter 3 is devoted to an exposition of two very different interpretations of Locke's writing on property. These interpretations are used to establish that so-called Lockean labour theories of property depend more for their plausibility on a concept of community than on labour. We claim that labour is too indeterminate a basis upon which to build a strong justificatory theory of intellectual property. The real relevance of Locke to intellectual property lies in the link he and other natural law thinkers made between property and the idea of positive and negative community, that is between a community in which the commons is owned by all and a community in which the commons is open to ownership by all. The second half of the chapter explores the connections between community, the intellectual commons and intellectual property.

Unlike Locke, Hegel is not concerned to know just the origins of property but also its evolutionary fate within the context of a social system. Property for Hegel is in the first instance a fundamental mechanism of survival for individuals. But it also has the potential to rupture community in various ways. Intellectual property particularly poses dangers of this kind.

Marx, more than Hegel, offers an explanatory perspective on property forms. Chapter 5 argues that his theory of class will not help us to understand much about intellectual property, but that his analysis of the competitive pressures facing individual capitalists will. Marx's obsession with the materiality of production leads him to ignore the importance of the abstract object to capitalism's processes of commodity accumulation. But his recognition of the importance of creative labour to capitalism's survival, combined with his understanding of capitalists as the individual subjects of the competition, allows us, we argue, to identify clearly the tasks of intellectual property.

Chapter 6 carries a serious charge against economists: they do not take the self-interested behaviour of individuals seriously enough – at least not when it comes to intellectual property. As a result the real-world costs of intellectual property are likely to be much higher than might be first thought. The source of these costs lies in the preventive strategies adopted by opportunistic actors in the marketplace. Intellectual property rights are a source of these strategies. Intellectual property more than other property forms leads to the problem of factions.

Implicit in Chapter 6 is the connection between intellectual property and power. The nature of this connection is analysed in Chapter 7. Property, we claim, is a sovereignty mechanism and in the case of intellectual property it has sovereignty effects. This chapter offers a more detailed analysis of the nature of the abstract object than is given in Chapter 2. Abstract objects are an important kind of capital. They also create 'person dependency' relationships. In doing so they make feasible certain kinds of coercion claims.

Abstract objects are a primary good. We should think about their distribution normatively. Chapter 8 asks how intellectual property rights fare under Rawls' theory of justice. The final chapter argues that proprietarianism is a creed that has come to dominate the evolution of intellectual property law. The chapter proposes a replacement for proprietarianism: instrumentalism. Instrumentalism conceives of intellectual property rights as a distinct kind of liberty-intruding privilege. Under the influence of proprietarianism, these privileges come to pose grave threats for negative liberty. The instrumentalism which is presented takes the form of a naturalistic empiricism that is guided by a principle of humanism.

A Note on the Subject Areas of Intellectual Property

For readers who are not familiar with the traditional core areas of intellectual property, an oversimplified description follows. These areas are usually governed by statute. While the content of these statutes is a matter of national policy, increasingly international conventions prescribe minimum standards of protection for intellectual property. Typically, intellectual property statutes create rights of personal property in the relevant subject matter. This means, for example, that a patent may be assigned or licensed. Some rights, such as patent rights, are of limited duration; other rights, trademarks being an example, are not. Copyright deals with the rights of authors in traditional cultural works like literary and artistic works. Examples of the rights that authors gain are the right to reproduce the work and the right to perform the work in public. Copyright protection has been progressively extended through an expansion of traditional rights (for example, computer software is protected as a literary work) and to new subject areas (for example, sound recordings and films).

Patent statutes protect inventions. Protection is conditional upon satisfying various criteria of which novelty and inventiveness are two important examples. Design deals with the appearance of articles in the industrial sphere. (The appearance of a toilet bowl can be the subject of design registration. The shape of a statue is a matter of copyright protection.) Trademarks protect signs that traders use to distinguish their goods or services from those of other traders. 'Signs' now has a broad meaning: it includes smells and sounds.

Unfair competition is a nebulous area. Article 10 *bis* of the Paris Convention For The Protection of Industrial Property (1883) as revised says that any act of competition contrary to honest practices in industrial or commercial matters constitutes an act of unfair competition. More than most areas of intellectual property, the law relating to unfair competition has evolved in very different directions in various countries.

Trade secret law provides protection for commercially valuable technical information which a person has chosen not to disclose. The same abstract object may be protected under more than one head of intellectual property protection. Algorithms are potentially protectable under patent, copyright and trade secret law. A sign may be a trade mark and an artistic work. The choice of protection for an object is a matter of business strategy. Each regime has different disadvantages and advantages. A product which is easy to reverse engineer (a machine, for example) is better protected by patent than by trade secret law since the latter does not offer rights against the independent originator. One problem with patent protection is that it is of limited duration. If the product is not easily reverse engineered (the recipe for Coca Cola, it is said, falls into this category) it is better to rely on trade secret protection because, provided certain conditions are satisfied, such protection is not limited by time.

Notes

1 The bundle of rights view of property is nicely captured by Kevin Gray in the following passage: 'When I sell you a quantum of airspace the whole point is that – apart from molecules of thin air – there is absolutely *nothing* there. The key is, of course, that I have transferred to you not a thing but a "bundle of rights", and it

is the "bundle of rights" that comprises the property.' K. Gray, 'Property in Thin Air', 50 *Cambridge Law Journal*, 252, 259 (1991).

2 For a discussion, see G.F. Gaus, 'Property, Rights, and Freedom', 11 *Social Philosophy and Politics*, 209, 211–216 (1994).

3 A. Reeve, *Property* (London, 1986), 10–12.

4 One of the reasons is that the attempt to do so leads rapidly into questions about the nature of philosophical analysis itself. For readings on this issue, see R. Rorty (ed.), *The Linguistic Turn* (Chicago, London, 1967).

5 W.N. Hohfeld, *Fundamental Legal Conceptions* (Westport, Connecticut, reprinted 1978).

6 Modern discussions include L.C. Becker, *Property Rights – Philosophic Foundations* (London, Boston, 1977); A. Ryan, *Property and Political Theory* (Oxford, New York, 1984); J.O. Grunebaum, *Private Ownership* (London, New York, 1987); J. Waldron, *The Right to Private Property* (Oxford, 1988); S.R. Munzer, *A Theory of Property* (Cambridge, 1990). For an overview, see A. Reeve, 'Property' in R.E. Goodin and P. Pettit (eds.), *A Companion to Contemporary Political Philosophy* (Oxford, 1993), chapter 31.

7 Sir William Blackstone, *Commentaries on the Laws of England* (1765; (1783 ed., reprinted by Garland Publishing, New York, London, 1978), Book 2, chapter 1, 2.

8 Ibid.

9 H. Grotius, *De Jure Belli Ac Pacis Libri Tres* (1625; F.W. Kelsey tr., New York, London, 1964), Book II, chapter 2, I.

10 Ibid.

11 Id. at Book II, chapter 2, II, 3.

12 For an interesting psychological account of the appropriation of ideas, see R.A. Wicklund, 'The Appropriation of Ideas' in P.B. Paulus (ed.), *Psychology of Group Influence* (2nd ed., Hillsdale, NJ; Hove, London, 1989). For an economic account of property rights which in part deals with their origins using some game theory, see D. Friedman, 'A Positive Account of Property Rights', 11 *Social Philosophy and Policy*, 1 (1994).

13 The study and development of formal arguments and language in the field of moral imperatives and concepts.

14 For a survey and discussion, see L. Lindahl, *Position and Change* (Dordrecht, Boston, 1977).

15 For a recent example, see S.R. Munzer, *A Theory of Property* (Cambridge, 1990).

16 As to why the latter view is logically flawed, see L. Lindahl, *Position and Change* (Dordrecht, Boston, 1977), 37.

17 A.M. Honoré, 'Ownership' in A.G. Guest (ed.), *Oxford Essays in Jurisprudence* (Oxford, 1961), 106, 134.

18 Theorists within the Scandinavian Realist tradition used the theory of performative utterances to give an account of the true nature of legal language. See K. Olivecrona, 'Legal Language and Reality' in R.A. Newman (ed.), *Essays in Jurisprudence in Honor of Roscoe Pound* (Indianapolis, New York, 1962), 151; K. Olivecrona, *Law as Fact* (2nd ed., London, 1971).

19 It was customary to refer to industrial and intellectual property rights. The term 'industrial' was used to cover technology-based subject areas like patents and designs. 'Intellectual property' was used to refer to copyright and its cultural subject matter. Many people now use 'intellectual property' generically to cover all the different parts of industrial and intellectual property. This modern convention is adopted here.

20 Both are the subject of international conventions. See the International Convention for the Protection of New Varieties of Plants of 2 December 1961 as revised and the Treaty on Intellectual Property in Respect of Integrated Circuits (Washington, 1989).

21 An example of a rather broad one couched in inclusive form is to be found in Article 2 (viii) of the Convention Establishing the World Intellectual Property Organization, signed at Stockholm on 14 July 1967. It provides that '"intellectual property" shall include the rights relating to:

literary, artistic and scientific works,
performances of performing artists, phonograms, and broadcasts,
inventions in all fields of human endeavor,
scientific discoveries,
industrial designs,
trademarks, service marks, and commercial names and designations,
protection against unfair competition,

and all other rights resulting from intellectual activity in the industrial, scientific, literary or artistic fields'.

22 R.A. Epstein, 'On the Optimal Mix of Private and Common Property', 11 *Social Philosophy and Policy*, 17 (1994).

23 L.C. Becker, 'Too Much Property', 21 *Philosophy and Public Affairs*, 196 (1992).

24 Works by North include D.C. North and R.P. Thomas, *The Rise of the Western World: A New Economic History* (Cambridge, 1973); D.C. North, *Structure and Change in Economic History* (New York, 1981); D.C. North, *Institutions, Institutional Change and Economic Performance* (Cambridge, New York, 1990).

25 For sources of important contributions in information economics, see D.M. Lamberton (ed.), *The Economics of Information* (Harmondsworth, UK, 1971); D.M. Lamberton (ed.), *The Economics of Communication and Information* (Cheltenham, UK, 1996).

26 A classical source of inspiration for this kind of work is J.R. Commons, *Institutional Economics* (New York, 1934).

27 See I. McLean, *Public Choice: An Introduction* (Oxford, 1991); D.A. Farber and P.P. Frickey, *Law and Public Choice: A Critical Introduction* (Chicago, 1991).

28 R.A. Posner, *Economic Analysis of Law* (4th ed., Boston, 1992) is emblematic of this approach.

29 One classical study is F. Machlup, *An Economic Review of the Patent System* (Study No. 15 of the Subcommittee on Patents, Trademarks, and Copyrights of the Committee on the Judiciary, U.S. Senate, 85th Congress, Washington, D.C., 1958). There are other important studies including E.T. Penrose, *The Economics of the International Patent System* (Baltimore, 1951). J. Schmookler, *Patents, Invention, and Economic Change* (Z. Griliches and L. Hurwicz eds., Cambridge, Mass., 1972); C.T. Taylor and Z.A. Silbertson, *The Economic Impact of the Patent System* (Cambridge, 1973). For a discussion of the economics of patents from an Australian perspective, see T. Mandeville, D. Lamberton and J. Bishop, 'The Use of Patent Information: Economics of Disclosure' in *The Economic Implications of Patents in Australia* (Canberra, 1981), 271. For a discussion of the impact of the patent system on developing countries, see A.S. Oddi, 'The International Patent System and Third World Development: Reality or Myth?' *Duke Law Journal*, 831 (1987).

30 For examples, see W.M. Landes and R.A. Posner, 'An Economic Analysis of Copyright Law', 18 *Journal of Legal Studies*, 325 (1989); W.M. Landes and R.A. Posner, 'Trademark Law: An Economic Perspective', 30 *Journal of Law and Economics*, 265 (1987).

31 For a survey, see Australian Law Reform Commission, *Designs* (DP 58, Australia, 1994), chapter 14.

32 See Industry Commission, *Report on Vehicle and Recreational Marine Craft Repair and Insurance Industries* (Australia, 1994), 123.

33 See the discussion of this in L. Kaplow, 'The Patent-Antitrust Intersection: A Reappraisal', 97 *Harvard Law Review*, 1815, 1823–1829 (1984).

2 Justifying Intellectual Property: Back to the Beginning

Why History?

History matters to philosophy. It would be nice if it did not, since this would simplify the task of philosophical analysis. There are at least three reasons why some history needs to be introduced to an analysis of intellectual property. Some philosophical frameworks, which might be chosen to do the job of analysis, necessarily draw on history. Applying Marx's theory of historical materialism (with some mechanical simplicity) one might claim that intellectual property is a superstructural phenomenon corresponding to the industrial (or perhaps post-industrial) phase of development of capitalist societies.[1] Such an explanation could only be made plausible by historical evidence.

History also matters to an economic or consequentialist analysis of intellectual property. These kinds of approaches would justify the creation of intellectual property rights on the basis that such rights helped to fulfil, for example, some stipulated goal, such as welfare, economic growth, cultural protection, reward for creativity and so on. For such approaches the real data of history would be a preferred source for understanding the effects of intellectual property rather than *a priori* theory. Finally, a historical perspective can, for the kinds of reasons which Quentin Skinner gives in relation to political philosophy, deepen our understanding of the philosophical dimensions of intellectual property.[2] Skinner's methodological argument is that the present meaning of the central concepts of political philosophy can only be understood through a linguistic analysis that tracks these concepts through their respective historical time lines and uncovers both the social context of their users and the matrix of assumptions surrounding their use. The kind of combined philosophical, historical and linguistic game analysis that Skinner has in mind has yet to be undertaken in the context of intellectual property. It is not undertaken here. This is clearly a task for specialists. But Skinner's general methodological claim provides another reason why a philosophy of intellectual property cannot turn its back on history.

Having built a case for a philosophy of intellectual property needing at least some history, we must now circumscribe our use of the historical materials for present purposes. Clearly, the national history of any one intellectual property regime such as copyright or the patent system could be the subject of a separate work. Even if one confines the historical investigation to enacted law and judge-made law in Europe, there is a sheer bulk of historical material going back centuries. 'Intellectual property' is a twentieth-century generic term used to refer to a group of legal regimes which began their existence independently of each other and at different times in different places.[3] England, for example, is often given the credit for having the first copyright statute, the *Act of Anne* of 1709. The Venetians are thought to have had the first patent statute.[4] And in any case the history of intellectual property law does not begin with statute. Copyright and patents in England evolved out of a complex system of prerogative, privilege and monopoly. Similarly, in many European countries, including Russia, there was a complex system of royal decrees and privileges that regulated the industrial arts.[5]

Two tasks govern the selection of historical materials in this chapter. The first relates to the legal categorization of intellectual property. One possibility is that we may gain some philosophical insight into intellectual property from the way in which English property law classified intellectual property. The law's own internal taxonomic structures may help us to understand the character of intellectual property rights, especially if this legal character is itself based on some pre-existing philosophical idea or influence. This possibility should not be discounted. The legal classification of intellectual property as incorporeal rights, we shall see, leads straight into the philosophical notion of abstract objects. The fusion of this notion with the property concept becomes important to the argument, given in Chapter 7, that the basis of power in modern economic systems lies in the control of abstract objects.

The second use we make of the legal historical materials is to examine the justifications to be found within early English law for copyright and patents. Naturally, the philosopher is not confined to these justifications. This material is used to support the proposition that early justificatory approaches to intellectual property were distinctly instrumental. The final chapter of the present volume sees more use being made of this historical material to mount a normative argument to the effect that an instrumental attitude should inform theory development within intellectual property.

Before commencing there are some more general observations to be made about the role which history can play in a critical evaluation of intellectual property systems. History is one distinctive kind of story-telling and intellectual property is an area in need of many more critical historical stories. One purpose of such stories would be to help evaluate the orthodox forms of justification for intellectual property. The history which is being contemplated here is actually a series of histories about the way in which different societies have, in terms of their institutional organization and norms, encouraged and harnessed human creativity, both scientific and non-scientific. To illustrate: a fundamental form of argument used to justify the creation of intellectual property rights is that such rights provide incentives for persons to engage in the activity covered by the particular right. Patent rights, according to this argument, encourage invention. History may tell us whether property rights are the only route to take for a society that wants to encourage invention and innovation. Imperial China is an example of a society that achieved spectacular outcomes in science and innovation,[6] yet it did not rely on intellectual property rights or a customary equivalent.[7] History may teach us that the connection between intellectual property, science and economic development is contingent and local rather than necessary and universal.

There are other purposes that such critical historical investigations could serve. It would make our examination of intellectual property less Eurocentric. What evidence there is suggests that intellectual property is a protean concept which has been configured in different ways by different societies. Lowie's anthropological work reveals that the concept of incorporeal property, and in particular patents and copyright, was highly developed amongst the Andaman Islanders, the Kai, the Koryak and the Plains Indians.[8] These societies were, in contrast to western approaches, more concerned to restrict the transferability of such rights.

Histories of intellectual property rights would also guard against an overreliance on economic story-tellers for an understanding of intellectual property. The signs which conventional economic analysts leave for others to follow in relation to property generally do not explicitly deal with the linkages between values and property, or with themes of power, domination, exploitation and control, themes so familiar to the historian. Property rules, more than most rules, are rooted in the fundamental morality of a given society. Western copyright laws, for instance, reflect a view of art that promotes the importance of individual creativity and individual rights, a view which has no real oriental parallels.[9] At a time when western forms of intellectual property are being transplanted to non-western countries, the signs of economic story-tellers need to be read critically by those who are adopting these forms.[10] Decisions about the adoption of foreign legal models have to be made with, as it were, informed consent. Critical historical story-telling can help those receiving intellectual property legal traditions gain a better understanding of their full consequences.

Classifying Intellectual Property: Rome Speaks

Most students of intellectual property are told of the distinction between corporeal (roughly, tangible) and incorporeal (roughly, intangible) property and that intellectual property rights are an example of incorporeal rights. One immediate analytical puzzle that this gives rise to is the very possibility of corporeal rights, since all rights would seem to be best thought of as incorporeal. (It is difficult to plough a right.) A judicial answer to the puzzle is to say that this is a loose but common way of talking and that the distinction is not between the nature of the rights but between the nature of the objects to which the right refers.[11] All rights are incorporeal, while some property is not.

The distinction between corporeal and incorporeal things is to be found in the classical period of Roman private law.[12] Classical Roman law, we know from the *Institutes of Gaius*, divided all law into the law relating to persons, things or actions. The distinction between corporeal and incorporeal occurs in the law of things (*res*). It is stated by Gaius in the following way:[13]

> 12. Further, things are divided into corporeal and incorporeal. 13. Corporeal things are tangible things, such as land, a slave, a garment, gold, silver, and countless other things. 14. Incorporeal are things that are intangible, such as exist merely in law, for example an inheritance, a usufruct, obligations however contracted.

The distinction, then, is one between tangible and intangible objects.[14] The distinction is not an old one since the words *corporalis* and *incorporalis* are not to be found till the time of the Empire.[15]

From where did the Roman jurists obtain the distinction?[16] This question is one for the classicists. One possibility is Stoicism.[17] Stoicism had a wide influence on Roman culture and philosophy, including legal culture, and the distinction is to be found within Stoic thought.[18] It is possible, therefore, that the Roman law category of incorporeal things derived from the Stoic notion of incorporeals.[19] Within Stoicism, four things were said to be incorporeal: time, space, the void and *lekta* (the meaning of words or sentences).[20] That the Stoics should have had the category at all is at first sight surprising, given that theirs was a philosophy of uncompromising materialism. God and the soul were for them corporeal entities. Only corporeal entities were real.[21] Incorporeal things were not existent, but rather subsistent. They subsisted by virtue of human mental life. They were things superimposed by the mind onto the corporeal world.[22]

The category of incorporeal things in a materialist philosophy is an intriguing juxtaposition. One of its analytical features is that it would have allowed the Stoics to give an account of universals without, as Plato did, committing themselves to the existence of abstract Ideas or Forms.[23] For Plato, universals like the number one, the property of squareness or moral terms like justice existed as eternal forms. Within Stoic metaphysical theory, only particulars existed. Universals were a convenient fiction which *subsisted* as incorporeal things, these things being essentially mental figments.

We should bear in mind that modern intellectual property rights relate to the grant of property rights in some *thing* as well as constituting a set of relations between individuals. But what is the nature of this thing? It cannot be a physical object for, as every law student is told, the fact that I own a physical copy of a book does not entail that I own the copyright in that book. Furthermore, I may own the copyright without owning a physical copy (for example, the letter I have written and sent is owned by someone else). By recognizing intellectual property rights, is the law forced also to recognize 'spooky' entities – universals? Or can Stoic thought offer us a more sensible account of property rights in incorporeal things?

The Stoic incorporeal category of most interest here is that of meaning (*lekt*a). Meaning is conceived to be something expressible, although it is not to be confused with the material expression of a sentence in writing or speech, for example the words on a tablet or spoken in a play. *Lekta* are signified meanings which are logically distinct from their physical representation or communication. Since *lekta* are incorporeals they cannot act in the world. They are causally inert. Meanings can become causal factors once they form part of people's beliefs.[24] At the point at which the incorporeal expressible enters a person's beliefs it becomes a corporeal force. Here, then, is one view of the metaphysical character of the legal category of incorporeal things. Before one can claim an intellectual property right, whether it be copyright, a patent right, a design and so on, there has to be some concrete specification of the subject matter. This process of specification can involve formalities (for example, the registration of a patent) or it can be informal (simply creating information that can be the subject of trade secret protection). This specification of subject matter does two things. It produces signifiers (the physical representations). It also generates an entity with specific meaning which, in the language of the Stoics, amounts to the creation of an 'expressible'.[25] An expressible is an abstract entity. It is also a convenient mental fiction. It subsists as a construct of the mind. An abstract object does not exist in the corporeal world. Once the abstract object attains corporeality by becoming embodied belief, at least in the Stoic scheme of things, it can play a causal role in the social and productive relations of people. At the same time, because it affects human conduct, it becomes a potential candidate for legal regulation.

To summarize, one view is that mental constructs are the stuff of intellectual property relations. Intellectual property rights are rights in our mental projections. An alternative is to adopt some kind of realist explanation of these abstract things. Shortly stated, this would involve arguing that abstract entities are real entities, just like law books and tennis balls. Following a realist line, abstract objects would have to be assigned an independent ontological status and given either an immanent (that is, Aristotelian) or transcendental (that is, Platonic) account of their existence. Either account has philosophical support, but this realist way of looking at abstract objects drives intellectual property law ever deeper into metaphysics. The law now has to contemplate the independent existence of unobservable entities.

Roman law, by inventing the category of *res incorporales,* plants its property law squarely in the realm of the metaphysical. English law, as we shall see in a moment, made use of this category in order to add a largely flexible category to its property law. Before moving on, though, we should make clear that the idea of incorporeal things in Gaius and Justinian refers to legal rights. Rights are used by both to include those rights we would think of as property rights as well as contractual rights. The strong implication from Justinian is that incorporeal things have corporeal counterparts. Incorporeal things are thought, in other words, to relate strongly to corporeal objects. The link between incorporeal rights and incorporeal objects, or what we have called abstract objects, only came to the fore in English property law when various intellectual property forms were classified as choses in action and these were carefully distinguished from any property rights in chattels.[26] Intellectual property rights are incorporeal things, but this came to mean incorporeal rights which relate to abstract objects.

From the very start the category of incorporeal things creates legal uncertainties. In *The Institutes,* Gaius in some places includes obligations as *res incorporales* and in other places does not.[27] On the basis of the distinction one might expect ownership (*dominium*) in a physical object to be a *res incorporales* since ownership is concerned with rights and rights are an intangible. But, as writers of Roman law routinely point out, dominium is to be found in the category of *res corporales.*[28]

What seems to happen is that the object is substituted for ownership, or perhaps object and ownership are thought of as substitutes.[29] Modern Roman law writers do not devote a great deal of attention to the distinction except to point out its logical flaws.[30] None do so with the impatience of the 19th-century jurist Austin. He dismisses the distinction as completely useless, saying that it is 'either imperfect, or else big with contradiction'.[31]

While the Roman scheme of property law conflates object and ownership, other rights, such as rights of way, are no longer seen concretely in terms of an actual path, but rather are viewed as intangible rights. Some writers use the corporeal/incorporeal distinction to support a claim that classical juristic thought was generally manifesting a tendency towards greater abstraction.[32] Whether this claim is true is another matter, but we can say that in the context of property law the recognition of a category of *res incorporales* and the formal classification of some rights as intangible at least leaves open the possibility for the development of a more abstract juristic mode of thought about the property concept.

The distinction lay dormant until the rediscovery and revival of Roman classical law by Irnerius and his followers in 11th-century Bologna. From here Roman law began a new journey of conquest and entered at various different times, and to varying degrees, the legal systems of Europe. *Res incorporales*, with its unexplored potentiality, found a place in the legal language of both civil systems and the common law.[33] Incorporeal things, or rather the category, found its way into English law only to be fused with an equally opaque legal category, that of the chose in action.[34] This latter category of personal property, more than most, was ready to lose the 'thinglikeness' which characterized mediaeval attitudes to the property concept and thus paved the way for the modern juristic discovery that property is not a thing but a set of relations between people.

Calling intellectual property rights choses in action does not bring immediate illumination. The reason, put shortly, is that doctrinal scholars have concluded that a chose in action is a class best understood in terms of the description of its members, rather than a definition capable of a self-selection of members.[35] Often a chose in action is explained by saying that it is not a chose in possession, but a thing recoverable by action, like a debt.[36] However not all rights of action are choses in action. The chose in action seems to have more than the usual degree of vagueness associated with legal predicates. The classification of apparently simple cases, like the owner of a chattel out of possession, have been the subject of debate.[37] The distinction between corporeal and incorporeal makes its presence felt in the category of chose in action, although it does not add much in the way of clarity. A chose in possession is said to refer to corporeal or tangible things while a chose in action is linked to intangible property, that is something which cannot be claimed by taking physical possession.[38]

Why do intellectual property rights come to be called choses in action? The answer has to do with chance, history and the internal dynamics of the English legal system rather than the application of logic. The process of classification has been a prolonged one, for even at the beginning of the 19th century there was going on in England a quiet debate about whether or not, for instance, copyright really was a chose in action.[39]

Early in its history the common law had a rule against the assignment of choses in action.[40] The primary reason for this was that choses in action were thought to be highly personal obligations not appropriate for transfer and in any case their transfer might provoke too much litigation.[41] At the time that patents and copyright came into being the rule about the non-assignment of choses in action was being substantially undermined by the courts of Equity. This made it easier to fit copyright and patents into the category. It was commercially necessary for these forms of property to be assignable and the prohibition on assignment was being undermined. The other factor influencing their classification was their incorporeal character.[42]

Things might have turned out differently. Holdsworth, for example, argues that, had Equity not modified the consequences of the rule against the assignment of choses in action, then intellectual property rights would have been treated as incorporeal hereditaments.[43] One view might be that whether intellectual property rights are classified as choses in action or incorporeal hereditaments matters not, for both are categories of property. There is perhaps a difference in the level of abstraction which each category represents. The incorporeal hereditaments which Blackstone lists (easements and profits à prendre are two examples) have a strong territorial ambit.[44] They, for the most part, in one way or another relate to bounded real property. The chose in action is better suited to lose the traces of territoriality and tangibility that exist in relation to other property forms – what Pollock termed the 'thinglikeness' of English property. These new forms of personal property were in one sense less personal, for they did not bind communities together in the same strong way that was true of customary and feudal forms of property. Rather these new forms make possible anonymous, impersonal connections between owners and strangers, connections which in the 20th century broke free of the usual territoriality of property relations and became genuinely global.

The magnitude of the psychological and conceptual shift which took place through the rise in importance of the chose in action should not be underestimated. Maitland and Pollock both argue that much of English real property law can best be understood by a mediaeval incapacity to separate the transfer of rights from the transfer of things.[45] There was, even in the case of incorporeal hereditaments like rights of way and offices, a tendency to ascribe to them a 'thinglike' character and to analogize their property nature to land. Maitland, for example, suggests that practices like attornment, which surrounded the transfer of incorporeal hereditaments, reveal that these hereditaments were considered really to be things rather than rights.[46]

Through linking the Roman law category of the incorporeal thing with the category of chose in action, English law produced a highly flexible concept of personal property. It was flexible precisely because its extension was not limited by some set of precisely specified attributes. Its indefiniteness was a source of functional strength for the property system. The result was that it was capable of being extended into many different areas of market and social relationships.[47] It was a concept that had no real equivalent within the Continental civil law system.[48]

There is one final observation to make. On one view our short story of the career of incorporeal things seems to support the idea that property law in its long evolution has been progressively dematerialized, made more abstract or, in Pollock's terms, has lost its 'thinglikeness'. This conclusion would be easy enough to draw, but should we draw it? What happens in our story is that a Roman law category is used by English juristic hands to fashion a practical solution to a practical problem. A person with ideas has in a broad sense assets. In order that the person may make a living in a market society those intangible assets have somehow to be recognized as property rights so that they can be commercially exploited. Some of the crucial conceptual apparatus to this end was provided by Roman law. The English common law, renowned for its pragmatism, ventured deep into metaphysical territory and added the abstract objects of intellectual property to the list of incorporeal things. By doing so it extended its reach over material objects. Artists, authors and inventors have to turn their intangible assets into material ones in order to survive economically in the world. Once the law recognized property in abstract objects, the significance of the materiality which governed property relations in the physical world grew stronger and not weaker. It grew stronger because through abstract objects many more material objects, both in number and in kind, could be reached by individual property owners. The abstract object became a way of gaining control over the material object. One patent could relate to an indefinite number of physical objects. The corporeality of intellectual property is, legally speaking, never very far away and manifests itself in various requirements which impose a condition of materiality on the abstract object.[49]

Justifying Intellectual Property

Abstract objects are the 'things' that mediate property relations between individuals in the case of intellectual property. What is the justification for creating property rights in what, after all, is the perfect example of a resource which cannot be exhausted through use? In the case of tangibles a person can deprive another by taking the thing. But the nature of abstract objects permits of their simultaneous use and so deprivation of the object through use cannot take place.

English law had first to confront this question of justification in the context of patents and copyright. In each of these contexts the answer was worked out within a heavily Christianized legal tradition and a discourse that was influenced by natural law theories of property. Within this tradition the justification issue was argued differently for patents and copyright. In order to illustrate these claims we shall restrict ourselves to a discussion of *Millar* v. *Taylor* and the *Act of Anne* in the case of copyright and, in relation to patents, the *Statute of Monopolies* and the *Case of Monopolies*.[50] This is admittedly a small number but then some cases and statutes reveal much about the broader legal universe of the times. The two cases, amongst the most famous in English law, are rich in philosophical argument. They show clearly the jurisprudential frame of reference that was used to work through the justification issue.

Copyright

We will begin with copyright. There are a number of excellent sources for the history of English copyright and so here we shall only make the briefest observations about this history before going on to the material we have selected for analysis.[51]

The printing and production of books in England in the 15th century was carried on by a craft guild known formally as the Stationers. Like all craft guilds it had a serious interest in monopoly profits and a commensurate fear of competition. The combination of these eventually led members of the guild to obtain in 1557 a royal charter of incorporation.[52] Queen Mary was happy to accommodate the Stationers. Giving the control of printing to the Stationers' Company provided another means by which the spread of seditious and heretical information could be controlled (although it should be said that the Crown did not make much early use of the Stationers, preferring to rely on rougher methods such as torture and killing).[53]

The use of privilege to control the book trade in 16th-century England occurred because of a complementarity between two sets of self-interest. The Crown saw that the control of printing was vital to its political well-being and the Stationers regarded the privilege system as a way of maintaining their London-based monopoly and extending their influence regionally and across the border to Scotland. At this stage of copyright's history the author had only a cameo role. The central players were the Crown and the printing trade and neither was particularly interested in the rights of the author, or the value of a right of copy to the economy or to culture. Unless an author was lucky enough to secure a personal privilege, his position was weak, so much so that, if he allowed a manuscript to be publicly circulated, there was nothing to prevent a member of the Stationers' Company from registering the copyright and exploiting it. The right to print books belonged to those members of the Stationers' Company who registered the particular work and not to the author.

This system of privileges eventually became a ruin, in part because privileges were unevenly distributed throughout the industry, producing a conflict between those in the industry who had a large and profitable share of it and those who survived on its edges. The *Act of Anne* in 1709 replaced the privilege system. It was a revolutionary statute because it heralded the arrival of a public interest dimension to copyright. Its preamble linked copyright to the 'Encouragement of Learning'. By limiting the term of copyright protection the Act recognized the existence of the public domain.[54] The Act gave authors the 'sole Liberty of printing' in relation to books not printed and published. The whole flavour of the Act was instrumental and practical. Copyright's role was to encourage writers to produce, thereby serving the larger purpose of encouraging and adding to learning. The monopoly control of the Stationers over existing books was removed by limiting protection for such books to 21 years. Price control provisions for books were introduced and the interests of universities explicitly protected.

The arrival of the *Act of Anne* was not the cause of great rejoicing amongst the Stationers and, in the decades that followed, the statute was tested in the English courts. These 18th-century cases have a sharp contemporary relevance for, in deciding whether authors had rights that survived the *Act of Anne,* the courts had to confront the basis of copyright protection. Consequently, they were forced to travel into philosophical territory. The Stationers' litigation was part of a wider social debate over property rights in books or 'literary property'. This debate was one of the longest running and most keenly contested in late 17th and 18th-century British life.[55] Drawn to it were not only those with economic interests in the book trade but those within intellectual circles generally. There was a lot at stake. For some the real issue lay in the control of the dissemination of ideas.[56]

The debate in the courts took the form of a basic question over the existence of common law copyright after the author had published his or her work. The Stationers, reluctant to let their monopoly slip, argued that, independently of any statute, the common law gave authors a perpetual copyright (a copyright they could acquire from authors) and that this remained unaffected by either publication or the *Act of Anne*. Ultimately they lost this argument but, as they pursued it in the courts, English judges were given the opportunity to comment on the nature of the rights of authors in their works. Finally, in the case of *Donaldson* v. *Beckett*, a slim majority (six to five) decided that the *Act of Anne* had abolished the common law right.[57] Although this was not the last case in which an opinion was expressed on the matter, it fixed the line of thinking that saw copyright come to be considered as a creature of statute.

We turn now to an examination of the first case we mentioned at the beginning of this section. It precedes *Donaldson* v. *Beckett* and in many ways captures the essence of the debates over literary property. The 1769 case of *Millar* v. *Taylor* raised two questions. Did authors have at common law a right of copy? If so, had this common law right been taken away by the *Act of Anne*? The plaintiff Millar in this case was the registered proprietor of the poem 'The Seasons'. Taylor, without Millar's permission, had copies made of the poem so that he could sell them. The period of protection granted by the *Act of Anne* had expired. Millar's only hope of succeeding was to establish the existence of a common law copyright which remained unaffected by the statute. He succeeded in doing so. Three out of four judges decided the case in Millar's favour.

There are a number of different lines of justificatory argument offered by those judges who found in favour of a common law copyright. Mansfield CJ, after arguing that the source of this author's right is the same whether before or after publication, claims that the basis of the right lies in justice: 'it is just, that an author should reap the pecuniary profits of his own ingenuity and labour. It is just, that another should not use his name, without his consent.'[58] While other judges also appeal to justice they provide additional arguments. Willes J advances an instrumental argument. He links property to incentive. After conceding that it is 'not agreeable to natural justice' that others should reap the benefits of what they did not sow, he states the following argument: 'It is wise in any state, to encourage letters, and the painful researches of learned men. The easiest and most equal way of doing it, is, by securing to them the property of their own works.'[59] A third line of justification is presented by Aston J. He bases the existence of the right upon the fact that the author owns the produce of his mental labours.[60] This leaves open the question of why labour should have this property-conferring quality. Although Aston is not clear on this, he does later refer to the law of nature to support his claim that the invasion of this property right is against natural reason.[61] Aston's analysis seems to have an obvious Lockean lineage and he does in fact refer to Locke's discussion of property in Book II of the *Two Treatises of Government*, but only to say that Locke's discussion of property has no relevance to literary property.[62] Despite this, Aston's argument that the mental labours of the author create a property right bears, as we shall see in the next chapter, a remarkable similarity to Locke's analysis of the origins of property.

There are in short three lines of justification to be found in *Millar* v. *Taylor* which we can label as the justice justification, the incentive justification and the natural rights justification. They are clearly independent. Somebody might deny that property rights are an incentive to be creative and yet argue that justice requires the creation of property rights to reward creators. The incentive justification is instrumentalist in nature. Property rights are levers for obtaining socially beneficial activities. The natural rights justification depends for its plausibility on the existence of a law of nature and the existence of reason in humans to enable its identification. Although these justifications are worked out by the judges in the context of copyright they can equally apply to other areas of intellectual property. In later chapters each of these justifications will be subject to a more detailed evaluation. For the moment, we shall continue with the analysis of *Millar* v. *Taylor*, since it reveals much about the connections between copyright and natural law thinking about property.

One of the interesting features of *Millar* v. *Taylor* is the different way in which each judge makes use of natural law property theory. All the judges have to confront this intellectual tradition, partly because it is clear from the case that counsel in their arguments drew heavily upon it, and partly because it is the dominant tradition of their times. One of the lessons for the modern observer of this case, interested in the question of property and its justification, is that the outcome of the analysis is less dependent on the choice of ethical theory and more dependent on the characterization or description of community in relation to which the particular justificatory theory stands. This point emerges when the judgements are studied more closely.

Aston J and Yates J (the only judge to dissent) make use of the theories of Grotius, Pufendorf and Locke.[63] Yates explicitly links the development of the English law of personal property to natural law.[64] And yet, working within the same natural law framework, Yates and Aston derive opposite conclusions. Aston concludes that authors have property in abstract objects while Yates argues that, upon publication, this property right vanishes. There are a number of differences between them in the way they use the intellectual corpus of natural law, but the crucial difference is in the way each uses the concept of community. Aston argues that literary property belongs to an author from the moment that the author brings that work into being. He contrasts this with tangible property which he says commences in common ownership and comes to be individually owned through some act of occupancy. The following passage shows the contrast he makes between the two kinds of property:[65]

> And there is a material difference in favour of this sort of property, from that gained by occupancy; which before was common, and not yours; but was to be rendered so by some act of your own. For, this is originally the author's: and therefore, unless clearly rendered common by his own act and full consent, it ought still to remain his.

Aston, in this passage, is drawing upon the discussion of an issue of enormous importance for natural law theorists like Grotius, Pufendorf and Locke. These theorists were, in part, trying to provide an explanation for the evolution of private property. Did God grant the earth and its contents to the original community in common, by way of joint ownership? Alternatively, did this grant simply make the earth available for use, the questions of ownership to be determined by men at some later stage? The former conception of community – positive community – would make the acquisition of property by an individual heavily dependent upon the consent of others, since the individual is trying to acquire something that belongs to all. The latter conception of original community – negative community – provides greater scope for individuals to acquire property through their labour, because the individual is trying to acquire something which, although open to all to acquire, does not belong to any one individual.[66] The consent of others does not have the same strong role that it has in positive community.

Aston J approvingly cites Pufendorf, a defender of negative community, and argues that the author's mental labours provide the foundation for the right to property in literary works.[67] The fact that abstract objects can become property does not pose problems for Aston for, drawing on Pufendorf, he argues that the objects of property are settled over time. Natural law principles do not, in other words, inhibit the capacity of a society to adapt its positive rules of property to suit its new circumstances. Discovery, invention and art have added to the range of possible objects of property.

Like Aston J, Yates J draws on the general principles of property to be found in natural law theory, but he concludes the opposite to Aston; authors do not have a common law copyright beyond the *Act of Anne*. Occupancy cannot be the basis of this right, for abstract objects cannot be occupied.[68] The fact that abstract objects are valuable does not turn them into the property of individuals for 'mere value does not constitute property'.[69] Yates' rejection of common law copyright is partly based on the nature of abstract objects. They are, as he makes clear in the following passage, incapable of being possessed:

> But the property here claimed is all ideal: a set of ideas which have no bounds or marks whatever, nothing that is capable of a visible possession, nothing that can sustain any one of the qualities or incidents of property. Their whole existence is in the mind alone.[70]

The deeper part of Yates' argument lies in his clear assumption that ideas are open to all. The nature of ideas are such that, once they are published, they are incapable of sole use and enjoyment. The act of publication is necessarily 'a gift to the public', an entry of those ideas into the commons.[71] It does not follow from this that authors are not entitled to a reward for their efforts. Invoking the principle that every man is entitled to the fruits of his own labour, Yates agrees that authors are entitled to a reward, but this reward has to be subject 'to the general rights of mankind, and the general rules of property'.[72]

Yates makes a subtle and interesting use of natural law principles. It is because the law of personal property is based upon natural law foundations that there cannot exist a common law right of literary property. Property, he says, is founded upon occupancy and abstract objects cannot be occupied.[73] As Yates makes clear at the end of his judgement, the claim that such a right exists is completely inconsistent with the general principles of property. Justice does require that the author be given some reward. The legislature, by having enacted the *Act of Anne*, which grants the author a limited monopoly, fulfils the requirements of justice. The grant of the monopoly is justifiable because it is consistent with justice and it encourages learning and science. But the exercise of this monopoly is subject to the overriding requirement that it be consistent with the natural rights of others. Others have a right to make use of ideas and others have a right to trade in the subject matter of the monopoly privilege. The view of community which is implicit in Yates' judgement is not the strong conception of negative community that is present in Aston's analysis. Abstract objects remain a resource for all to use. They become part of a commons to which all have natural rights of access and use.

Millar v. *Taylor* turns out to be a revealing case on at least two levels. At one level the three different justifications which are to be found in the case for the existence of common law copyright have a modern relevance. Willes' incentive argument is a precursor of modern economic arguments which assume that the motivation towards creativity will be strengthened through the use of property rights in abstract objects and weakened by their absence.[74] Aston's natural rights justification is along similar lines to those offered by some modern libertarians for private property rights.[75] At another level, the case reveals that the course which a first order justificatory analysis of property is likely to run is deeply dependent upon the metaphysical scheme in which the analysis is housed and in particular upon the characterization and assumptions made about community. This dependence is so great that, within the same first order ethical theory such as natural law, different views of community lead to different conclusions about the justifiability of particular property arrangements.

One of the puzzles with the early cases on common law copyright is the apparently conflicting signals which they send. Holdsworth has pointed out that most English judges found in favour of a common law copyright and yet in English law an economic, pragmatic concept of copyright law ultimately triumphed.[76] Why this happened is worth exploring. After all, Locke's natural rights-based account of property rights was widely accepted in 18th-century England.[77] Most English judges took as their point of departure the strong connection between individual labour and the existence of a private property right, a connection which had been discussed by theorists of the natural law tradition. Very few judges took the view proposed by Pollock in *Jefferys* v. *Boosey* that copyright is 'altogether an artificial right'.[78]

Perhaps the economic concept of copyright law arrived in English law because of natural law principles rather than despite them. The right of every person to pursue a trade had long been a part of the common law and, more than most rights, enjoyed a fundamental status.[79] Judges who had to decide the issue of common law copyright could not but help contemplate the economic consequences of a perpetual monopoly in literary property. Rather than separating the interests of publishers and authors, they chose to limit the potentially absolute common law rights of authors by upholding the operation of the *Act of Anne*.[80] The triumph of the economic view of copyright turns out also to be an example of the way natural law property principles were adapted to fashion practical solutions to meet changing economic and technological circumstances. In adopting an economic concept of copyright, English law was not really rejecting a natural rights justification for copyright. Rather, it took the principles of natural law and gave them a practical interpretation which saw authors gain some reward for their labours and others be allowed to pursue their natural right to freedom of trade. It was an interpretation that ultimately suited the expanding industrial economy of the second half of 18th-century England.

Patents

Significantly, there was never a serious argument that inventors should enjoy the same perpetual right as authors. The rights of inventors, it was settled, depended on Crown privilege or an Act of Parliament.[81] The reason for this probably was that inventions were thought to be too important in terms of their social utility to tie up in the hands of their inventors. Those judges who argued in favour of common law literary property were left with the task of trying to distinguish property in inventions from property in books.[82] This is a difficult analytical job, for invention and authorship both involve the labours of the mind. Why should one form of labour ground a natural right of property, while the other grounds nothing at all unless the state decides to award a privilege in the form of a patent? The philosophical answer which English law adopted is that authors create something while inventors merely uncover what is already there.[83] This is not particularly convincing. The idea that inventors create nothing confuses the pre-existence of the laws of nature with their novel application. The latter does demand creative labour. Despite the creative element in invention, it remains true that English law was highly instrumentalist in its treatment of patents. Patent rights for centuries never escaped the language of privilege. There was more judicial disagreement over whether this was also true of copyright, but eventually copyrights, like patents, were thought to be privileges rather than natural rights.

Patent law, like copyright law, has its beginnings in the prerogative-based privilege system of mediaeval England. The sovereign could, on the basis of its prerogative power of grant, make grants of all kinds including grants of interests in land, offices of various kinds and franchises. The range of this power of grant was extensive, but in relation to the grant of monopolies it had to be exercised with care. The problem was that it was not. For successive English sovereigns, the grant of monopoly powers became a convenient source of revenue. Holdsworth neatly captures the money-making attitude with which sovereigns tended to treat what in theory was a limited power to grant monopolies.

> James I was always hard up; and for a consideration he was prepared to grant many privileges both of the governmental and of the industrial varieties. ... Of the second of these varieties of grants the following are a few examples: grant of an exclusive right to export calfskins; grant of an exclusive right to import cod and ling; grant of an exclusive right to make farthing tokens of copper.[84]

The reason that the power to grant monopolies had to be exercised with great care by the sovereign was that, as the *Case of Monopolies* was to make plain, the power was a very circumscribed one. It was clear that the royal prerogative was subject to Magna Carta and the common law, both of which were aimed, in terms of ideals, at the protection of the negative liberties of subjects.[85] Prerogative-based monopolies were a particularly strong form of interference in negative liberties because they prevented individual subjects from pursuing certain kinds of trades altogether. Conventional property rights did not hold the same danger for negative liberty because they operated to protect the property holdings that an individual might amass during the course of pursuing a trade or business. They did not prevent others from following a trade or business.

The response of the common law courts to the grant of monopolies was to give the principle of freedom of trade a primary status, even where the consequence of doing so was to interfere in the freedom of contract.[86] The courts, however, had to wait for an opportunity to declare the law on monopolies for they had no jurisdiction to assess the validity of an exercise of the royal prerogative.[87] They were given the jurisdiction to deal with monopolies by proclamation from the Queen in 1601, and in 1602 one of the most famous cases in English law, *The Case of Monopolies,* was heard by the Queen's Bench.[88] The story of this case has been told often enough.[89] Our interest is in the arguments used in the case to support the conclusion that, with some exceptions, monopolies were contrary to the common law.

The case involved the acquisition by Darcy of a patent that created exclusive rights to provide playing cards in England, which meant amongst other things the exclusive right to sell and import playing cards. Darcy sued Allen arguing that Allen had sold cards and therefore defrauded Darcy of the benefit of the patent. There were several successful arguments that were put forward by Allen's counsel concerning the general issue of whether Darcy's monopoly was good.[90] One line of argument related to employment. Monopolies which prevented others from working were against the interests of the commonwealth. Under the common law every subject had the right to lawful trade.[91] Another line of argument was straightforwardly economic. Monopolies ultimately were for private gain and this meant they had certain undesirable qualities. Amongst other things they raised prices. They also tended to impoverish those who prior to grant of the monopoly were able to pursue the trade but, once a monopoly in it was granted to someone else, could no longer do so. Both the common law and the 'equity of the law of God' condemned this feature of monopolies.[92]

One clear and major theme in the case is that monopolies are a profound interference in the liberty of subjects to trade and so for that reason are void at common law. The prerogative power to create privileges could not be exercised so as to injure subjects of the realm.

Allen's counsel argued that there was one exception to this in the form of monopoly patents. In those cases where useful trades and inventions had been brought into the commonwealth by a person, 'the King may grant to him a monopoly patent for some reasonable time, until the subjects may learn the same, in consideration of the good that he doth bring by his invention to the commonwealth: otherwise not'.[93] Here is a clear indication of what is generally acknowledged to be the purpose of the patent system in England at this time – to encourage the transfer of valuable trades and technologies to England. The Crown would, if it were exercising its prerogative properly, grant monopolies only to those persons who had invented something or had brought an invention or trade from abroad.[94] It was therefore not just discovery that was being rewarded at this stage, but also entrepreneurship in importing foreign discoveries. The crucial objective of the patent system was in effect to promote the growth of human capital. Once the relevant knowledge had been diffused throughout the society the Crown could not renew the monopoly, for that would be to undermine trade.[95]

Apart from this instrumentalist line of justification for the patent system there was another important line of argument based on religious morality which provided reasons for limiting the role of monopolies. Allen's counsel sought in the case to demonstrate that the monopoly in question was against the law of God. His argument was that it was an ordinance of God that men labour so that they and their families could survive. The labour of men gave rise to various trade skills and this was part of God's design. Anything which prohibited a man from pursuing his chosen trade was not only an interference in his liberty but also a breach of the laws of God. Although this argument is shortly put, it probably had considerable persuasive effect on its judicial audience, for it drew on a Church teaching which had condemned monopolies in the strongest possible terms. There were several reasons why the Church had labelled many monopolies a sin.[96] The ability of the monopolist to dictate price contravened just price theory.[97] Monopolies were seen to have a speculative economic character and so became part of the general moral criticism directed against usury. Many monopolies related to food. The monopolist's capacity to create scarcity in basic necessities could not be, it was thought, in the public welfare.

The argument that monopolies are against the law of God makes labour of central importance. The labour of others within a Christian community becomes a reason for not unnecessarily creating or extending the role of patents. It is precisely because patents interfere in the labour of others that they are a privilege. Their creation has to be consistent with the rights of others to labour, for, as Allen's counsel argues, the capacity of men to labour is part of God's design. Patents have the potential to interfere in this design and so whoever has the power to create them must act responsibly. The king's prerogative (used to create patents) is 'no warrant to injure any subject'.[98]

The instrumentalist attitude which dominated the approach of the common law courts to monopolies made its way into the *Statute of Monopolies* (1623). Section 1 of the Statute made clear that monopoly privileges had not performed their intended function of promoting the 'publique good' and so declared all monopolies to be contrary to the laws of the realm and so therefore void. There was one exception. The declaration in section 1 did not extend to the grant of a patent to an inventor of a manner of new manufacture.[99] The grant was conditional upon it not being contrary to law or 'mischievous to the state' in some way. The Statute made clear that patents belong to inventors by virtue of a privilege and not a natural right of some kind. The opening section stated that monopolies are contrary to the 'auncient and fundamental lawes' of the realm. By implication, if they are to be tolerated it is only if they contribute to the public good. The Statute was in many respects a straight piece of economic policy.[100]

The reluctance of the legislature to encase patents in the language of natural rights is perfectly understandable in the light of the Crown's abuse of the privilege system. Even in those countries such as America and France where the concept of natural rights was exercising a revolutionary political influence, the degree of that influence on patent rights seems to have been qualified, if the early patent law in those jurisdictions is some kind of guide. Classical natural rights, such as the right to liberty, were not thought to carry expiry dates. However, from the beginning, patent rights were seen in these two countries as rights which could be readily shaped, limited and finally extinguished by positive law.[101]

Conclusion

We are now in a better position to appreciate why the justification for patents was so highly instrumental within English law and why copyright, after some argument, went the same way. It was uncontroversial within the society of the time that individuals had to exist by their labour. This was part of God's design. Inventors and authors, like others, laboured and were entitled to a reward, but the reward which they could be given consistently with God's design was no more than a temporary privilege. Anything more would be too great an interference with the labour of others and therefore against the law of God and the fundamental laws of the realm. At best an inventor or an author could expect some kind of temporary advantage over others. The character of this advantage was a privilege. It could never amount to anything more because that would constitute too great a threat to the negative liberties of others, particularly in the area of commerce and trade. The right of free trade was a fundamental common law right. It meant, in theory at least, that people had a right of entry into the labour force. Temporary privileges in abstract objects had, it was thought, the long-term effect of increasing the industry of others. Such privileges were consistent with fundamental law and God's design. Natural property rights in abstract objects never could be. Natural property rights in the physical objects which one's labour had produced were consistent with the divine plan.

The interesting feature of the instrumentalist justification for copyright and patents is that it is worked out in the context of a natural law tradition, a tradition which at first sight might be thought not to be sympathetic to such a treatment of the mental products of one's labour. That such a justification emerged shows that, when it comes to justifying intellectual property, the crucial choices are between not first order ethical theories (natural law versus utilitarianism) but rather the concept of community and the metaphysical scheme upon which that concept of community is dependent. As it happens, the modern emphasis on the question of justification is at the level of first order ethical theory. This does not mean that concepts of community are irrelevant to the question of justification. Rather, it suggests that they are the silent drivers of the debate.

Notes

1 This is not to say that Marxists would necessarily approach intellectual property in this way. There are, within the traditions that Marx inspired, complex and subtle treatments of law. See, for instance, K. Renner, *The Institutions of Private Law* (O. Kahn-Freund ed., A. Schwarzchild tr., London, 1949); E.B. Pashukanis, *Law and Marxism: A General Theory* (C. Arthur ed., B. Einhorn tr., London, 1978). For a Marxist treatment which uses copyright law to build some of the elements of its theory of law, see B. Edelman, *Ownership of the Image* (E. Kingdom tr., London, Boston, Henley, 1979).

2 For a flavour of this debate which seems to take place mainly in intellectual history, see J. Tully (ed.), *Meaning and Context: Quentin Skinner and his Critics* (Cambridge, 1988). See also D. LaCapra and S. Kaplan (eds.), *Modern European Intellectual History: Reappraisals and New Perspectives* (Ithaca, N.Y., 1982).

3 The use of the term 'intellectual property' to refer to both industrial property and copyright seems to have first occurred in the 1950s. See A. Bogsch, *Brief History of the First 25 Years of the World Intellectual Property Organization* (Geneva, 1992), 8.

4 S. Ricketson, *The Law of Intellectual Property* (Sydney, 1984), 860–861.

5 See F. Machlup and E. Penrose, 'The Patent Controversy', X, *The Journal of Economic History*, 1, 2 (1950). On Russia, see J. Vojacek, *A Survey of the Principal National Patent Systems* (London, 1936).

6 See J. Needham, *The Grand Titration* (London, 1969). See also the volumes in

the series J. Needham, *Science and Civilization in China* (Cambridge at the University Press, 1954 v.1 –).

7 This raises the question of how Imperial China was able to achieve such an impressive track record in innovation in the absence of intellectual property rights. This is a matter for historians of science and technology. But there is little doubt that intellectual property did not play a role. There was no legal or customary equivalent to intellectual property in Imperial China. See W.P. Alford, 'Don't Stop Thinking About ... Yesterday: Why There was No Indigenous Counterpart to Intellectual Property Law in Imperial China', 7 *Journal of Chinese Law*, 3 (1993).

8 R.H. Lowie, *Primitive Society* (New York, 1920), 235-243.

9 See A. Hauser, *The Social History of Art* (S. Godman tr., London, 1951) volume 1, 65–66.

10 The most obvious example of this globalization is the Agreement on Trade-Related Aspects of Intellectual Property Rights contained in Annex 1C of the Final Act Embodying the Results of the Uruguay Round of Multilateral Trade Negotiations, Marrakesh, 15 April 1994.

11 This is how Windeyer J deals with the problem in *Pacific Film Laboratories Pty. Ltd.* v. *Federal Commissioner of Taxation* (1970) 121 C.L.R. 154 at 168.

12 The expression 'classical period' is used by writers to refer to the period of the Principate – from Augustus (27BC) to the beginning of the reign of Diocletian (284AD). See F. Schulz, *Classical Roman Law* (Oxford at the Clarendon Press, 1951), 1.

13 *The Institutes of Gaius* (F. De Zulueta (ed. and tr.), Oxford at the Clarendon Press, 1946), Book II, 12–14. The distinction is similarly put in *Justinian's Institutes* (translated with an Introduction by Peter Birks and Grant McLeod, Ithaca, New York, 1987), 2.2:

> Some things are corporeal, some incorporeal. 1. Corporeal things can actually be touched – land, a slave, clothes, gold, silver, and of course countless others. 2. Incorporeal things cannot be touched. They consist of legal rights – inheritance, usufruct, obligations however contracted. It is irrelevant that an inheritance may include corporeal things. ... The point is that the actual right of inheritance is incorporeal ... .

14 The modern distinction between tangible and intangible is between things which can be perceived by the senses and things which are merely creations of the mind. In Roman law tangible seems to have meant things which could be touched and used. See P. Warmelo, 'The Institutes of Justinian as Students' Manual' in P.G. Stein and A.D.E. Lewis (eds.), *Studies in Justinian's Institutes in Memory of J.A.C. Thomas* (London, 1983), 164, 169.

15 W.W. Buckland, *The Main Institutions of Roman Private Law* (Cambridge at the University Press, 1931), 91. Buckland observes that the words were rarely used outside juristic work.

16 Modern Roman law texts do not address the question since they are concerned with the law rather than its philosophical origins.

17 John Austin is confident that the distinction is borrowed from the Stoics and Epicureans. See, J. Austin, *Lectures on Jurisprudence* (5th ed., London, 1885), Lecture XIII. Austin is not alone in his belief. See also P. Colquhoun, *A Summary of the Roman Civil Law* (London, author's preface 1851), vol. 2, 13, section 931 for the suggestion that the distinction came from the Stoics.

18 For a general treatment of the influence of Stoicism on Roman thinking and culture, see E.V. Arnold, *Roman Stoicism* (London, 1911, reissued 1958).

19 That the Stoics had the distinction we know from Sextus Empiricus. See Sextus Empiricus, *Adversus Dogmatico*, ii, 11–13, in *Sextus Empiricus* (R.G. Bury tr., London, Cambridge, Mass., 1935), vol. 2, 247–249.

20 The word *lekta* is translated by Rist as 'things meant'. See J.M. Rist, *Stoic Philoso-*

phy (Cambridge, 1969), 152–153. Also translated as 'that which can be expressed' or 'what is meant'. See G. Watson, *The Stoic Theory of Knowledge* (Belfast, 1966), 41.

21 For a general discussion, see D.E. Hahm, *The Origins of Stoic Cosmology* (Columbus, Ohio, 1977).

22 For a discussion of this, see G. Watson, *The Stoic Theory of Knowledge* (Belfast, 1966), chapter 2. See also J.M. Rist, *Stoic Philosophy* (Cambridge, 1969), chapter 9.

23 For an argument that the Stoics had a theory of universals, see D. Sedley, 'The Stoic Theory of Universals' in R.H. Epp (ed.), *Recovering the Stoics*, XXIII, Supplement, *Southern Journal of Philosophy*, 87–92 (1985).

24 F.H. Sandbach, *The Stoics* (London, 1975), 92.

25 See G. Verberke, *The Presence of Stoicism in Medieval Thought* (Washington, D.C., 1983), 22–33.

26 In English law a patent is a chose in action. See *In re Heath's Patent* [1912] W.N. 137. This right is completely separate from the right of property in the physical thing made under the patent. See *Edwards & Co.* v. *Picard* [1909] 2 K.B. 903, 905.

27 See W.W. Buckland, *A Text-Book of Roman Law from Augustus to Justinian* (3rd ed., revised by Peter Stein, Cambridge, 1963), 186. On the failure of Gaius to follow through the distinction, see R. Zimmermann, *The Law of Obligations* (Cape Town, Wetton, Johannesburg, 1990), 26.

28 W.W. Buckland, *A Text-Book of Roman Law from Augustus to Justinian* (3rd ed., revised by Peter Stein, Cambridge, 1963), 186.

29 Nicholas suggests that because only corporeal things could be owned there was no need for a clear distinction between ownership and its object. The effect is that object and ownership come to be thought of as interchangeable terms. See B. Nicholas, *An Introduction to Roman Law* (Oxford University Press, 1962), 107.

30 The distinction is said not to be logical because it equates ownership with the objects of ownership. See B. Nicholas, *An Introduction to Roman Law* (Oxford University Press, 1962), 107. See also H.F. Jolowicz and B. Nicholas, *Historical Introduction to the Study of Roman Law* (3rd ed., Cambridge, 1972), 412–413; W.W. Buckland, *A Text-Book of Roman Law from Augustus to Justinian* (3rd ed., revised by Peter Stein, Cambridge, 1963), 185–186; W.W. Buckland, *The Main Institutions of Roman Private Law* (Cambridge at the University Press, 1931), 91–92.

31 J. Austin, *Lectures on Jurisprudence* (5th ed., London, 1885), Lecture XLVI, 777. Austin's criticism is founded on the fact that within Roman law the meaning of corporeal things is extended to include acts and forbearances in addition to objects of the senses. If forbearances are part of corporeal subject matter then there is a contradiction, for the intangible is ranked with the tangible. If not, says Austin, then an object of the distinction is omitted.

32 See H.F. Jolowicz and B. Nicholas, *Historical Introduction to the Study of Roman Law* (3rd ed., Cambridge, 1972), 412. But for a contrary view, see F. Schulz, *History of Roman Science* (Oxford at the Clarendon Press, 1946), 130–131.

33 On the influence of Justinian's *Institutes* in England, see A. Watson, 'Justinian's Institutes and some English Counterparts' in P.G. Stein and A.D.E. Lewis (eds.), *Studies in Justinian's Institutes in Memory of J.A.C. Thomas* (London, 1983), 181-186.

34 Within English property law a distinction is made between real and personal property. Real property is linked to interests in land while personal property is defined negatively to refer to property which is not real property. Personal property is subdivided into chattels personal and chattels real. Chattels real are an anomalous category whereby, for historical reasons, leases were classed as personal property. Chattels personal are further subdivided into choses in possession and choses in action. It is this latter category that houses many statutory forms of intellectual property such as patents and copyright. Typically, statutes classify the relevant right as personal property, relying on the legally established meaning of

that term. For Australian examples, see section 13(2) of the *Patents Act 1990*, section 196(1) of the *Copyright Act 1968* and section 20 of the *Plant Breeder's Rights Act 1994*. For a discussion of English personal property law, see A.P. Bell, *Modern Law of Personal Property in England and Ireland* (London and Edinburgh, 1989). For an Australian discussion, see J.W. Carter *et al*, *Helmore Commercial Law and Personal Property in New South Wales* (10th ed., Sydney, 1992).

35 O.R. Marshall, *The Assignment of Choses in Action* (London, 1950), 33. See also pages 6–8, where ten different definitions of a chose in action are listed.

36 *Halsbury's Laws of England* (4th ed.) vol. 6, 2, para. 1.

37 See O.R. Marshall, *The Assignment of Choses in Action* (London, 1950), 8–16.

38 A.P. Bell, *Modern Law of Personal Property in England and Ireland* (London, Edinburgh, 1989), 21–22.

39 See H.W. Elphinstone, 'What is a Chose in Action?', 9 *Law Quarterly Review*, 311 (1893); C. Sweet, 'Choses in Action', 10 *Law Quarterly Review*, 303 (1894); F. Pollock, 'What is a Thing?', 10 *Law Quarterly Review*, 318 (1894); S. Brodhurst, 'Is Copyright a Chose in Action?', 11 *Law Quarterly Review*, 64 (1895); T.C. Williams, 'Property, Things in Action, and Copyright', 11 *Law Quarterly Review*, 223 (1895); C. Sweet, 'Choses in Action', 11 *Law Quarterly Review*, 238 (1895).

40 See O.R. Marshall, *The Assignment of Choses in Action* (London, 1950), chapter 3.

41 Known as the objection to maintenance. See *Lampet's Case* (1612) 10 Co. Rep. 46b at 48a; 77 ER 994 at 997. It was thought that assignment would encourage maintenance, that is, the promotion by intermeddlers of litigation. This was both a crime and a tort.

42 See E. Jenks, *A Short History of English Law* (6th ed., London, 1949), 281.

43 W.S. Holdsworth, 'The History of the Treatment of Choses in Action by the Common Law', 33 *Harvard Law Review*, 997 (1920).

44 Sir William Blackstone, *Commentaries on the Laws of England* (1765; 1783 ed., reprinted by Garland Publishing, New York, London, 1978), Book 2, chapter 3.

45 F. Pollock and F.W. Maitland, *The History of English Law* (2nd ed., Cambridge at the University Press, 1898, reissued 1968), 124–125.

46 F.W. Maitland, 'The Mystery of Seisin' in *Select Essays in Anglo-American History* (edited by a committee of the Association of American Law Schools, Cambridge at the University Press, 1909), 591–610.

47 Austin argues that indefiniteness is the essence of property. He writes, though, as if it were true of property in all jurisdictions. See J. Austin, *Lectures on Jurisprudence* (5th ed., London, 1885), Lecture 48.

48 For an excellent discussion of the differences in approach to property between common law and civil law systems, see 'Introduction' by O. Kahn-Freund (ed.) in K. Renner, *The Institutions of Private Law* (A. Schwarzschild tr., London, 1949).

49 For example, patent applications need to be accompanied by specifications that describe and define the invention. Invention itself is often defined in terms that resonate of the material. The *Statute of Monopolies* refers to 'any manner of new manufactures' and this language is carried over into the Australian *Patents Act 1990* by s.18(1)(a) which defines an invention as 'a manner of manufacture within the meaning of section 6 of the *Statute of Monopolies*'. Copyright statutes generally also impose a requirement of material form in relation to works.

50 *Millar* v. *Taylor* (1769) 4 Burr. 2303, 98 E.R. 201; *Act of Anne* 8 Anne, c. 19 (1709); *The Case of Monopolies* (1602) 11 Co. Rep. 84b, 77 E.R. 1260: *Statute of Monopolies* 21 Jac 1 c. 3 (1623).

51 An excellent source of primary materials is E. Arber (ed.), *A Transcript of the Registers of the Company of Stationers of London 1554–1640 A.D.* (London, 1875–94, privately printed, 5 volumes). Examples of specialist texts include C. Blagden, *The*

Stationers' Company: A History, 1403–1959 (Cambridge, 1960); L.R. Patterson, *Copyright in Historical Perspective* (Nashville, 1968); G. Putnam, *Books and Their Makers During the Middle Ages 1476–1600* (New York, 1962); H. Ransom, *The First Copyright Statute* (Austin, 1956).

52 Reproduced in E. Arber (ed.), *A Transcript of the Registers of the Company of Stationers of London 1554–1640 A.D.* (London, 1875–94, privately printed, 5 volumes), vol. 1, xxviii. The Charter begins as follows:

> The King and Queen ... Know ye that we, considering and manifestly perceiving that certain seditious and heretical books rhymes and treatises are daily published and printed by divers scandalous malicious schismatical and heretical persons, not only moving our subjects and lieges to sedition and disobedience against us, our crown and dignity, but also to renew and move very great and detestable heresies against the faith and sound catholic doctrine of Holy Mother Church.

53 Ibid at xxvii.

54 L. Ray Patterson and Stanley W. Lindberg, *The Nature of Copyright* (Athens, London, 1991), 29–31.

55 The titles relating to the debate have been reproduced in 42 volumes in S. Parkes (ed.), *The English Book Trade 1660–1853* (New York, London, 1974). Of particular interest are the following titles: 'English Publishing, the Struggle for Copyright and the Freedom of the Press: Thirteen Tracts, 1666–1774'; 'The Literary Property Debate: Seven Tracts 1747–1773'; 'The Literary Property Debate: Six Tracts 1764–1774'; 'The Literary Property Debate: Eight Tracts, 1774–1775'.

56 For a judicial view to this effect, see the dissenting judgement of Yates J in *Millar* v. *Taylor* 98 E.R. at 229–250.

57 (1774) 4 Burr. 2408, 98 E.R. 257. For the view that the House of Lords in this case did not hold that authors had a common law copyright in the first place, see L. Ray Patterson and Stanley W. Lindberg, *The Nature of Copyright* (Athens, London, 1991), 36–46.

58 98 E.R., at 252.

59 Id., at 218.

60 Id., at 221.

61 Id., at 222.

62 Id., at 220–221. Aston J thinks this because Locke's theory applies to 'the necessaries of life'. Further, theories like Locke's depend on some act of occupancy, a physical act of attachment. Aston seems to be suggesting that occupancy is not relevant to acquiring property in literary works.

63 Aston J at 98 E.R., 220 refers explicitly to Locke's discussion of property in *The Second Treatise of Government* (1690). He also refers to Grotius' discussion of the origins of property in *De Jure Belli Ac Pacis Libri Tres* (1625) and Pufendorf's *De Jure Naturae et Gentium Libri Octo* (1672). See 98 E.R. at 220–221. Yates makes explicit use of Pufendorf at 98 E.R., 231 and 233. Willes J refers to the metaphysical arguments which he says have exercised the 'ingenuity of the bar' and alludes to 'supposed modes of acquiring the property of acorns'. See 98 E.R. at 218. This is perhaps a reference to Locke's discussion of property which does mention acorns. (See, J. Locke, *Two Treatises of Government* (P. Laslett (ed.), Cambridge, 1988), Book II, chapter 5, section 28.) In any case Willes chooses to sidestep an explicit discussion of the natural law tradition by claiming that this discussion related only to physical objects. Mansfield J draws on natural principles and moral justice to justify his conclusion. He makes no explicit reference to Grotius, Pufendorf or Locke.

64 98 E.R., 229.

65 Id., at 221.

66 Grotius is somewhat ambiguous on the question of the nature of the original community. In *Mare Liberum* he begins by saying that there are some things 'which

every man enjoys in common' without specifying the nature of this common ownership. Later he suggests that in the beginning 'common' simply meant a complete absence of ownership rather than an ownership by all. See H. Grotius, *Mare Liberum* (1608; R. Van Deman Magoffin tr., New York, 1916) at 2, and 22–25. See also H. Grotius, *De Jure Belli Ac Pacis Libri Tres* (1625; F.W. Kelsey tr., New York, London, 1964), Book II, chapter 2 for a discussion of the origin and development of private property. There Grotius cites Justin saying that all things were the common and undivided possession of all men. Grotius then follows this with the claim that 'each man could at once take whatever he wished for his own needs'. This is consistent with negative community. On the use of negative and positive community by natural law writers, see the commentary by K. Haakonssen on Thomas Reid, *Practical Ethics* (K. Haakonssen ed., Princeton, New Jersey, 1990), 323–326. For an excellent discussion of natural law theories of property, see S. Buckle, *Natural Law and the Theory of Property* (Oxford, 1991).

67 For Pufendorf's claim that the original community is negative, see S. Pufendorf, *De Jure Naturae et Gentium Libri Octo* (1672; translation of 1688 ed. by C.H. and W.A. Oldfather, New York, London, 1964), IV. 4. 3.

68 Blackstone points out that occupancy was 'taking possession of those things which before belonged to nobody': Sir William Blackstone, *Commentaries on the Laws of England*, (1765; 1783 ed., reprinted by Garland Publishing, New York, London, 1978), Book 2, Chapter 16, 258.

69 98 E.R., at 230.

70 Id., at 233.

71 Ibid.

72 Ibid.

73 Id., at 230. Occupancy was crucial to the explanation of both Grotius and Pufendorf for the emergence of private property. The following passage from Grotius illustrates the point: 'When property or ownership was invented, the law of property was established to imitate nature. For as that use began in connection with bodily needs, from which as we have said property first arose, so by similar connection it was decided that things were the property of individuals. This is called "occupation", a word most appropriate to those things which in former times had been held in common.' See H. Grotius, *Mare Liberum* (1608; R. Van Deman Magoffin (tr., New York, 1916), 25.

74 On the importance of property rights generally, see D.C. North and R.P. Thomas, *The Rise of the Western World: A New Economic History* (Cambridge, 1973).

75 R. Nozick, *Anarchy, State, and Utopia* (Oxford, 1974).

76 See W.S. Holdsworth, *A History of English Law* (2nd ed., 1937, London), vol. 6, 379. The same might be said of the United States where the US Supreme Court in *Wheaton* v. *Peters* 33 U.S. (8 Peters) 591 (1834) extinguished common law copyright.

77 On Locke's influence, see P. Larkin, *Property in the Eighteenth Century* (Dublin, Cork, 1930).

78 4 H.L.C. 815, 10 E.R. 681 at 729.

79 The right to freedom of trade is described by Yates J in *Millar* v. *Taylor* as a natural right. See 98 E.R. at 250. The *Case of Monopolies* discussed later in this chapter is also authority for this proposition. Examples of other cases which assert the fundamental nature of this principle are *The Case of the Tailors, &c. of Ipswich* (1614) 11 Co. Rep. 53a, 77 E.R. 1218 and *Norris* v. *Staps* (1616) 11 Co. Rep. 53a, 80 E.R. 357.

80 On the need to separate these interests, see L.R. Patterson, *Copyright in Historical Perspective* (Nashville, 1968).

81 *Jefferys* v. *Boosey* (1854) 4 H.L.C. 815, 10 E.R. 681 at 745.

82 For some attempts, see *Millar* v. *Taylor* 98 E.R. at 216 and 226.

83 'If Milton had not written *Paradise Lost* it would never have been written: if Watt had not discovered the use of high-pressure steam, someone else would have done so.' See Halsbury, *The Laws of England* (London, 1912), vol. 22, p. 127, para. 267.

84 W.S. Holdsworth, 'The Commons Debates 1621', 52 *Law Quarterly Review*, 481, 487 (1936).

85 An early case declaring the common law freedom of trade is *Davenant* v. *Hurdis* (1599) referred to in *The Case of Monopolies* 77 E.R. at 1263.

86 See *Nordenfelt* v. *Maxim Nordenfelt Guns and Ammunition Company* [1894] A.C. 535, per Lord Watson at 552; see also *Trego* v. *Hunt* [1896] A.C. 7, *per* Lord Macnaghten at 24.

87 See K. Boehm, *The British Patent System, I: Administration* (Cambridge at the University Press, 1967), 15.

88 (1602) 11 Co. Rep. 84b, 77 E.R. 1260. Also reported as *Darcy* v. *Allen* (1602) Noy 173, 74 E.R., 1131; *Darcy* v. *Allen* (1602) Moore K.B. 671, 72 E.R. 830.

89 See W.S. Holdsworth, *A History of English Law* (2nd ed., 1937, London), vol. 4, 349–353.

90 The submission of the Defendant's Counsel is reported in Noy, 173, 74 E.R. 1131.

91 See 77 E.R. at 1263.

92 Id.

93 74 E.R. at 1139.

94 For a clear statement of this, see *The Clothworkers of Ipswich Case* (1615) Godbolt, 252, 78 E.R. 147. For some of the training conditions that were imposed on early patents, see E.W. Hulme, 'The History of the Patent System under the Prerogative and at Common Law', 12 *Law Quarterly Review*, 141–154 (1896).

95 *The Clothworkers of Ipswich Case* (1615) Godbolt, 252, 78 E.R. 147.

96 A classical but general description of the impact of religious thought and ethics on commerce is R.H. Tawney, *Religion and the Rise of Capitalism* (West Drayton, Middlesex, 1938 ed.). See also D.J. Gerber, 'Prometheus Born: The High Middle Ages and the Relationship Between Law and Economic Conduct', 38 *Saint Louis University Law Journal*, 673, 720–725 (1994).

97 For an account, see R. De Roover, 'Monopoly Theory Prior to Adam Smith: A Revision', 65 *Quarterly Journal of Economics*, 492, 500 (1951).

98 74 E.R. at 1139.

99 Section 6.

100 W.R. Cornish, *Intellectual Property* (2nd ed., London, 1989), 67.

101 For a discussion of early US patent legislation see B.W. Bugbee, *Genesis of American Patent and Copyright Law* (Washington, D.C., 1967). In France the decrees of the Assemblée Nationale in 1791 concerning patents, while using the language of natural rights, required that the inventor's idea be useful and also limited the right to a specified period of time. See Bugbee at 153.

3 Locke, Labour and the Intellectual Commons

Does a person have a natural right of property in those abstract objects that she or he discovers or creates? The common law ultimately did not declare such a right. The answer to our question might still be a philosophical 'yes'. One philosopher, probably more than any other, has been linked with a natural rights theory of property. The influence on political philosophy of John Locke's short discussion of property in Chapter V, Book II of the *Two Treatises of Government* (1690) has been profound.[1] Locke on property has a totemic status. It is not surprising, therefore, that modern theorists discuss a 'Lockean labour theory' of intellectual property.[2]

The purpose of this chapter is to evaluate the application of Locke's writing on property to intellectual property. By way of preview, it is argued that labour has a comparatively minor, somewhat functional role in so-called 'labour theories of property' with which Locke is commonly linked. The real value of Locke's writing on property is that it shows us that the coherence or truth of an argument that relies on natural rights to justify intellectual property rights primarily depends on a concept of community and an accompanying metaphysical scheme. Appeals to labour in labour theories of property are essentially exhortations to keep certain metaphysical assumptions and a concept of community in place.

Locke is a philosopher who does not lack interpreters.[3] No attempt is made to add another interpretation or yet another version of a labour theory of property. The remainder of this chapter is divided into four sections. The first section offers a brief description of Locke's purposes and claims in Chapter V of the *Second Treatise*. Readers familiar with Locke will want to skip this section. The second section discusses some of the conflicting interpretations of his property theory. Sections 3 and 4 link these interpretations to intellectual property.

Locke's Purposes in 'Of Property'

Heretical though the suggestion seems, perhaps Locke does not have a theory of property. Chapter V of the *Second Treatise* is a short chapter. If there is a theory of property in any full-blown sense, it is sparsely presented. Locke begins the chapter by referring to a 'very great difficulty': if God gave the earth to 'Mankind in common', how can any individual have property in any thing?[4] The remainder of the chapter elaborates an answer to this question.

Chapter V plays a crucial supporting role in Locke's theory of Civil Government. The *Two Treatises*, it is well known, are an attack on absolutist monarchical government.[5] Locke attacks a specific argument for absolutist monarchy as presented by Robert Filmer in his *Patriarcha: or the Natural Power of Kings* (1680). Filmer had developed the idea that Adam had complete authority over the world, an authority that kings, being Adam's heirs, could claim. Locke opens the *Second Treatise* with the claim that he has shown Filmer's idea to be impossible. This leaves a problem. If the legitimacy of political power is not to be found in Adam's patriarchal heritage, where is it to be found? Of necessity, says Locke, we must find 'another rise of Government, another Original Political Power, and another way of designing and knowing the Persons that have it, than what Sir *Robert F.* hath taught us'.[6]

This then is the mission of the *Second Treatise*. How does Chapter V fit in? The answer lies in the problems which Filmer sets for natural law theorists and Locke's desire to use the framework of natural law for his theory of civil government. Filmer had charged natural law thinkers like Grotius with incoherence and inconsistency. How could natural law, which proclaimed the existence of a commons, lead to a state of private ownership? Did this not entail the mutability of the immutable? If the consent of all the commoners was required for individual acts of appropriation from the commons, how could this consent be obtained from *all* the commoners?

In order to show that Filmer's blows against natural law were not mortal, Locke was forced to construct an argument within natural law that showed that equality and the commons could coexist with individual apprcpriation and property rights.[7] Having done that, Locke could return to his principal task of providing a theory of government and the right to resistance. Locke's solution to the problem of the God-given commons and private appropriation starts with the assumption that 'every Man has a *Property* in his own *Person*'.[8] This assumption leads Locke to claim that an individual's labour also belongs to that individual. And in turn this produces the following condition of origination for property: 'Whatsoever then he removes out of the State that Nature hath provided, and left it in, he hath mixed his *Labour* with, and joyned to it something that is his own, and thereby makes it his *Property*.'[9]

Locke adds two further conditions. The first states that labour only originates a property right to the object to which it is joined 'where there is enough, and as good left in common for others'.[10] The second limit on acquisitiveness is derived by Locke from God's purposes. God made things for people to enjoy and not to spoil or destroy.[11] From this Locke deduces the following: 'As much as any one can make use of to any advantage of life before it spoils; so much he may by his labour fix a Property in.'[12] Locke recognized that this second condition would not serve, in a money economy, to limit large property holdings because men could, through the process of exchange, amass non-perishable wealth. There is more than a touch of unreality about this part of Locke's discussion. One could, according to Locke, acquire fabulous wealth through stocks and money but it was morally reprehensible to allow a bag of plums to go to waste. With breathtaking swiftness he glides over the connections between property, wealth, political and social power and the implications of this for a theory like his which claims that men are naturally equal and have a natural right to property. In Locke's defence it might be said that he does not seem to relish the introduction of money.[13]

For what reason does man acquire property rights through labour? The answer lies in God's purposes. God commanded men to labour so that they might enjoy the conveniences of life: food, shelter, clothes and a comfortable way of living.[14] Locke does not assume that all men will be interested in labouring; it was to the 'Industrious and Rational' that God had given the commons.[15] Labour was to function as a certificate of title. Locke thought that labour needed to be rewarded, for he characterizes labour in negative terms.[16] Summarized, Locke's core propositions are these:

1 God has given the world to people in common.
2 Every person has a property in his own person.
3 A person's labour belongs to him.
4 Whenever a person mixes his labour with something in the commons he thereby makes it his property.
5 The right of property is conditional upon a person leaving in the commons enough and as good for the other commoners.
6 A person cannot take more out of the commons than they can use to advantage.

Proposition 4 does not of itself provide a justification for property rights. Claiming that labour begins property still leaves the question of why labour rather than intention or possession should be the basis of property rights. Locke has several answers as to why labour should serve this role. The connection between labour and property exists by virtue of divine command, or natural law, or both. Locke suggests that property rights are a just reward for the industrious. He does not use the language of just deserts explicitly, although he does later talk of 'just *Property*'.[17] Locke also argues that the labour of individuals adds value to a product and confers a general social benefit. Using the example of land, he claims that the person who encloses ten acres and produces from them the same amount that can be obtained from 100 acres in the commons has increased the 'common stock of mankind'.[18] This argument begins to move in a utilitarian direction.[19]

Interpreting Locke

There are different interpretations of Locke on property. In the case of two well-known ones, those of Tully and Macpherson, the interpretive lines are so flatly contrary that the reader of both can ask whether the same text was being read. For Tully, Locke's philosophy represents 'a philosophy of religious praxis'.[20] It ultimately justifies, not the right of private property, but the commons. For Macpherson, Locke is one of capitalism's most faithful ideological servants. His service is to provide 'a moral foundation for bourgeois appropriation'.[21]

Perhaps the problem with Locke's text is that it encourages contrary interpretations. Monson, in a perceptive analysis of the philosophical scholarship on Locke, argues that the problem stems from the fact that Locke counterpoises so many basic concepts – obedience to state versus right to revolt, unlimited appropriation versus duty to preserve others, majority rule versus inalienability of consent – that almost any theory is derivable from the text.[22] If Monson is right, and the numerous interpretations of Locke's work suggest he may be, then Locke's text in all probability allows for a range of justificatory models of property, including intellectual property, to be built. Certainly those scholars seeking to build a Lockean justificatory theory of intellectual property have yet to discuss the hermeneutical free play of Locke's text and the strategic freedoms it offers interpreters and model builders.

The purpose here is to show that the load which labour can carry in a justificatory theory of intellectual property depends on two factors: a conception of community and the relation of that community to the intellectual commons. Although labour is frequently appealed to by judges in intellectual property matters, the metaphysical framework which gives the appeal its normative force is rarely brought out into the open. Similarly, when nation states argue that the international protection for intellectual property ought to be improved to protect the labour of their citizens, the appeal to labour is simply an indicator that a particular conception of community and the intellectual commons is being advanced. Under the cries of theft there is an agenda related to the metaphysics of community. In order to demonstrate these claims, we need to discuss Tully's and Macpherson's respective interpretations of Locke.

Tully's quest is for the theological Locke. The basis of Locke's theory of property is the special relationship between God and man. Tully labels this 'the workmanship model' and draws on the following passage from Locke for support:[23]

> For Men being all the Workmanship of one Omnipotent, and infinitely wise Maker; All the Servants of one Sovereign Master, sent into the World by his order and about his business, they are his Property, whose Workmanship they are, made to last during his, not one anothers Pleasure.

The notion of man doing God's business is crucial to the theological Locke. It allows him to argue that man has a definite purpose in the world and forms the basis of rights and obligations for man. By consulting reason man discovers that he has obligations in the state of nature. The first of these is that he is under a duty of self-preservation. This duty, says Tully, depends on the workmanship model: God made all men and as maker has the rights to which men have a corresponding duty, that of self-preservation and the preservation of others.[24] The right to property is deduced from the right of preservation and the right to engage in activities leading to preservation. Natural property rights to the items of subsistence are a necessary consequence of the natural rights of preservation.[25]

The existence of natural property rights poses a problem because they have to be consistent with the existence of an original common and an original community. Tully argues that the intellectual discourse in which Locke writes contains two versions of community and property. One version of property, articulated by Grotius, Filmer and Pufendorf, confines the meaning of property (*dominium*) to private property. Private property implies a right of exclusive possession. The world is given to people in common, but crucially 'in common' means that the world 'belongs originally to no one and is open to all'.[26] Property simply means the right of exclusive possession to the objects which people take from the commons. There is no right to be included in the commons, merely a right to control over what one takes from the commons. The conception of community which underpins this version of the commons and property is negative community.

Negative community has a historically prior opposite – positive community – the second version. Going back to Aquinas, the term *'dominium'* refers to exclusive possession. It is also used by Aquinas to refer to the capacity to use natural things for self-preservation. This 'use right' exists in relation to a commons which is owned by all, rather than a commons which is open to all to procure or appropriate. By Locke's time there is a clear choice to be made concerning property and the commons. Negative community is defined in terms of a commons belonging to no one, parts of which may be appropriated. Positive community is defined in terms of a common which belongs to all. All have a right to be included in the use of it. It is this positive, inclusive concept of property which Locke sets out to defend, according to Tully. The very great difficulty which Locke takes on by choosing to defend a concept of positive community is how individuals can make use of the commons without having to obtain the consent of all the commoners. Lack of consent to taking denotes robbery.

Locke's solution, Tully argues, is to 'redefine positive community'.[27] A person's inclusive right to the commons does not include a right to everything in the commons, but merely the right to be included in the commons for the purpose of exercising the natural rights of survival and subsistence. Property refers to the right to use the commons and those objects extracted from the commons – a usufructory right. Describing the means of extraction leads Locke into his famous discussion of how labour begins property. By using labour as the starting-point for property, Locke overcomes the problem of how individuals might be said to acquire property in objects from the commons without obtaining the consent of the rest of the commoners. Labour provides the individual commoners with a way of using the commons for their purposes.

On Tully's analysis of Locke, labour of itself does not produce a right of property. More controversially, Locke, according to Tully, provides a justification not of private property but of 'the English Common'.[28] The common is there to serve God's purposes for man and labour enables man to particularize the commons and realise God's purposes.[29]

Macpherson, on the other hand, discovers the capitalist Locke. Locke's 'astonishing achievement' is to derive from natural law a right of property while simultaneously removing those natural law conditions which traditionally qualify the exercise of that right. The result is an argument which supports unlimited appropriation. The spoilage limitation is overcome by the invention of money. By shifting from a system of barter to a currency system, men can hoard money without fear of infringing the spoilage limitation because money, unlike fruit, does not spoil. Furthermore, argues Macpherson, this capital formation is sanctioned by Locke within the state of nature, for the consent to the introduction of money takes place there. [30]

The sufficiency limitation, which requires men to leave enough and as good for others, is removed by Locke, in part, by arguing that it is taken care of by the introduction of money. Locke also argues that the appropriation of land in excess of this limit results in productivity gains which would not occur if the land were left unappropriated. Everyone, in short, is better off if the 'enough and as good' condition does not apply to land. The private ownership of land will deliver greater wealth to all, thereby ensuring men's natural right to subsistence.[31] Macpherson considers a third implied limitation: one can only appropriate that which one has personally laboured for. This, Macpherson suggests, does not count as a constraint for Locke because he assumes that persons can acquire property through the labour of their servants.[32] The property-conferring nature of labour can be transferred to others for wages.

For Macpherson, Locke seems something of an evil genius. Starting from the assumptions of the natural law tradition, Locke produces a justification for unlimited capitalist appropriation. There is no hint in Locke that labour and its products is in some broader sense a joint enterprise between the individual and the society in which he labours. For the capitalist Locke, individuals labour under a law of appropriation that is not qualified by those traditional obligations of preservation that the Thomist tradition ascribed to property owners in a positive community.

Both Tully's and Macpherson's discussions reveal that the commons is a normatively loaded construct. Depending on the set of initial conditions that are specified for it, very different explanations and justifications for the beginnings of private property can be developed. Tully's discussion suggests that within 17th-century political discourse the choice of community in relation to the commons was, at the most fundamental level, one between positive and negative community. This same choice, we shall see, faces those who argue for various arrangements of intellectual property.

Locke on Intellectual Property

When he wrote on property, Locke probably did not have intellectual property in mind. It was the ownership of physical rather than abstract objects that occupied his attention. In any case, as we have briefly tried to show, his writing on property was part of a wider philosophical agenda on the nature of government. Despite the very different historical context in which his views on property were formed, those thinking about intellectual property have made use of his work. Generally speaking, people who use Locke's theory tend to concentrate on labour and the mixing metaphor. To a large extent this focus on labour is misplaced. Labour is either too indeterminate or too incomplete a basis on which to base a justification of property. It may work reasonably well in some cases, for example making a dolls house or growing a crop, but its usefulness runs out with forms of work that are characterized by the presence of many interdependent relations (the design of a computer program or building a skyscraper).

Labour does not, for instance, have a dominant role in the discussion of the origin of property rights to be found in Grotius or in that of Pufendorf. Labour has a role in both, of course, but this role is crucially dependent upon a metaphysic of community. Pufendorf, more clearly than Grotius, depicts the original community as negative and then proceeds to argue that, when men left this 'original negative community of things', they 'by a pact established separate dominions over things, not indeed, all at once and for all time, but successively, and as the state of things, or the nature and number of men seemed to require'.[33] It is also true for Grotius that the emergence of private property is based on agreement and a metaphysic of community.[34] Labour is not the dominant category of explanation in Grotius' explanation of the beginnings of private property. Similarly, it is somewhat misleading to depict Locke as a labour theorist of property.[35] This is too simple a view of the natural law tradition in which Locke worked.

The desire to link a theory of intellectual property back to Locke probably has much to do with reasons of ideological legitimacy. Locke remains a powerful totem. The remainder of this section illustrates how one can generate different 'Lockean' theories of intellectual property by utilizing different parts of Locke's conceptual legacy. Theories which claim to be Lockean usually do so because of the use they make of the mixing metaphor and the fact that the property rights they establish are not dependent for their existence upon positive law.

By concentrating on Locke's mixing metaphor and at the same time ignoring the religious metaphysical scheme which Locke uses to give the metaphor a more precise meaning, one can derive a strong justificatory theory of intellectual property. 'Strong' is used to refer to the extensional reach of the theory. Very few abstract objects, if any, would escape individual ownership. In outline an argument for such a theory would have the following form. A strong justificatory theory would have to ignore a possible distinction between those abstract objects which are creations (for instance, the Mutant Ninja Turtles, Bilbo the hobbit and Sherlock Holmes) and those abstract objects which exist independently of us and are discovered (electrons, quarks and large primary numbers are all candidates for this category).[36] We might call this a distinction between real and invented abstract objects. It gives rise to many metaphysical issues which we set aside. Creation and invention in a strong justificatory theory would be subsumed under the general category of intellectual labour. One possible direction in which such a theory could go is to claim that there is no such thing as the intellectual commons. Abstract objects, whether discovered or created, are always the product of individual intellectual labour and, therefore, the property of the intellectual worker responsible for their generation. Intellectual property legislation that sets limits on the private ownership of such objects invades the natural right of the owner. The crucial step in this argument is the assumption that there is no intellectual commons. Locke's analysis of property starts with the existence of the commons. It is God's gift. The challenge Locke faces is to explain the shift from the earthly commons to private property. If, as is possible, there is no equivalent of the earthly commons for abstract objects, building a case for the ownership of such objects becomes easier. The challenge under a strong Lockean labour theory of intellectual property is to justify how such objects could ever be part of an intellectual commons, that is, the shift from private property to the commons. The challenge comes about because, while acts of individual labour allow the commoners to demarcate a part of the physical commons which they need for their survival, acts of labour that relate to abstract objects potentially prevent the emergence of an intellectual commons. Labour, once joined to the abstract object, allows an individual to bar its journey to an intellectual commons. Putting it another way, it prevents the creation of a common pool of these objects.

Alternatively, the strong theory might concede that there is an intellectual commons and define it as the set of discoverable abstract objects (and therefore unowned objects). On the strong theory such objects could be annexed by individual labour. They could not be removed or taken from the commons in the way that physical objects can be. Rather, a person would through an act of intellectual labour identify such objects and through that act of identification acquire property in them.

As in the case of the removal of physical objects from the earthly commons, Locke's two provisos, the sufficiency limitation and the spoilage limitation, apply to regulate the removal of abstract objects from the intellectual commons. When the sufficiency limitation is applied literally to physical objects it has the consequence that no objects may be removed from the commons. Any disturbance of the commons means that a condition requiring enough *and* as good be left for others cannot be strictly satisfied.[37] But perhaps the provisos do not apply with such severity to abstract objects. A piece of fruit may spoil but a formula, by its abstract nature, cannot. The 'enough and as good' requirement might also be satisfied. Abstract objects are not consumed in use. In one sense they never leave the intellectual commons. In addition, abstract objects seem to exist in large numbers. The nature of the molecular world, for example, seems to be such that the synthesis of one perfume leaves other manufacturers with lots of other possibilities. If the world of abstract objects is a more or less infinite set of equivalents then it follows under the strong theory we have been discussing that any given appropriation by an individual of an abstract object would be allowed.

Potentially this justificatory line of argument has radical implications for existing intellectual property regimes. It suggests that a much larger scale of appropriation of the intellectual commons is justifiable. Typically, intellectual property regimes have not included ideas and discoveries as objects of property rights. There would, in principle, be no reason why the basic ideas of science, for example the second law of thermodynamics, could not be owned by those who laboured to produce them. Similarly, copyright has traditionally not protected ideas. But on a strong justificatory natural rights model of intellectual property there would be no reason in principle why originators of ideas could not claim copyright protection for them.

A social system that operated with a strong labour-based natural property rights view of intellectual property could be expected to concentrate heavily on the propertization and appropriation of the intellectual commons. Courts in such a social system could be expected to concentrate solely on the presence or absence of labour when considering the issue of property in abstract objects. Similarly, legislatures could be expected to recognize many new forms of intellectual property. The task of positive intellectual property law would be to secure the labour-based pre-legal rights of individuals.

The persuasiveness of the strong natural rights theory of intellectual property depends on a number of assumptions. One central assumption is that abstract objects are, or can be, the product of labour.[38] One counter to this, although an implausible one for materialists, is to run a supernaturalist argument in relation to abstract objects. Abstract objects, it might be said, have an external source like God, spirits or a platonic heaven and do not therefore involve individual persons in work. On this view people are the passive recipients of ideas and do not labour for them. Needless to say that the metaphysical nature of this counter would itself be highly controversial.

There are less controversial ways in which to problematize the strong argument for property rights in abstract objects. The strong form assumes that Locke's sufficiency and spoilage provisos do not apply to abstract objects. Is this true? Might not ideas (one form of abstract object) spoil? As abstract objects ideas cannot spoil, but the opportunities that they confer may. Ideas for the improvements to the catapult were only of use while the catapult remained a weapon of siege. Perhaps ideas can spoil in the sense that, once appropriated, their time span of useful application in many cases is limited. Those who appropriate ideas with a view to doing nothing with them arguably infringe Locke's spoilage proviso.

There are circumstances in which the sufficiency limitation might also apply to limit any natural right in abstract objects. Assume that it is true that the stock of abstract objects is infinite and that it consists of many abstract objects of comparable utility. Can the sufficiency limitation operate in this case? One reason for thinking that it can is this: even where the stock of abstract objects is infinite, the human capacity to exploit that stock at any given moment is conditioned by the state of cultural and scientific knowledge which exists at that historical moment. Human capabilities set limits on the abstract objects that may possibly be exploited. The set of usable abstract objects may also be further reduced because some ideas or knowledge may be necessary gateways to others. Non-Euclidean geometries, for instance, were essential to the breakthroughs in theoretical physics in the 20th century. Contrary to the view that societies are awash with information, it may be that, at various points in history, societies may face a shortage of supply of abstract objects. Under such conditions of shortage, those who claim property rights in abstract objects may well fail to leave enough and as good for others.

There are other problems with the strong justificatory form for intellectual property. The connection it posits between labour and the object of the property right is not straightforward. Can labour precisely designate the object of the right it is meant to begin? Nozick, in a somewhat teasing fashion, raises an aspect of this problem when he asks whether, by mixing my tomato juice with the ocean, I can claim property rights in the ocean. There is a serious problem here. If labour is to form the basis of a natural property right there must be some way in which to demarcate precisely the object of the property right. Locke's two provisos, the spoilage proviso and the sufficiency proviso, do not necessarily help here, for they operate primarily to set limits on the extension of property rights to objects. But what is it that defines the boundaries of the object of property? Labour creates the property right, but what identifies the object of that property right? This issue does not arise in a central way for Locke since his examples of objects of property, such as game or acorns, suggest to the reader that objects have natural boundaries. The issue of boundaries does arise for Grotius when he discusses whether the sea can be privately owned. Private ownership could take place through occupation, but only objects with definite limits could be occupied.[39] The sea, like the air, could not be occupied.[40] Therefore it was not capable of private ownership. Both Grotius and Pufendorf spend time discussing the link between occupation and the physical object of occupation. They are clearly aware that, even in the case of physical objects, the action of labour needs to be supplemented by custom and convention in order to settle the object of occupation. They do not, of course, discuss the fanciful examples put forward by Nozick. This is hardly surprising since the existence of boundaries is to a large extent dependent on shared understandings and conventions. No one in the natural law tradition would seriously have contended that one could own a planet by clearing a space on it. This, amongst other things, would have seemed, on the face of it, inconsistent with God's purposes.

If a labour theory of property has problems in accounting for the boundaries of physical objects, those problems are magnified when it comes to abstract objects. In Chapter 7 we will see that the problem is a severe one. Abstract objects have the potential to reside in one physical object or many. Their extension to the physical world depends on their definition. A literary archetype (an abstract object) is potentially 'seen' in many individual works. The action of writing begins an abstract object. But how does one limit the proprietary scope of that abstract object? The action of labour does not of itself provide the answer, for it simply begins the process. Within the natural law tradition the answer was largely provided by a religious metaphysical scheme. A labour theory of property, if it is to provide an answer as to how abstract objects might be limited and defined, has to start by adopting some metaphysical scheme in order to avoid labour becoming a major source of indeterminacy within the theory itself.

Taking a strong labour theory of property rights seriously may, paradoxically, threaten the legitimacy of individual property holdings. In a market society the value of objects one has produced is set by the subjective demand of others in the market.[41] How can labour ground a natural right to market value if that value is determined not by individual labour but by the demand activity of others? If the right relates, not to the value but to the object, the boundary problems mentioned in the previous paragraph arise. Concentrating on the labour of individuals might extinguish the possibility of private ownership of abstract objects altogether. Within an interdependent, differentiated society the labour of any one individual is made possible by the labour of others. If we define a direct contribution of labour in terms of a contribution that enables the production of an abstract object, this forces a recognition of the fact that many ostensibly individually owned abstract objects are in reality collectively owned by virtue of joint labour. It is perhaps because a full acknowledgment of the labour of others has such profound implications for the possibility of private ownership that Grotius and Pufendorf were careful to emphasize, in their accounts of the origins of private property, the role of agreement and convention. Property in their theories has a strong conventional element. In Pufendorf's words, 'the proprietorship of things has resulted immediately from the convention of men, either tacit or express'.[42]

So far our criticisms have been aimed at a strong justificatory form of the labour theory of property. This is not the only kind of theory of intellectual property that might be extracted from Locke's text. On one view of Locke the role of labour in the formation of private property is confined to that period of the state of nature where there is abundance. Olivecrona takes this line, arguing that the 'age of abundance' comes to an end because of population pressures and the introduction of money.[43] In the age of scarcity distinct communities exist and the distribution of property becomes primarily conventional, settled '*by Compact* and Agreement', to use Locke's words.[44] Positive law and convention, informed by utilitarian considerations, determine the shape of property law. Intellectual property laws would on this approach be positive laws justified by utility and designed to serve the goal of maximizing welfare of the community in question.

The strong form of the labour theory of intellectual property is consistent with modern theories that portray rights as pre-social entities. This emphasis on the independence and naturalness of rights is to be found in Nozick's theory of state and rights. For Nozick, the state is an invention, but individual rights are not, or at least they are not an invention of the state. Rather, they set limits on the kind of state we are justified in inventing. For Nozick the primary task of the state is to secure individual property rights rather than interfere with them. The implications of this kind of theoretical approach for the reform of intellectual property are radical. One might be led to the conclusion that intellectual property rights should be held by individuals in perpetuity: where legislatures limit the duration of intellectual property rights or enact compulsory licensing provisions, as they do in the case of patents and copyright, they commit theft.

Modern supporters of natural property rights tend to play down the historical tradition on which they rely, because this tradition does not establish the sanctity of property rights. They remain a regulatory phenomenon. Locke states that governments have the power to regulate property.[45] This power has to be exercised consistently with the goals of natural law, but at the same time governments have, when making regulatory decisions, leeways of choice.[46] There is also enough evidence to suggest, Macpherson's interpretation notwithstanding, that Locke's right of property is primarily an instrumental right. It is deduced from the rights to life and self-preservation and is 'always subordinate to the latter'.[47] This then clearly allows for the possibility that the natural right of property may be modified by positive law, provided always that any such law itself remains consistent with natural law.

Ultimately, looking to Locke as the theoretical fountainhead of a strong labour theory of intellectual property is not sustainable. Locke's mixing metaphor, once it is stripped of its metaphysical context, generates too many indeterminacies and problems to provide a justification for intellectual property. The lesson from Locke on property is that we should take the metaphysical context of labour theories of property and their accompanying schemes of community seriously. Labour should not hold centre stage.

Community and the Intellectual Commons

The Intellectual Commons

There are probably a variety of metaphysical schemes which might be used to support a theory of property. There is less choice when it comes to offering a generic characterization of community. Essentially the choice is the same one that faced Grotius, Pufendorf and Locke. This is a choice between negative and positive community. What follows is an analysis of the relationship between these two conceptions of community and the intellectual commons. A final opening remark: we have seen that some of the elements of Locke's property theory might be used to advance the conclusion that there should be no intellectual commons. There are, we have seen, problems with this extreme conclusion, problems of indeterminacy based on the nature of labour. Without further argument we shall assume that some version of the intellectual commons will be necessary to a theory of intellectual property.

How might we describe the intellectual commons? One way in which to think about it is to say that it consists of that part of the objective world of knowledge which is not subject to any of the following: property rights or some other conventional bar (contract, for instance); technological bars (for example, encryption) or a physical bar (hidden manuscripts). Our definition emphasizes the idea that the intellectual commons is an independently existing resource which is open to use. Open to use does not mean, however, that abstract objects in the intellectual commons are necessarily accessible. Moreover the fact that an abstract object is not in the intellectual commons and therefore not open to use does not mean that it is inaccessible. Some examples are needed to illustrate.

The Tale of Genji was completed probably by the first quarter of the 11th century in Japan. By now it is part of the intellectual commons. While this tale remained in Japanese it was accessible, at least on one level, only to those who could read Japanese. Much of modern theoretical physics is open to use (that is, in the intellectual commons) but is accessible to only a small number. Hieroglyphics, while part of the intellectual commons, might at some point in its history have been accessible by no one. Accessibility to the intellectual commons depends on a commoner having the relevant capability and competence (for example, to be able to read and understand Japanese). The openness to use of an abstract object depends on its subsisting in the intellectual commons. Intellectual property rights can take an abstract object out of the intellectual commons, but this does not mean that it becomes inaccessible. Competent and capable persons can still gain access to the object provided they pay the relevant licence fee. Intellectual property rights place restrictions on the use of an abstract object, but this is a separate matter from the accessibility of the object to agents. This, as we have said, relates to the agent's capacities and competencies.

Our characterization of the intellectual commons makes use of the idea of an objective world of knowledge. This at best would seem quaint to a post-modernist and in any case it seems to suggest that abstract objects exist. Actually the use of objective knowledge can be consistent with the claim that abstract objects only subsist. The objective world of knowledge is a concept developed by Karl Popper as part of his epistemological project.[48] Popper divides the world into world one, world two and world three: world one is the physical world; world two is the world of our conscious experience; world three is the world of objective knowledge and this equals the logical contents of books, libraries, computer memories and so on. *Objective knowledge* for Popper simply means that truths about this world are independent of our subjective preferences. World three remains a human construction. Language provides a useful illustration of these two points. Humans invent language. Having invented it, certain truths about language hold independently of their wishes. I may want it to be the case that all languages have a subject predicate structure but the truth of the matter is independent of my desires. Abstract objects have their place in world three. Clearly different ontological accounts can be given of them. Their objective status does not settle their metaphysical status.

The intellectual commons, then, consists of those abstract objects which remain open to use. It is a resource which by its nature is inexhaustible but not necessarily accessible. So far the intellectual commons has been portrayed as a global entity constructed by the collective labours of all humanity over all time. One implication which might be readily drawn from this model of the intellectual commons is that it is a resource open to use by all. This is by no means the only way in which the intellectual commons can be presented. Seeing the other possibilities is helped by a comparison with the common in English law.

The commons is a distinctive legal concept within English property law.[49] By Locke's time the commons in English law already had a complex legal form. When Locke speaks of the common it is this legal conception that he has in mind.[50] The commons refers to rights of common held by persons in relation to another's land.[51] These rights include rights of pasture, rights of digging turf (common of turbary) and rights of fishing (common of piscary). Rights of common are confined to specific groups such as the inhabitants of a village or a manor or town. Most importantly for our purposes, the concept of common does not refer to the public ownership of land. Common land is land that is already owned by a person against whom the commoners have rights.[52] Those who have rights of common have a right of access to the commons for those purposes connected with the exercise of their rights; there is no general right of access by commoners and no general right of access by members of the public.[53] The concept of the commons in English law is a deeply territorial, group-specific one. It does not refer to something to which all humanity has rights of entry or even something to which all the citizens of one state have entry.

Rights of entry to the intellectual commons can also be limited to some group smaller than all of humanity. Some countries might lay claim to a distinctive intellectual commons which their citizens have, over time, generated. The cultural intellectual commons is something which is often linked to a specific group, this group being defined by reference to a criterion such as race or territory. Within the context of international law at least, the idea of a distinct international cultural heritage has only embryonic beginnings.[54] The idea that there are objects that belong in a global cultural commons is an idea which has been discussed, but has in no way replaced the belief that the cultural commons is predominantly national or regional.[55] Just as countries recognize and protect their cultural commons, so they may lay claim to the existence of a distinctly territorial scientific/technological commons which is open only to those who are related to the territory or group. The belief in a territorial scientific commons may help to explain the reluctance of western countries to concede to developing countries the claim that technology is the common heritage of mankind.[56] Yet at the same time there is no doubt that some technology is now the common heritage of mankind.

The scope of the intellectual commons, we have seen, can be narrowed by being linked to the activities of different kinds of groups. The intellectual commons can be divided up in different ways according to place, time and content. There can also be different assumptions about the nature of community in the intellectual commons. At a fundamental level the decision comes down to a decision between positive and negative community. This decision, we shall see, has direct implications for the content and scope of intellectual property laws.

Four Types of Community

The purpose here is to show the different choices to be made concerning positive and negative community and the implications of this for intellectual property, particularly its scope of appropriation. As part of this exercise we shall be drawing on Pufendorf in order to illustrate the analytical possibilities implicit in positive and negative community. The use of Pufendorf, though, is not part of an exegetical venture and should not be taken as such. Finally it needs to be remembered that for Pufendorf, Grotius and Locke the challenge is to explain the origins of private property in a world in which things begin their existence in common. Our purpose is different. It is to show that the evolutionary possibilities of intellectual property law depend heavily on how one models the relationship between the intellectual commons and community.

Pufendorf, unlike Grotius, spends time discussing the distinction between positive and negative community. In one passage he describes negative community as a 'community of all things' in which 'all things lay open to all men, and belonged no more to one than to another'.[57] Negative community is a state in which things are open to anybody to make the subject of exclusive belonging. Air, for example, can be captured, compressed and bottled. By contrast positive community is a state in which things (for example, land or a fishing ground) are jointly owned by some group. In positive community there are joint rather than individual owners of common things. Pufendorf, in describing the difference, says that common things in positive community 'differ from things owned, only in the respect that the latter belong to one person while the former belong to several in the same manner'.[58]

Positive community is for Pufendorf clearly a product of consent. It is not the state in which people found themselves. Rather it was created by people to suit their purposes. 'And so things were created neither proper nor common (in positive community) by any express command of God, but these distinctions were later created by men as the peace of human society demanded.'[59] Pufendorf's discussion of positive community shows that it does not include all in the ownership of things but only 'those for whom the thing is said to be common'.[60] Positive community for Pufendorf is an exclusive state. It excludes those who are not part of the ownership agreement. In the case of negative community the position is different. There is no ownership agreement in place. No one is excluded by virtue of an agreement and so acquiring the ownership of something is open to all. Once acts of ownership take place in negative community, it too becomes exclusionary in nature. But at least in the beginning we might see it as an inclusive form of community, for ownership is open to all.[61]

Taking Pufendorf's distinction between negative and positive community and then applying the inclusive/exclusive distinction to both produces a matrix of four basic types of community: inclusive positive community, exclusive positive community, inclusive negative community and exclusive negative community. These four types of community have the following stipulative meanings assigned to them.

Inclusive positive community represents a broad vision of human community, for it includes all humans; that is, there is only one group.[62] Inclusive positive community is a global vision of community in which all have the right to use the commons for their individual welfare.[63] The commons acts as a kind of global resource which belongs to all to use. This form of community is perfectly consistent with individuals holding private property. Under conditions of inclusive positive community all individuals have a right to use the commons as a resource and may generate property rights in those things made by using the resources of the commons.[64] The commons itself does not fall into appropriation, for that would be to destroy it as a resource for all.

Exclusive positive community is the ownership of things in the commons by a group of some kind; that is, a group smaller than all of humanity. Those who are not part of the ownership group are necessarily excluded.

Inclusive negative community, like inclusive positive community, encompasses all individuals. It is, following Pufendorf, a community in which the acquisition of things lies open to all. The principal difference between it and inclusive positive community is that, in the case of the former, the commons does not belong to anyone. But anyone may capture and own a part of it.

Exclusive negative community represents some subset of inclusive negative community. The ownership of things in the commons is open to all the members of some group, rather than just all.

There are many forms of community. It seems the worst kind of reductionism to posit four types. But our claim is not this. There are as many kinds of community as there are moral traditions, shared understandings and ways of life. Different communities also make very different normative and legal arrangements for the distribution and use of property. However all communities have to make decisions about the scope of the commons and the relationship of those in the community to the commons. Our four basic types of community represent alternative models of the way that relationship might be constructed. The existence of these four models is perfectly consistent with the existence of many communities, all differing in the detail of their moral and property norms. Two communities, for instance, might both adopt a model of an inclusive negative community, but have very different views on what may be taken out of the commons. The fact that in negative community things lie open to all does not necessarily mean that all things are open to ownership.[65] Furthermore, as we saw earlier, the intellectual commons itself may have different boundaries drawn around it, based on content, time and place. So, for example, the intellectual commons might be limited to the culture of a particular people, or a place such as North America, and this form of the intellectual commons might be linked to exclusive positive community.

When it comes to the regulation of the commons, all property regimes are underpinned by some version of one of the four basic types of community we have identified. Which model serves any given property regime is a question of fact. Pufendorf, for instance, makes it clear that the original community was negative and that this is a matter of fact, not moral argument.[66] Humans are free to change this arrangement provided always that whatever they choose is consistent with natural law.

Our analysis of the commons and community then raises two separate questions. Which vision of community drives the property arrangements for the intellectual commons? Are there moral arguments for preferring one type of community over another when it comes to making decisions about the relationship between community and the intellectual commons? The first question is primarily a question of fact. The intellectual commons is a resource, a resource which consists of abstract objects. Every community has to make decisions about the use of this resource. There is no escaping this. Decisions about who is to have rights of access and use of the intellectual commons are decisions that are constitutive of community.

The second question we posed is moral in kind. Are there reasons to choose one kind of community rather than another when it comes to making regulative arrangements in relation to the intellectual commons? Answering the second question is going to be difficult outside the context of any given community, its goals and predicaments. This is not to say that there are no philosophical methods for generating an *a priori*, context-independent answer as to which model of community and commons is morally desirable. One might use, as John Rawls does in his analysis of justice, a combination of ideal theory and abstract contractarianism, in order to arrive at some universal answer. Another route to a universal answer might be through the method of dialectical reasoning employed by Plato. Choosing either one of these methods would involve us in a debate with their communitarian critics.

Another way of approaching our second question is to ask whether there are any philosophically grounded reasons for thinking that one vision of community is preferable to another when it comes to decisions about property that involve the use of the intellectual commons. This approach does not aspire to demonstrate a philosophical truth, but rather seeks to build a philosophical case for a position by providing reasons for thinking it to be correct. At the same it remains open to the possibility that the philosophical case may be rebutted by experience. But, equally, experience may help to show that the philosophically grounded case is correct.

Our question, then, is whether there are reasons to favour one of the models of community we have identified when it comes to making decisions about the relationship between community and the intellectual commons. One assumption we make without defending it is that communities have an interest in encouraging the creativity of their members. A way to proceed to an answer is to come to some understanding of the role that the intellectual commons has in aiding creativity of all kinds. If, as we shall suggest, the intellectual commons has a vital role to play in the creative process then one way in which to decide amongst the various basic types of community is to ask which one best serves to cultivate an intellectual commons. Of course it may be that the intellectual commons does not just serve to promote creativity, but also has a more general role in the economic survival and evolution of communities. In other words there may be more reasons than just the encouragement of creativity to maintain the intellectual commons as an open resource. The next section confines itself to a discussion of the link between creativity and the intellectual commons.

Creativity and the Intellectual Commons

The link between the commons and creativity is not to be found in Locke. Tully claims that Locke has a view of man as a maker of things, but he then goes on to say that Locke was seeking to emphasize man's creative achievements.[67] This is probably a mistake on Tully's part because the concept of creativity does not gain wide currency until the

20th century. It does not appear as a fully fledged notion until the Romantic movement of the 18th century.[68] Until that period man's status was that of labourer while the role of creator is exclusively occupied by God. According to Locke, the clear implication is that men are workers and labourers in the commons, rather than creators. With Marx, as we shall see in Chapter 5, the creativity of humans is fully recognized, but the full expression of that creativity only occurs outside of private property rights and capitalism.

One problem is that the concept of creativity has for a long time been the province of psychology rather than philosophy. It may be a concept that is not responsive to philosophical treatment.[69] On one view creativity is simply a psychological phenomenon best consigned to the philosopher's category of the context of discovery. This seems too limited a view. And, in any case, the philosophical work on the importance of tradition in the context of the philosophy of science suggests that it may be possible to develop a coherent philosophical account of creativity.[70]

One common view of creativity is to see it as a highly individual process or act. This view, if analysed, would have for its ontological base some version of individualism. Roughly this is the idea that the dominant forces in social life are individuals and their decisions, rather than groups, forces of history, institutions and so on.[71] Linked to this ontology is a standard view of the nature of individuals which emphasizes their rationality and independence. Individuals are whole and they extend themselves in various ways to make up parts of social life. On this view creative acts would be the expressive acts of individuals following their own interests. On the other hand, one can also completely subordinate the individual in an analysis of creativity. Such an analysis is conditional upon denying individuals their ontological primacy. Individuals in a sense become derivative creatures, dependent for their make-up upon various collectivities and impersonal forces. Individuals still create, but their role becomes that of a conduit for some greater whole.

Neither view of the ontology of creativity is particularly attractive. It is incomplete at best to say that creativity is exclusively an individual act or alternatively that it is the manifestation of greater forces outside of the individual. The first view ignores the importance of tradition. Creativity is tied to tradition. Authors, composers, musicians and scientists move in traditions and cultures which they react to or against. Equally a story about creativity which sees it as an outcome of tradition or other social forces ignores the capacity of individuals to step outside of social norms. Creative individuals are in one respect rule breakers. They develop ways of looking at the world that have no immediately recognizable fit with the pre-existing norms or ways of thinking in a given area. A better way of thinking about creativity is to say that it involves individuals in dual and contrary roles. When the act of creation is complete, the individual steps forward to claim the role of inventor, pioneer, innovator, genius and so on. Yet the link between tradition and creativity suggests that, in the creative process, individuals play out another role, that of the borrower and copier. When intellectual property rights are claimed, right holders often lose sight of the duality of roles they have occupied, preferring to think of themselves exclusively in terms of creator and demanding protection against other borrowers and copiers. Intellectual property law, because of its focus on individual ownership, helps in fact to embed an individualistic notion of creativity.

This sketch of creativity assumes a different ontology from the two just described. It endorses some version of individualism, for it recognizes an autonomous capacity of individuals to create. But it also implies that individuals only reach this capacity with the help of others, for in the role of borrower the creator sits at the table of others. The ontology which best fits with this view of creativity is the one that Philip Pettit develops and defends under the distinctive label of holistic individualism.[72] Roughly his argument is that social ontology has two axes. The vertical is concerned with the extent to which individuals are patterned social objects, patterned from above by structures, forces and so on. The horizontal axis is concerned with the extent to which individual capacity depends on interaction with others. Pettit defends one form of individualism on the vertical axis and holism on the horizontal axis. This ontology fits neatly with our view of creativity and so we will adopt it for our ontological base. It helps to provide the analytical justification for our claim that creators are involved in dual and contrary roles.

As we have seen, individuals engaged in the creative process need the interaction of others. The presence of others can manifest itself in various ways. It can be a personal presence or a notional presence in the form of the creator accessing the works of other individuals. Presence can also take a diffuse form as it does in the case when individuals work in ways which have been determined by tradition. The intellectual commons has a vital role in the interactive process. It consists of abstract objects embodied by others in works, works which individuals draw upon in the process of creating their own. Abstract objects are the beliefs, arguments and theories of others. They are, as it were, the disembodied presence of others. By its nature the commons is an inexhaustible resource which grows richer in content through use. Its influence is hard to map in some straight-line fashion.

The kinds of arrangements which are made to regulate the access of individuals to the commons would affect creativity in different ways. Restricting access to the commons would probably have a negative impact on creativity, at least for those individuals denied access. The general argument we have developed makes this a plausible claim. Ultimately, though, assessing the truth of this claim is a matter of experience over time. We can deepen the plausibility of our claim by means of an example drawn from the history of science. The dominant motif in much of the scholarship in this area has been that the fate of scientific theories is heavily affected by social and cultural factors.[73]

Some history of science is deeply suggestive of the possibility that even temporary bars to the intellectual commons might have adverse long-term effects on scientific understanding and creativity. Goldberg's comparative study of the response to, and spread of, the theory of relativity in four different countries illustrates how different social structures caused vast differences in the understanding and spread of the theory. In Germany between 1905 and 1911, relativity became a focal point of discussion because of the combative and competitive nature of German academic scientific life, as well as the migratory behaviour of its academicians. No one university was able to dominate scholarly discussion for any length of time and the comparative free flow of information and ideas within an intellectually competitive environment ensured a variety of critical responses. This variety was in the case of Germany the reason for the eventual acceptance of the theory of relativity.[74] The French response to relativity in the same period came in the form of a superior silence. The reason lay in an institutional arrangement which made it possible for one man, Poincaré, to dominate thought about the theory.[75]

Although Goldberg is centrally interested in the diffusion of relativity theory, his work suggests, on the assumption that variety of response in a given field is a key indicator of creativity at work, that a strong link exists between scientific creativity and institutional structures that promote the communication of scientific ideas. Such a claim is also consistent with those analyses of creativity which see its essence lying in the act of cross-fertilization or recombination of different frames of reference, ideas and theories.[76] Without access or with only limited access to ideas, creativity in the form of cross-fertilization is not likely to flourish. One might extrapolate from this kind of work that creativity in science especially might be dramatically affected by choices about the structure of the intellectual commons in which science is to work.

A summary of the point we have arrived at is this. The intellectual commons is crucial to creativity. We can depict it as a resource. It is much more than this, but that is another matter. It is an unusual resource in that it grows in strength through use and exploitation. In other words, as the contents of the world of unpropertized *objective knowledge* (abstract objects) expand that world becomes more valuable for problem solving. Experimenters, whether they are artists or scientists, have more abstract objects that are open to use. Progress with the solution of complex, polycentric tasks improves.

If this is right, there are at least two objectives a society should consider when it comes to considering arrangements for the intellectual commons. First, the existing intellectual commons should not be depleted. More rather than less abstract objects should remain open to use. (The question of access, we have noted, is a separate matter.) This suggests the existence of preservationist duties with respect to the commons. Second, the intellectual commons should continue to be enlarged. More rather than less abstract objects should be added to it. This suggests that duties of nurture relate to the intellectual commons.

The next stage of the argument suggests how we might proceed in making decisions about community and the intellectual commons. The point has already been made that there is not likely to be a satisfactory universal answer to this question.

Choosing Community and Common

One way in which to decide about the appropriate property arrangement for the intellectual commons is on the basis of self-interest. Self-interest forms the basis of certain kinds of ethical theory. It also is a central assumption of rational choice explanations of individual behaviour and the social patterns that such behaviour causes. In the past, self-interest seems to have been at play when agents have had to choose negative or positive community. The history of certain resources under international law and the evolution of the common heritage of mankind principle in international law are both instructive in this respect. When Grotius, a defender of negative community, argued for the principle of freedom of the seas, 'he provided a useful ideology for competition over material resources in the non-European world'.[77] Grotius' *Mare Liberum*, which articulates the principle of freedom of the seas, was, we know, a legal brief composed to justify the capture of a Portuguese galleon by a vessel of the Dutch East India Company.[78] Debates over the concept of community to govern use of various resources still continue to be heavily influenced by perceptions of economic self-interest. The deep sea-bed, for instance, is a natural resource. Amongst other things it contains mineral deposits. Over the years the status of this resource in international law has been the subject of considerable debate.[79] Clearly those countries like the United States which have the technological capacity to exploit the sea-bed have a great deal to gain from the legal implementation of a regime for the sea-bed which sees it as part of the commons in the context of negative community. Under such a regime all states would have the rights of commoners to appropriate the resources of the sea-bed but only some would be capable of exercising those rights. Those agents who are not integrated into negative community, in that they lack capacity to exploit it, are left with the effort of arguing for a share of the proceeds of the commons on the basis of some distributivist principle, or alternatively depending on some principle of charity. The inclusiveness of individual agents in the negative commons and community only relates to the existence of rights of use or appropriation which all are said to have. This inclusiveness does not extend to making one a part-owner of the commons.

It is hardly surprising that developing countries that lack the industrial power to exploit natural resources like the sea-bed have argued that positive forms of community should underpin the legal regimes that govern the exploitation of such resources. Positive community offers commoners the rights of joint ownership. Any one individual commoner has to seek the consent of the others to exploit the resource or cooperate with others in the exploitation of the resource. No such cooperation is required in negative community. The contest between negative and positive community emerges clearly in relation to the sea-bed and the principle of 'the common heritage of mankind'.[80] The problem has been that the common heritage principle like the commons needs some supporting vision of community so that its implications in terms of rights and obligations of states can be identified.[81] Developing countries have naturally sought to inject some vision of positive community into the principle. On the other hand, in different economic contexts, developing countries might support the idea of negative community. Those developing countries which had a rich variety of plant genetic information might favour negative community if they had the economic and technological capability of profiting from the transformation of such information into a tradeable commodity.

Self-interest might guide agents to other kinds of decisions about the community and the intellectual commons. Obviously enough, much depends on whether the self, as it were, includes more than just economic gains in its thinking. In any case, even if self-interest is calculated purely in economic terms, rational agents may decide in favour of positive community. Assume for a moment that the claim that the intellectual commons supports creativity is right, and assume further that agents, in this case states, want to encourage creativity of all kinds. Then one means to that end is to ensure that the choice of community serves to preserve the commons. Is there a reason for thinking that either positive or negative community will better serve the goal of preserving the intellectual commons? The answer to this question is largely an empirical matter. Without arguing the matter in full, positive community does probably establish some kind of duty of care to preserve the commons. It seems to do so in Locke's theory. For Locke, once the proviso concerning enough and as good for others is not satisfied in the state of nature, then property must revert to common ownership.[82] Nor is the situation so strikingly different in civil society. Property in civil society is now a matter of positive regulation, but governments have to carry out that regulation bearing in mind that persons retain their natural rights of life, liberty and the means of preservation.[83] Individuals continue to have a right to participate in the resources of the community. Rights of common ownership along with private property rights are one important way in which the natural rights of individuals over resources are preserved. Preserving the commons seems to be part of the prudential duties of governments.

Negative community contains more dangers for the existence of the intellectual commons, both its present existence and its future enlargement. There are two kinds of dangers. One kind involves more individual raids being carried out on the existing commons. Property strikes against the commons manifest themselves in various ways. The scope of patentable subject matter, for instance, increases. A second kind of danger is that individuals find ways to prevent abstract objects from making it into the intellectual commons. So, for instance, individuals find ways of switching protection for abstract objects from systems of limited duration to systems of indefinite duration. (An example is the use of trademarks to protect shapes once design protection for those shapes has run out.) Both these dangers increase under proprietarianism, something we discuss in the final chapter.

The adoption of negative community has the possible consequence that large parts of the intellectual commons can be appropriated over a period of time. There are two reasons for suggesting it is only a possible consequence. First, some things may be inherently incapable of being appropriated. This is just the point which Grotius makes with respect to the sea and why on his argument it remains in the commons. Second, negative community need not logically entail the appropriation of the intellectual commons, if there are regulatory conventions or principles which in some way set limits on the permissible scope of appropriation. In the case of intellectual property, distinctions like those between ideas and expression in copyright and discovery and invention in patent law have just such a regulative role.

The dangers of negative community for the intellectual commons come when technology makes new kinds of appropriation possible or when the regulatory conventions protecting it for one reason or another cease to work. The intellectual commons then becomes a hunting ground for the economically strong and the technologically capable. An example from patent law helps to illustrate the kinds of appropriations that might become allowable under conditions of negative community. Most patent law systems operate with a distinction between discovery and invention. Discoveries, unless they are part of some novel process, are not generally patentable. So, for example, human DNA sequences, because they are sequences of information that occur in nature, would not normally be patentable. They would form part of the intellectual commons. If, however, for some reason the principle that discoveries were not to be patentable were no longer followed, then, under conditions of negative community, human genes could become the subject matter of individual appropriation.[84] It is less clear that this would happen under conditions of positive community. Before it could happen, it would require the consent of all the commoners since the human genome would itself be jointly owned. Linking positive community to the intellectual commons would have the effect of reducing predatory moves against the commons by individuals. The cooperation of other individuals would be necessary before individuals could make any such moves.

It is not possible to be sure about the fate of the intellectual commons under either negative or positive community. Our general claim is that, under conditions of negative community, the existence of the intellectual commons is more likely to be threatened, more likely to be propertized. If we accept that the intellectual commons is vital to the goal of maintaining and encouraging creativity, we have one reason for choosing to link positive community to the intellectual commons: it is more likely to preserve the commons. Those who argue for an extension of intellectual property rights and link that extension to negative community may ultimately be suggesting a self-defeating strategy. The extension of intellectual property rights under conditions of negative community may provide individuals with strong incentives to act in non-preservationist ways when it comes to the intellectual commons. A reversal of the economist's common pool problem takes place.[85] Common pool problems deal with valuable objects/assets that are open to capture. In the case of physical objects such as fish the absence of property rights leads to a depletion of the resource. First possession rules.[86] People overfish because there is no incentive to do otherwise. Some scheme of well defined property rights in such a case can have a preservation effect with respect to the resource in question, provided the scheme makes people calculate the costs of overfishing. In the case of abstract objects under conditions of negative community, property rights provide an incentive to appropriate the commons or prevent abstract objects from making it into the commons. The stronger the property rights the more marked this effect. Self-interest combined with conditions of competition make this behaviour the only rational course of action. (We expand on this argument in Chapters 5 and 6.) Under conditions of negative community, property rights in abstract objects no longer have a strong preservation or nurturing effect. Depending on their scope they may in fact, for reasons we give in Chapter 6, have a destructive effect. The intellectual commons faces a different kind of tragedy to its physical counterpart.

So far we have explored the role that self-interest might play in choices about community and the intellectual commons. But there are other kinds of arguments which might be explored – in fact probably a long list of them. Classical liberal principles suggest some *prima facie* reasons for choosing positive community when considering the link between community and the commons. For many, if not most, liberals it is axiomatic that the state should be neutral as between conceptions of the good life. The state is only to intervene in order to prevent harm to others. Private property is central to liberalism's promise of allowing different visions of the good life to flourish. The institution of private property gives individuals control over those resources needed to implement their particular version of the good life. One possibility, within market societies, is that property holdings may be concentrated in the hands of a few. This is a problem to the extent that control over property by a few entails the control over the means of implementing different individual visions of the good life. The problem of a concentration of ownership may be more of a problem in those societies where negative community is regularly chosen over positive community. Positive community, because it mandates the cooperation of the commoners, may be a better option in relation to those resources like the intellectual commons which we think should have the status of a universal and permanently accessible asset.

Conclusion

Locke is important to the intellectual property theorist but not because he provides a labour theory of justification for intellectual property rights. First, his analysis shows the indeterminacy of labour as a basis for a theory of property rights. Labour only offers an apparently stable basis for theorizing in Locke's work because of Locke's metaphysical assumptions. Locke, and the natural law tradition of which he was a part, remind us that the choices over property forms are choices about the nature of community. When it comes to intellectual property it is, we have argued, positive community we should be inclined to choose. The intellectual commons has to be nurtured by a continuing process of accretion. Negative community is more likely to interfere with or curtail this process.

Notes

1 References to Locke's *Two Treatises* are to John Locke, *Two Treatises of Government* (1690; P. Laslett, ed., Cambridge, 1988). The references are to Book I or II and the numbered sections of Locke's text.

2 J. Hughes, 'The Philosophy of Intellectual Property', 77 *The Georgetown Law Journal*, 287, 288 (1988); H.M. Spector, 'An Outline of a Theory Justifying Intellectual and Industrial Property Rights', 8 *European Intellectual Property Review*, 270 (1989); E.C. Hettinger, 'Justifying Intellectual Property', 18 *Philosophy and Public Affairs*, 31 (1989).

3 A good source for the critical literature on Locke is the four-volume work edited by Richard Ashcraft: *John Locke: Critical Assessments* (London, New York, 1991). Volume 3 contains the discussion of Locke's theory of property.

4 II, 25.

5 J. Tully, *A Discourse on Property* (Cambridge, 1980), 53. See also Laslett's Introduction to the *Two Treatises*, 75–76.

6 II, 1.

7 J. Tully, *A Discourse On Property* (Cambridge, 1980), 54.

8 II, 27.

9 Ibid.

10 Ibid.

11 II, 31.

12 Ibid.

13 II, 46, 50. See also J. Dunn, *Locke* (Oxford, 1984), 40.

14 II, 32.

15 II, 34.

16 II, 34, 37.

17 II, 46.

18 II, 37, 40.

19 A. Ryan, *Property and Political Theory* (Oxford, New York, 1984), 30.

20 J. Tully, *A Discourse on Property* (Cambridge, 1980), 174.

21 C.B. Macpherson, *The Political Theory of Possessive Individualism* (Oxford, 1979), 221.

22 C.H. Monson, 'Locke and his Interpreters' in R. Ashcraft (ed.), *John Locke* (London, New York, 1991), vol. 3, 13, 23–24. So, for instance, it is even possible to find in his work a contribution to feminism. See M.A. Butler, 'Early Liberal Roots of Feminism: John Locke and the Attack on Patriarchy' in R. Ashcraft (ed.), *John Locke* (London, New York, 1991), vol. 3, 639.

23 II, 6.

24 J. Tully, *A Discourse on Property*, (Cambridge, 1980), 4.

25 Id., 62–63.

26 Id., 71.

27 Id., 127.

28 Id., 130.

29 Id., 3.

30 C.B. Macpherson, *The Political Theory of Possessive Individualism* (Oxford, 1979), 209.

31 Id., 212.

32 Id., 220.
33 S. Pufendorf, *De Jure Naturae et Gentium Libri Octo* (1672; translation of 1688 ed. by C.H. and W.A. Oldfather, New York, London, 1964), IV, 4, 6.
34 H. Grotius, *De Jure Belli Ac Pacis Libri Tres* (1625; F.W. Kelsey tr., New York, London, 1964), II, 2, 5.
35 For some argument as to why, see S. Buckle, *Natural Law and the Theory of Property* (Oxford, 1991), 179–80.
36 A scientific realist would claim that theoretical entities of this kind exist. For a description of scientific realism, see N. Tennant, *Anti-Realism and Logic* (Oxford, 1987), chapter 2.
37 The consequences of applying Locke's sufficiency limitation to the physical commons has been the subject of some discussion. See, for example, R. Nozick, *Anarchy, State, and Utopia* (Oxford, 1974), 174–178; J. Waldron, 'Enough and As Good Left for Others', 29 *Philosophical Quarterly*, 319 (1979); J.H. Bogart, 'Lockean Provisos and State of Nature Theories', 95 *Ethics*, 828 (1985); J.J. Thomson, *The Realm of Rights* (Cambridge, Mass., 1990), 330–331. For an example of an argument that offers a counter to the usual problems with the proviso, see D. Schmidtz, 'The Institution of Property', 11 *Social Philosophy and Policy*, 42, 45–46 (1994).
38 See J. Hughes, 'The Philosophy of Intellectual Property', 77 *The Georgetown Law Journal*, 287, 310–314 (1988).
39 H. Grotius, *De Jure Belli Ac Pacis Libri Tres* (1625; F.W. Kelsey tr., New York, London, 1964), II, 2, 3.
40 H. Grotius, *Mare Liberum* (1608; R.V.D. Magoffin tr., New York, 1916), chapter V, 28.
41 See E.C. Hettinger, 'Justifying Intellectual Property', 18 *Philosophy and Public Affairs*, 31, 38 (1989).
42 S. Pufendorf, *De Jure Naturae et Gentium Libri Octo* (1672; translation of 1688 ed. by C.H. and W.A. Oldfather, New York, London, 1964), IV, 4, 4.
43 K. Olivecrona, 'Locke's Theory of Appropriation' in R. Ashcraft (ed.), *John Locke* (London, New York, 1991) vol. 3, 327–342.
44 II, 45.
45 II, 120.
46 J. Tully, *A Discourse on Property* (Cambridge, 1980), 48.
47 S.B. Dury, 'Locke and Nozick on Property', in Richard Ashcraft (ed.), *John Locke: Critical Assessments* (London, New York, 1991), vol. 3, 495, 506.
48 K.R. Popper, *Objective Knowledge* (Oxford, 1972), chapter 3.
49 G.D. Gadsden, *The Law of Commons* (London, 1988).
50 See II, 35. See also Laslett's notes on pp. 288–289.
51 *Halsbury's Laws of England* (4th ed.), vol. 6, para 505.
52 Id., para 504.
53 T. Bonyhady, *The Law of the Countryside: The Rights of the Public* (Milton Park Estate, Abingdon, 1987), 131.
54 The UNESCO Convention for the Protection of the World Cultural and Natural Heritage (1972), which requires states to cooperate in the preservation of cultural heritage, suggests that states may have to recognize duties towards some global cultural commons.
55 See Council of Europe, *International Legal Protection of Cultural Property* (Strasbourg, 1984).
56 For a discussion of the common heritage of mankind, see page 65 of this volume.
57 S. Pufendorf, *De Jure Naturae et Gentium Libri Octo* (1672; translation of 1688 ed. by C.H. and W.A. Oldfather, New York, London, 1964), IV, 4, 5.
58 Id. IV, 4, 2.
59 Id. IV, 4, 4.

60 Id. IV, 4, 2.

61 This is how Buckle interprets Pufendorf. See S. Buckle, *Natural Law and the Theory of Property* (Oxford, 1991), 94.

62 It is not the broadest possible vision of community since the reference to humans makes it vulnerable to the charge of speciesism.

63 Tully claims that Locke redefined positive community along these lines. See J. Tully, *A Discourse on Property* (Cambridge, 1980), 126–129. For some objections to Tully's interpretation of Locke, see S. Buckle, *Natural Law and the Theory of Property* (Oxford, 1991), 183–187.

64 J. Tully, *A Discourse on Property* (Cambridge, 1980), 127.

65 Here we do not follow Pufendorf since he took the view that in negative community 'all things lay open to all men'. See S. Pufendorf, *De Jure Naturae et Gentium Libri Octo* (1672; translation of 1688 ed. by C.H. and W.A. Oldfather, New York, London, 1964), IV, 4, 5.

66 Ibid.

67 J. Tully, *A Discourse on Property* (Cambridge, 1980), 121.

68 See P.O. Kristeller, 'Creativity and Tradition', XLIV *Journal of the History of Ideas*, 105 (1983).

69 For philosophical discussions of creativity, see D. Dutton and M. Krausz (eds.), *The Concept of Creativity in Science and Art* (The Hague, Boston, London, 1981). See also A. Koestler, *The Act of Creation* (London, 1964).

70 The standard work is T.S. Kuhn, *The Structure of Scientific Revolutions* (2nd ed., Chicago, 1970).

71 P. Pettit, *The Common Mind* (New York, Oxford, 1993), chapter 3.

72 P. Pettit, *The Common Mind* (New York, Oxford, 1993).

73 See, for example, T.S. Kuhn, *The Structure of Scientific Revolutions* (2nd. ed., Chicago, 1970); R.K. Merton, *The Sociology of Science* (Chicago, 1973); S. Goldberg, *Understanding Relativity: Origin and Impact of a Scientific Revolution* (Oxford, 1984).

74 S. Goldberg, *Understanding Relativity: Origin and Impact of a Scientific Revolution* (Oxford, 1984), 185.

75 Id., 220.

76 A. Koestler, *The Act of Creation* (London, 1964); A. Koestler, 'The Three Domains of Creativity', in D. Dutton and M. Krausz (eds.), *The Concept of Creativity in Science and Art* (The Hague, Boston, London, 1981), 1, 2.

77 R. Tuck, *Natural Rights Theories* (Cambridge, 1979), 62.

78 See the Introductory Note by J. Brown in H. Grotius, *Mare Liberum* (1609; R.V.D. Magoffin tr., New York, 1916).

79 For an overview, see O. Schachter, *International Law in Theory and Practice* (Dordrecht, Boston, London, 1991), chapter XIII.

80 The General Assembly of the United Nations has passed a declaration stating that the sea-bed is the common heritage of mankind. See UNGA Res. 2749 (XXV), 17 December 1970 containing the Declaration of Principles Governing the Sea-bed and the Ocean Floor, and the Subsoil Thereof, beyond the Limits of National Jurisdiction.

81 For discussions of the common heritage of mankind principle in international law, see B. Larschan and B.C. Brennan, 'The Common Heritage of Mankind Principle in International Law', 21 *Columbia Journal of Transnational Law*, 305 (1983); C.C. Joyner, 'Legal Implications of the Concept of the Common Heritage of Mankind', 35 *International and Comparative Law Quarterly*, 190 (1986); O. Schachter, *International Law in Theory and Practice* (Dordrecht, Boston, London, 1991), chapter XIII.

82 J.L. Mackie, *Ethics* (Harmondsworth, 1977), 176.

83 J. Tully, *A Discourse on Property* (Cambridge, 1980), 166

84 For a discussion of the issues, see G. Winter, 'Patent Law Policy in Biotechnology', 4 *Journal of Environmental Law*, 167 (1992); R.S. Eisenberg, 'A Technology

Policy Perspective on the NIH Gene Patenting Controversy', 55 *University of Pittsburgh Law Review*, 633 (1994); R. Moufgang, 'Patenting of Human Genes, Cells and Parts of the Body? – The Ethical Dimensions of Patent Law', 25 *International Review of Industrial Property and Copyright Law*, 487 (1994).

85 H.S. Gordon, 'The Economic Theory of a Common Property Resource: The Fishery', 62 *Journal of Political Economy*, 124 (1954); A.E. Friedman, 'The Economics of the Common Pool: Property Rights in Exhaustible Resources', 18 *UCLA Law Review*, 855 (1971).

86 For an analysis of the problems of first possession, see D.D. Haddock, 'First Possession Versus Optimal Timing: Limiting the Dissipation of Economic Value', 64 *Washington University Law Quarterly*, 775 (1968).

4 Hegel: The Spirit of Intellectual Property

Introduction

Like Locke, Hegel wrote on property. To a far greater extent than Locke, Hegel's analysis of property and his political philosophy are integrated parts of a dense metaphysical system. No attempt is made here to develop an account of the complex interlinkages between the various parts of Hegel's philosophical system. This is a matter for Hegel's interpreters.

This said, Hegel is too important to ignore when it comes to a treatment of property. Hegel is a philosopher of 'big' ideas. His idealist metaphysic is aimed at an explanation of the world and its major phenomena, such as being, freedom, consciousness and the state. It is precisely because Hegel was dedicated to the task of building a philosophical system that would confer an understanding of major existential, metaphysical and social issues that his philosophy continues to be an important source of ideas and influence for contemporary theorists.[1] This chapter, then, is part of a tradition which looks to Hegel's work in order to acquire a distinctive explanatory perspective on the particular object of analysis – in the present case the institution of property in the form of intellectual property.

Unlike Locke, Hegel is not primarily interested in defending a particular normative structure of community (for example, positive inclusive community). Instead his aim is to reveal the role that community plays in the evolution of individual freedom. The challenge in this chapter is to try to identify the distinctive role and effects that property in abstract objects might have in that epic historical journey. To this end we concentrate on Hegel's explanation of the role of property in those systems that he identifies as being active in the development of the individual will and the state. There is in Hegel a full-blooded analysis of property as a phenomenon of system. The question we ask is whether this analysis offers any insights into the phenomenon of intellectual property in the context of modern societies. Our reading of Hegel suggests that intellectual property may have negative effects on community.

Philosophy, says Hegel, is 'the exploration of the rational'.[2] But knowledge of the rational requires the identification and elaboration of forms: he rails against those who are preoccupied with the substantive and ignore the fact that philosophical knowledge is based on a unity of form and context.[3] The reference to form does not signal the adoption by Hegel of Plato's theory of Forms, a theory which claims that knowledge is based on eternal objective forms of which earthly reality is but a poor imitation. Hegel's problem with Plato's metaphysical scheme is that it leads political philosophy into stasis. Greek ethical life is portrayed as static and one-dimensional. There is no room for the subjective, personal impulse that would inevitably bring change to Plato's objective, rigidly ordered, ethical and political world.[4] Hegel confronts what he implicitly claims that Plato does not – the brute fact that there is change in the world. The construction of any philosophical system must stay open to that fact.

In Hegel's *Philosophy of Right*, change takes the form of a series of transitions: personality to morality, morality to ethical life, family to civil society, civil society to state. Personality, morality and so on are concepts, but for Hegel concept has a special strong sense; concept includes its actualization. A concept is fit for philosophical science when it is combined with its determinate expression in the world. Hence Hegel's claim that philosophy has no truck with '"mere concepts"'.[5] A sociological reading of Hegel is possible because he is concerned with the manifestation of concepts in the world.[6] In the *Philosophy of Right* these concepts take on the form of systems which, critically, undergo a process of evolution and transformation. Hegel, through his speculative method of philosophy, outlines the forms of those systems important to the 'idea of right' and then maps the direction of their evolution.[7] The family goes through dissolution and merges with civil society while civil society is made up of independent and interacting systems such as the system of need.[8] In short, concepts are concretely embodied in the world in the form of social systems.

Within legal philosophy, Hegel's arguments concerning property do not enjoy a great following. There are occasional explorations of his philosophical system, carried out mainly for the purpose of showing how his arguments relate to the justification for property.[9] Hegel is sometimes said to be offering a distinctive personality theory of property, one which can be contrasted with a Lockean labour theory of property.[10] In the case of certain intellectual property rights such as copyright, which deals with artistic works, dramatic works or literary works, the link between property rights and personality intuitively seems strong. Thus one tempting strategy is to make Hegel's personality theory serve the task of justifying at least those intellectual property rights in which personality is creatively involved.

There are two reasons why this approach is not adopted here. First, there is a serious question whether the contrast between Locke's theory of property and Hegel's theory ought to be framed in terms of labour versus personality.[11] For the theological Locke, the whole point of the connection between labour and property is that it allows individuals to fulfil God's purposes. Property for Locke serves personality. For Hegel, 'property is the *embodiment* of personality'.[12] That embodiment begins with the taking of something not in the possession of others, or, in Locke's terms, taking from the commons. The difference between the two theories perhaps lies less in the specifics of their respective accounts of property and more in the different metaphysical schemes that property is made to serve. Secondly, discussions of Hegel's work which utilize his theory for justificatory purposes also tend to overlook the critical nature of his philosophy, especially with respect to property. Hegel does see a contradiction in individual property ownership (using individual subjective will, which makes something mine, depends on participation with others in a common will that it be mine).[13] Gillian Rose puts it this way:

> The fundamental paradox of Hegel's thought is that he was a critic of *all* property forms, but his central notion of a free and equal political relationship is inexplicable without concepts of property ... and hence incomplete without the elaboration of an alternative property relation.[14]

The rest of this chapter is divided into two sections. The first delivers a general discussion of Hegel's work on property, including some remarks he makes on intellectual property. Property theorists tend to concentrate heavily on what he said in the *Philosophy of Right*. We shall follow this practice. The second section links the general discussion of property to Hegel's theory of state and examines the implications of this analysis for the phenomenon of intellectual property.

Hegel's Property

Central to the *Philosophy of Right* is the concept of a will which undergoes a series of evolutionary transitions. These transitions begin with a will unmediated by social relations and culminate in the generalized will that has located itself in the context of the state and world history. Will is defined in terms of the unity of two moments of the ego, one 'the pure thought of oneself' and the other 'the finitude or particularization of the ego'.[15] Hegel completes the definition by saying that will is

> the *self*-determination of the ego, which means that at one and the same time the ego posits itself as its own negative, i.e. as restricted and determinate, and yet remains by itself, i.e. in its self-identity and universality. It determines itself and yet at the same time binds itself with itself.[16]

In essence, will is thought made articulate in one of two contrasting dimensions. The contrast is between thought in an abstract, universal mode and thought in a particularistic, determinate mode of operation. Operating in these modes, both of which presuppose self-consciousness, the task of the will is to achieve absolute freedom.[17] Freedom is not used by Hegel in the liberal sense of lack of constraints on the volitional agent, but rather is a realized state of being of the agent, a state of being which is situated in a given historical context. Freedom is not, on Hegel's account, just a suitable institutional arrangement for individuals. It also involves their participation in a historical process, a process which shapes their perception and realization of freedom. The task of the will is carried out in several stages. In the first stage will is conscious of itself as personality, and seeks to impose itself on the external world.[18] Will must also exist in the form of particular, subjective morality before it finds its ultimate liberation in the state. Hegel's main account of property is to be found in the first stage of the will's development when will manifests itself as personality.

The mind for Hegel is free and its personality begins when it has self-knowledge unhindered by any restriction.[19] This universal but bare form of freedom is not enough, for personality has to achieve some more concrete form of existence in the world. This is where property makes its entrance. The more concrete form happens through the appropriation of things, there being an 'absolute right' to the appropriation of things.[20] Included in the category of things are 'mental aptitudes, erudition, artistic skill'.[21] These 'inner possessions', once externalized, become things capable of legal possession. These statements on property may easily be interpreted as an argument for the existence of private property. Hegel does, after all, talk of an absolute right of appropriation, and argues that will becomes objective in private property. But this interpretation loses sight of Hegel's explanatory, evolutionary perspective. He is concerned with the beginnings of mind or will in the external, physical world. Persons inescapably have to make decisions about the external world. This is a situation that has the character of both immediacy and confrontation.[22] Personality begins to lift itself out of this situation by claiming the 'external world as its own'.[23] Property represents the first stage of this actualizing process. It is one of the first acts of free will in which the will as personality takes on a concrete, free form. However property, for Hegel, does not primarily exist to satisfy ordinary needs, desires or cravings, although he concedes that it can easily appear so.[24] The underlying reality is that 'property is the first embodiment of freedom'.[25]

Why Hegel says this is more readily understandable when his concept of will is exposed a little more. Hegel does not reject private property. He is critical of Plato for doing so in the *Republic*. To reject property is to misunderstand the true nature of freedom. Freedom has a subjective element, an element which Plato's state denies its citizens. Their freedom is the objective freedom that comes from conformity to a set of rules cognized and promulgated by those possessing moral wisdom and objective knowledge – the Philosopher Kings. Hegel's constant claim is that the modern state must recognize subjective freedom.

What is the role of property in the attainment of subjective freedom? One suggestion has been that private property is the institution which allows the exercise of subjective freedom, where subjective freedom means the satisfaction of individual wants and desires.[26] Another is that the making of property claims contributes to the development of personality. It invites recognition by others which, if given, helps to foster a moral and social dimension in the personality of the property claimer.[27] There is more to add here, however. It is certainly true that, for Hegel, property plays a crucial role in defining an arena of social life in which desires rather than law are the prime determinants of choice and activity. But property also has a more fundamental role. Hegel's argument, although encased in complex language, carries a simple message: property is essential to individual survival in the world where survival refers not just to biological survival but also to the ability to cope with life in the context of one's given social system. Living in the world, the exercise of our abilities in life, requires certain things of us if we are to survive and one of these is the accumulation of property. Mine and thine is not only a division that personality needs to make, in order to take its place in the world as a moral free-willing individual entity or particularity, but it is also an institutional form which individuals need in order to make their way in the world.

Hegel's absolute right of appropriation does not entail rights of absolute appropriation. Like others before him, Hegel posits the case of the extremely needy individual and the 'rightful property of someone else'. There is in this situation a 'right of distress'.[28] The needy individual is entitled to take those resources he requires for survival. Hegel's argument is simply that, where the denial of property involves the denial of life, a person is truly being deprived of his freedom of will.[29] Property, essentially, retains for Hegel a deeply instrumental character. Good for Hegel is 'freedom realized, the absolute end and aim of the world'.[30] The abstract right of property is subordinate to this end; it has no independent validity.[31]

This first part of Hegel's explanation of property focuses on its importance for the individual personality. Although it resembles a psychological account of personality and property, it is closer to a teaching of an understanding of property and personality. It is an account of the way the free-willing mind, imagining itself to be infinite and universal, confronts an external reality that restricts it. The beginnings of coping with that restriction are the beginnings of property.

As Hegel's philosophical description of right unfolds, a crucial shift takes place in the presentation of property. His perspective shifts from that of the individual looking into the world to that of the philosophical scientist looking at the patterned manifestations of objective spirit in the world.[32] Property from this perspective appears differently. It becomes systemic in character and is now to be understood through its functional links with state and civil society. Hegel's analysis of property shifts into what in modern terms we might call a sociological mode of analysis. Personality requires the concept of property; the presence of others means that the concept of property has to assume a role in addition to the one it has in individual psychology. Property ceases to be just the extension of personality and becomes the subject-matter of contract.[33] Contract law necessarily draws in the state. Property becomes the subject-matter of interaction between personalities and the state.

Hegel envisages that the free mind may place almost anything into the category of thing. There is no prior determination of what can and cannot be the subject of property. Personality is left free to range over the world. Thus the patenting of animal life forms, or DNA segments, or plant varieties involves things that are all potentially capable of appropriation. There is no obvious normative argument in Hegel against such developments, merely an explanation of their nature. Property is whatever the will chooses to occupy, although the nature of the thing in question can determine the effectiveness of the occupation. Some things, such as food, can be completely appropriated. Others, such as the elements, cannot be. Mastery of things in the sense of occupying them, Hegel thinks, is always likely to be incomplete.[34] Our equipment, cunning and dexterity also condition the activity of occupation.[35] For highly scientific/technological societies guided by cunning, very little is likely to remain free from appropriation.

Property, because it is the product of will, can be abandoned or alienated through an act of will.[36] However there is a proviso: the thing must be 'external by nature'.[37] The proviso serves to support Hegel's immediately succeeding proposition that 'those goods, or rather substantive characteristics which constitute my own private personality and the universal essence of my self-consciousness are inalienable and my right to them is imprescriptible. Such characteristics are my personality as such, my universal freedom of will, my ethical life, my religion.'[38] There is a rough parallel with Locke's wide use of property to include life and liberty. For Hegel, personality is something that belongs to oneself. Taking possession of oneself occurs through a process of self-development.[39] The concept (here used to refer to potentiality) of oneself as free and self-determining is made actual through conscious self-development. Self-ownership is not, however, inevitable. Mind, because it is free, may fail to live up to its potential. There is also the possibility of the alienation of personality.[40] (It seems, for Hegel, that something which by nature is not external can be made so.) Similarly for Hegel intelligence, morality and rationality can also be alienated by giving somebody else power over one's conduct. The regaining of personality and its characteristics involves negating just those actions which make it external and therefore capable of possession by somebody else.

Hegel's discussion of this is based around individual will and the capacity to retrieve personality. For Hegel, personality can either be alienated volitionally or presumably through force, slavery being an example. In both cases individuals have knowledge of the externalizing process. High-technology societies raise another possibility. Through computer technology, information about individuals can be pooled to create a personality profile of a given individual, a kind of electronic doppelgänger which can be put to a large range of uses. This electronic doppelgänger is an externalization of which the individual to whom it relates may have very little knowledge or control. The implication of this in Hegelian terms is straightforward: it represents a loss of freedom. Potentially at least, if this electronic doppelgänger comes to mediate relations between ourselves and the institutions within our social system, our personality has been appropriated – it is no longer ours to control. Once again the clear implication of Hegel's argument is that property functions as a survival or defence mechanism. The free-willing mind occupies things in the world, including personality, so that others will not do so and rob it of its powers of determination and self-development.

Hegel's claim that 'property is the embodiment of personality' has led some to forge a link between his theory and artistic objects. It is a tempting path to go down. Hughes, for example, argues that poems, stories, novels and musical works are 'natural receptacles for personality' while other objects such as 'patents, microchip masks and engineering trade secrets' are not obviously manifestations of individual personality.[41] This argument interprets personality as some sort of essence which in varying degrees is 'poured' into objects.

One problem with this argument is that it assumes that justification rather than explanation is Hegel's primary aim. We have seen, however, that property – all property – is part of the explanation for the way personality begins to actualize itself in the world. In order to achieve this end individuals have the right of placing their 'will into any and everything'.[42] Hegel's explanation of this process is a highly functional one. Will finds itself in the world, subject to restrictions, and has to make decisions. Property at first instance becomes a survival mechanism. Artistic forms and objects have no privileged status in this respect. The imposition of artistic form is simply one means by which we can take possession of something.[43] Personality is not a springboard, at least for Hegel, for special rights for artists and other creators. Thus Hegel's analysis of property offers the possibility of a potent critique of authors' rights systems.

Copyright is a term which, historically speaking, refers to legislative systems which were premised on the assumption that the interests that authors had in the protection of their works were economic interests – the interests of *owners*. European civil systems over time evolved legislative systems that operated with a broader conception of the interests of *authors*. Authors were thought to relate to their work *qua* creators as well as *qua* owners. The practical effect of this was that European systems began to develop rights such as the right of the author 'to claim authorship of the work, and to object to any distortion, mutilation or other modification, or other derogatory action' in relation to their works.[44] One major philosophical source of this distinctive juristic turn in authors' rights is said to be Kant.[45] Kant's specific suggestion in relation to authors was that they enjoyed rights over their work by virtue of their personality. In his words, an author's right is 'an innate right, inherent in his own person'.[46]

Kant's comparatively few remarks on the connection between personality and the nature of the rights of authors were taken up by German scholars who articulated and defended an authors' right jurisprudence.[47] While the juristic literature on moral rights is vast, much less attention has been devoted to a general philosophical evaluation of authors' rights jurisprudence. It is not clear, for instance, how rights for authors fit with the broader Kantian metaethical system, for it is a system which through its formal principle of universalization seeks to avoid the possibility of special pleading by moral agents.

In any case, Hegel's analysis of the link between property and personality sets some problems for any Kantian personality-based justification for moral rights. Within a Kantian justification for authors' rights, those rights are seen as claims that the author can make over the fate of a work because the claim is not just a claim over the work, but simultaneously a claim to the protection of the author's personality. The author's work is simultaneously an expression of his or her ideas and an expression of personality. The consequence of taking such a view is that authors enjoy a distinct set of rights. To put it more provocatively, a certain class of personality (authors, artists) becomes entitled to make claims that other property-owning moral agents cannot. The motor vehicle enthusiast who 'pours' his personality into the restoration of an old car does not have moral rights over the car once he sells it. Hegel's argument, we have seen, is that private property is an essential part of the process in which personality realizes itself in the world. There is no suggestion by him that through this process some personalities acquire special entitlements. Why should the law recognize special rights for artistic personalities? The reply – that rights of paternity and integrity help to protect important works, that they help to stimulate the production of unique and distinctive works (and therefore more economically valuable works) and that they serve to preserve the accuracy of a society's cultural record – is not really a reply that is centred on the importance of works to the artistic personality. Such a reply recognizes that personality rights of authors are important because they serve some other goal, like the production and preservation of art. But this is not a justification based on the intrinsic importance of personality. To use Kantian language, it treats protection of the authorial personality as an important means to some other end. The question we began with remains. What is it about artistic personality that justifies rights peculiar to that personality? When we begin to think about this in the context of Hegel's analysis of the role of property, the answer that authorial personality simply gives rise to these rights is far more problematic than it first appears. Within Hegel's system property, whether in physical or abstract objects, is equally important to the survival and flourishing of personality in the world. Kant's brief remarks on the subject of authors and books suggest that it was only authors (and presumably artists) that gained these distinctive rights. Scientists and inventors who also produce abstract objects were not rewarded with personality rights. Equally there is no authors' rights tradition within patent law. On what basis should we discriminate between producers of physical objects, or between producers of different classes of abstract objects? In making such discriminations, do we not devalue the contributions of some and elevate those of others? The subjective freedom of some creators is ranked higher than that of others or those who are not recognized as creators. Hegel's systemic account of property does pose a more serious critical challenge to authors' rights jurisprudence than is commonly realized.

Hegel does make some observations that deal with intellectual property. Products of the mind which are 'peculiarly' ours may when externalized be produced by others.[48] Hegel does not see this as a problem but rather as a good. An individual, by coming into possession of externalized thoughts, whether in book or inventive form, comes into contact with 'universal methods of so expressing himself and producing numerous other things of the same sort'.[49]

Hegel seems to tread the classic utilitarian path when he suggests that the best way of progressing science and arts is to protect scientists and artists from thievery. He is at the same time sensitive to the possible problems of this solution. The whole purpose of intellectual products for Hegel is that they be recognized by others: that is, that they become the basis for learning by others. This recognition by others (perhaps re-cognition) relies on previous patterns of thought, ideas being accessible. In the social process of the transmission of knowledge 'well-established thoughts' are reworked and given new individual form. At any given moment individuals are engaged in personal, incremental contributions or modification of this stock of knowledge. Existing forms of knowledge are revised by individuals of different generations and so are thus both propagated and perhaps advanced for the benefit of others. To what extent can individuals appropriate even temporarily this flow of knowledge and claim property rights in these reworked forms? Hegel thinks there is no 'precise principle of determination' to answer this question.[50] Communities then presumably, through experience, have to work out legal boundaries within their intellectual systems that ensure those systems serve the learning needs of others and future generations. There is in this part of Hegel's analysis a recognition of the importance of an intellectual commons.

But while this is all that Hegel says on the subject of intellectual property directly, his theory of state, we shall see in the next section, helps us to understand the organic role of intellectual property and the dangers that intellectual property rights may pose for community.

The State, Civil Society and Intellectual Property

The idea of state remains one of the most complex and heavily criticized parts of Hegel's political philosophy.[51] Our present interest in his concept of state is necessarily limited to its connections with property.

One traditional view of freedom, linked to (amongst others) Hobbes and Locke, is that individual subjective freedom is to be found outside of the state. The price of this freedom, represented by an uncertain and anxious life in the state of nature, is too high. The creation of the state involves restrictions on freedom but life is safer, more certain. By contrast, for Hegel the state represents the highest form of freedom an individual can attain. Individuals no longer conceive of themselves in terms of abstract freedom, a condition in which they are free-willing agents confronting restrictions, but rather see restrictions in the form of duty as a form of objective freedom. The potentiality which begins with subjective free will and personality becomes concrete actuality in the state.[52]

There are, Pelczynski has argued, three aspects to state in Hegel: civil society, the strictly political state and the political state.[53] Civil society is a more complex notion than in Marx, where it refers to the competitive, antagonistic relations of individuals in the world of business. For Hegel, civil society includes not only the relations that accompany self-interested individualism, but also the organizational and legal infrastructure which supports those relations. This infrastructure has to have a source, and in Hegel's terminology it is the strictly political state.

The political state is an obscurer but crucial part of Hegel's concept of state. It is obscure, Pelczynski argues, because Hegel does not make it clear that he is offering a third and distinct concept of state. This concept is full of moral significance. It refers to 'the whole population of an independent, politically and "civilly" organized country in so far as it is permeated by "ethical life" and forms an "ethical order" or "ethical community".'[54] Vital to this third concept of state is the concept of ethical life (*Sittlichkeit*).[55] The concept has its source point in the Greek idea of *polis*. Ethical life implies a set of shared values but it also includes the distinctive attitudes and approaches to life of a given community, the common spirit which expresses itself in the daily life and practical affairs of a community. Ethical life refers to some deep element or idea that inspires a community way of life.

Hegel, like John Locke, assigns to the state the task of defending the property of its citizens. The state's function is to provide the laws which recognize and guarantee to individuals their property claims. In *The German Constitution* he writes that a 'multitude of human beings can only call itself a state if it be united for the common defence of the entirety of its property'.[56] But in the *Philosophy of Right*, probably because of his dialectical methodology, Hegel drives his analysis of state deeper than many liberal thinkers. The state for Hegel is an amalgam of three subsystems: the political, the civil and the ethical. These three systems operate in a kind of tense unity which is the source of the modern state's strength. Civil society represents the dangerous subjectivity of strong individualism while the ethical represents the enclosure of that subjectivity by the community, its public morality and attitudes. The synthesis of these contrary forces within a legal and institutional framework was for Hegel the secret of the state's success.

The stability of the state depends on each of these systems carrying out their function without any one achieving a dominance over the other. Hegel was particularly sensitive to the possibility that civil society or some of its elements might come to dominate the political state. He saw in the individualism of civil society the potential destruction of ethical life and therefore community.

Here we are not interested in Hegel's proposals for the political structure of the state but rather the implications of his argument for property. Within civil society are to be found those institutions necessary for the security of property, such as the law courts and the police. We have also seen that private property is a vitally important feature of individual development of the personality in civil society. But property for Hegel also seems to be an institution which embodies contrary forces. He sees logical difficulties in relying on Kant's principles of universalization to establish the morality of claims to private property.[57] Property, he suggests, is opposed to universality, and if it is equated with it, it is superseded.[58]

The existence of private property for Hegel is crucially dependent upon universal bonds created between persons interacting in the ethical dimension of the state. The security of my property is dependent on the conformity of the citizenry to those ideals which form part of the ethical life of the state. If this occurs then, in the context of civil society, I have real freedom to pursue my affairs. Civil society has its dangerous side, for it is there that subjective impulse is given the freedom to reign. Hegel was all too aware that this subjective impulse could become a predatory force which would threaten freedom and the state itself:[59]

> Of course it is the almost unanimous view of the pragmatic historians that if in any nation private interest and a dirty monetary advantage becomes the preponderating ingredient in the election of Ministers of state, then the situation is to be regarded as the forerunner of the inevitable loss of that nation's political freedom, the ruin of its constitution and even of the state.

While the interests of the wealthy and the propertied are legitimate within Hegel's state, the public authority of the state was not to be the private property of these or any other interests.[60] The danger lurking within civil society is that it can rob or weaken the ethical life of the state and it is the ethical life of the state which makes it a community. So much is clear from Hegel. Less clear, though, is that one profound source of danger to community comes from civil society's pursuit of property. The state has a very clear role in serving individuals as members of civil society, but at the same time the state has for Hegel an obligation to preserve the ethical life of the state. Satisfying the subjectivism inherent in the property claims of individuals runs the risk that the state simply becomes the compliant arm of civil society and for Hegel the ascendancy of civil society within the state is ruinous.

Intellectual property, through its nature and form, acts to increase the pressure which civil society brings to bear on the political state. The reason is simple enough. Individuals begin to realize the strategic business advantages which a proprietary control over abstract objects gives them. With this realization the race to secure property rights in abstract objects begins. Civil society experiences an intellectual property consciousness. The vulnerability of abstract objects makes those elements of civil society most dependent on them put enormous pressure on the state to mint new forms of intellectual property protection. This process also has an international dimension. Individual owners of intellectual property want security of property, not just nationally, but in the context of trade of intellectual property rights in international markets.[61] As individuals acting within global and regional markets there are limits to their capacity to protect their interests. A natural solution is to turn to the services of a strong state and influence its decision-making processes to bring about the realization of a global property regime.[62]

The upshot of this process of creation and enforcement of property rights in abstract objects is that civil society and political society undergo an increasing interpenetration. The process of the production of law-based privileges in abstract objects promotes an integration of elements of civil society and the political state. What Hegel would say about this is uncertain and so what we say about the implications of the rise of privilege-based property forms in the state is necessarily speculative. The clear message from Hegel's political writings is that the state should not be the creator and guardian of privilege. Yet this is precisely the risk the state takes when it begins to champion the property interests of parts of civil society. Clearly there is a critical role for the state in protecting the property of its citizens, but this is a fundamentally different proposition from saying that the state should be the servant of propertied interests. The danger in the political state becoming a captive of proprietarian elements of civil society is that, in Hegelian terms, it impairs the state's capacity to protect the ethical life of the state. Individual participation in the larger ethical life of the community is the final stage of the individual's journey to freedom. But in a situation where civil society has pushed the state into a protection of selected property interests the ethical life of the community faces the danger of replacement by a group morality. Individuals, when they reach the summit of the state, do not find a broader community life in which to participate, but rather a narrow group morality. It is the morality of property owners. Marx's class instrumentalist analysis of morality is, on our view of Hegel, implicit in Hegel's system once civil society turns the state to its own uses and *Sittlichkeit* falls prey to the self-interest of property holders.

Hegel's analysis of state and property is also suggestive of another unsettling possibility when it comes to intellectual property: the evolution of intellectual property rights may exacerbate the problems of poverty and economic development rather than help them. Property which, at the level of abstract right, was a relation between a thing and an individual will becomes in civil society a formal and posited relation of recognition between individuals.[63] Hegel's description of civil society remains starkly functional. At one level, civil society can be described as the system of needs. Individuals have a social existence that is characterized by 'complete interdependence' in which the 'livelihood, happiness, and the legal status of one man is interwoven with the livelihood, happiness, and rights of all'.[64] Hegel's description of this stage of civil society is not particularly appealing in normative terms. Individuals have innumerable personal developmental possibilities and the pursuit of these simply 'breeds new desires without end'.[65] Needs become part of a self-generating process, in which the means to the satisfaction of needs becomes subdivided into further needs and means, the whole process being spurred on by the desire for equal satisfaction and a simultaneous desire for individual distinctiveness. Things that satisfy needs are the external products of the will of others. In civil society these individual products of subjective will become recognized as property. Property shifts from having a subjective pre-legal existence to a legal form of existence. Property rights, because they are posited by law, become part of the recognition patterns of individuals. Once law assumes a posited character then right, which at an individual level has been abstract, takes on a determinate form, one capable of greater determinacy of content through application to individual problems.[66] Civil society then is a functional combination of a system of needs with a system of law in which property constitutes the formal recognition of others and the embodiment of individual will in things.

Hegel's analysis seems to indicate that poverty is an inevitable byproduct of the system of needs in civil society. The reproduction of needs and means is a process which can go on endlessly.[67] The increasing particularity and division of needs produces a functional response – the division of labour.[68] Class systems also emerge. Individual survival and development within this system is conditioned by, amongst other things, a person's skill, something which, Hegel argues, is unevenly distributed by nature. If uninterrupted in its development, civil society becomes more complex, in the sense that more needs are generated for satisfaction. Simultaneously, however, Hegel asserts that 'dependence and want increase *ad infinitum*'.[69] The satisfaction of the needs of the poor (those lacking the requisite survival skills) is barred for two reasons. First, the possible objects of satisfaction have become the property of others. (Presumably in extreme cases a right of distress may operate.) Second, acquiring property now depends on contract and so satisfying needs through original modes of acquisition, such as taking possession, becomes no more than 'isolated accidents'.[70] Somewhat paradoxically, the systems complexity of civil society, if unchecked, produces poverty at the same time that it produces luxury and wealth.

The solution to this problem is not readily to hand. Public authorities and organizations, along with individual charity, can help the poor.[71] There remains a certain bleakness in Hegel's discussion of poverty. He hints that the problem in the context of civil society is structural, in that it is driven by overproduction, and to this problem Hegel sees no solution except that civil society is led to seek markets outside of itself.[72]

Implicit in Hegel's analysis is that the actualizing possibilities of individuals within civil society are conditioned by formal property relations. There is a negative and positive aspect to this. On the positive side the existence of formal property relations means that the embodiment of my will in things is recognized. The negative is that a pattern of formal recognition of property rights can limit my possibilities. The fact that others have property rights as well as the matrix of individual property relations within the social system means that some objects are put beyond my will. Contract can overcome this restrictive aspect of property in that I can acquire the property of others through agreement.[73] The basic point, however, remains unchanged. Property conditions the development potentialities of individuals and communities in both negative and positive ways. Intellectual property represents an extension of property rights to an almost indefinite range of objects – scientific ideas, art, the genetic codes of nature – all of which fall within intellectual property's ever expanding domain. This extension is full of possibility. On Hegel's systemic account of property in civil society, the prospects are likely to be negative. As we argued in Chapter 2, property in abstract objects increases the capacity of owners to place restrictions on the use of physical objects. The more objects that are removed from the possibility of direct occupation by personality, the greater the reliance by individuals on the contract mechanism to gain access. Contract, when it operates within the atomistic setting of civil society, is hardly likely to remedy unequal property distribution. The poor are unlikely to be able to bargain their way to a more equitable distribution of property, or even to negotiate just access and use. Civil society, through the self-generating system of needs, reaches higher and higher levels of production, but access to the benefits of this production becomes harder to achieve because more and more of the objects of production come to be guarded by property rights.

Intellectual property offers personality the possibility of a qualitative shift in its powers to extend itself into the world. Ideas, knowledge and all forms of information circulate in the world in a way that blocks of land and chattels do not. By the positing of property laws in abstract objects, the personality, in Hegelian terms, gains a proprietary hold over the production and distribution of physical objects in undreamt of ways. The very act of communicating an abstract object becomes the subject of a property relation. Moreover, since abstract objects are not territorially bound, it becomes meaningful for personality to begin to contemplate property laws that have a global reach. Through property, personality imposes itself on its immediate social world and local community. Through a global system of intellectual property law, personality has the potential to reach into other social worlds, other communities. The possibility of a global system of property to regulate relations between states is hardly a possibility that Hegel could have foreseen. Yet his theory does carry a warning for this kind of development. Within Hegel's system, property remains the embodiment of freedom because he clearly assumes that property relations occur within the context of a community which has its own distinctive ethical life. Property is a way of taking a participatory position in that life. This is not necessarily true of a global system of property that regulates access to the abstract objects of art and science. Property rights in abstract objects facilitate trade in culture between states. To the extent that such trade promotes the homogenization of culture it threatens the survival of local cultural forms and therefore local communities.[74] There is another problem. The very fact that the global system of property regulates access to abstract objects means that it has the potential to separate some individuals from those objects. This separation occurs when individuals cannot meet the demands of the commerce in culture and information that a global system of property rights in abstract objects creates. In short, a global system of property can easily become a force for destabilizing the pattern of local institutionalized cultural values and can separate creators from their creations or, in more Hegelian terms, for disrupting and perhaps destroying the ethical life of communities.

There is one final argument to make here and it relates to our earlier claim that intellectual property can exacerbate the problems of poverty and inequality within social systems. In sharp contrast to

Marx, the principles which Hegel identifies as conditioning the evolution of the state do not lead Hegel to prophesize about the final outcome of that evolution. Nevertheless we have seen that Hegel seems to think that poverty and its attendant miseries are a more or less permanent feature of social life. Hegel's complex metaphysic is suggestive of a deeper explanation for his belief and it is this explanation, implicit in his analysis, that we want to bring to the fore.

Work plays a crucial role in Hegel's analysis, as it does in Locke's political theory.[75] Work in the world is the form needed for the realization of spirit. For Hegel, spirit begins in a stage of ignorance and is led through stages of development and realization. The medium of this development is work, speech and activity. Through these things the spirit gains the recognition of others. The relevance of this metaphysic for property comes about in this way. Property, we have seen, when viewed at the individual level, is a need, a survival mechanism, for without it spirit cannot survive in the world and go on to develop. But property, in order to function in this way, must be institutionalized as a set of norms. Property has to become systemic in character, a task which both Locke and Hegel assign to the legal system. Property rights are formally defined and sanctioned by positive law. Law's function is not solely to institutionalize property norms although, given the negative potentialities of group life without property norms, described so vividly by state of nature theorists, it is, within political theory, clearly a primary (although quietly stated) task of law.

Modern sociological theory has emphasized law's general integrative function[76] and, although Hegel did not see law in these exact terms, we know that mechanisms for producing a stable and cohesive society were important to him.[77] The question we want to address here is how formal property fits into law's general task of societal integration, because by grappling with this question we obtain a better understanding of the possible adverse effects of property within society.

At first glance property does not seem to fit in particularly well with law's general task of social integration, precisely because, as a mechanism of self-defence, it promotes relations of separation. It prevents others from doing as we do. It presents a vision from inside, not outside the fence. But, within an abstract sociological schema, integration is simply the adjustments required to be made to the subunits of a system so that the system as a whole can function effectively.[78] In this sense formal property contributes to integration because institutionalized property norms provide individuals, including those outside the fence, with information about the expectations of others so that others can plan and predict action. But, because property does involve relations of separation, it does at least potentially pose dangers for the kind of communal integration that is involved in Hegel's concept of the ethical life of a state. There are, within most formal property systems, mechanisms for ensuring that property as a relation of separation is not insisted upon too strongly, for otherwise group life becomes increasingly unworkable. The basic mechanism here is that of permission, which when viewed internally and manipulated by lawyers assumes an almost endless variety of legal forms. So within the English context we have easements of light and air, prescriptive easements, negative and positive easements of rights of way, licences of various kinds and so on. The mechanism of permission in its many different guises acts within a social system to limit the potentially disintegrative effect of property on social life.

The integrative role of property is critically dependent on the condition of permission being elaborated and utilized within a given social system. The structural problem that seems implicit in Hegel's analysis is that the fulfilment of this condition within the context of civil society becomes increasingly problematic. Once there is a widespread realization by the members of civil society that it is control and monopoly of the abstract intellectual object which is the real source of economic wealth then, because individuals within civil society are universally driven by self-interest, the permission mechanism increasingly becomes the target of ownership forces. Permission to use the abstract intellectual object becomes conditional upon the capacity to pay for the use of that object. The possibility of creating many new property forms through law has the possible effect that the task of social integration becomes that much more difficult. Because of its individualistic and antagonistic nature, civil society is disposed to press home the advantages of new property forms at the expense of the value of communal integration and this in turn is not likely to do much which is positive for the problem of poverty. Participation in culture more than ever becomes conditional upon the payment of a fee to intellectual property owners. Intellectual property, when placed within Hegel's systemic analysis of property, turns out to be the potential assassin of community.

The deleterious link between property and community is pursued in more detail by one of Hegel's critics - Marx - and it is to his version of the story concerning property and community we turn in the next chapter.

Conclusion

Although he expressly mentions patents and recognizes the importance of the intellectual commons, Hegel does not present an analysis of property that explores the relationship between property and the commons. For Hegel, property represents the beginnings of a journey for individual will within its social environment. Intellectual property, like other forms of property, has a role to play in the development of the individual person. The danger of intellectual property lies in its utilization by civil society. Civil society, once it comes to realize the pecuniary advantages of intellectual property rights, presses the state to build ever more elaborate intellectual property systems, systems which ultimately become a global system. This, we have suggested, threatens the ethical life of individual communities. The abstract objects to be found in science and culture lie at the centre of many of the interdependencies to be found in community life. Civil society's relentless pursuit of these objects produces relations of separation and a force for the fragmentation of community. Once property in abstract objects becomes part of a global system, it no longer acts within communities to enable freedom but acts upon them to restrict freedom. Or at least this is one possible outcome of such a system.

Notes

1 A good example of this is the influence of Hegel's work on modern communitarians such as Michael Sandel, Michael Walzer and Charles Taylor. For an excellent account of the modern relevance of Hegel's philosophy, see C. Taylor, *Hegel and Modern Society* (Cambridge, 1979) chapter 2, sections 6, 7, 8 and chapter 3.

2 G.W.F. Hegel, *Philosophy of Right* (1821; T.M. Knox tr., Oxford at the Clarendon Press, 1952, 1st ed., 1967 reprint), 10. References in square brackets are to the Knox translation. References without brackets are to page numbers.

3 Id. 2.

4 Id. 10.

5 Id. [1].

6 The perceptive observation that Hegel's political philosophy has some affinity with modern sociology comes from Z.A. Pelczynski, 'Hegel's Political Philosophy: Some Thoughts on its Contemporary Relevance', in Z.A. Pelczynski (ed.), *Hegel's Political Philosophy: Problems and Perspectives* (London, 1971), 230, 238. Ryan makes the observation that Hegel's analysis of property and politics can be read sociologically. See A. Ryan, *Property and Political Theory* (Oxford, New York, 1984), 118–19.

7 For an account of how Hegel's propositions are to be read speculatively, see G. Rose, *Hegel Contra Sociology* (London, 1981), 48–49.

8 G.W.F. Hegel, *Philosophy of Right* (1821; T.M. Knox tr., Oxford at the Clarendon Press 1952, 1st ed., 1967 reprint), [181] and [187].

9 See, for example, J. Hughes, 'The Philosophy of Intellectual Property', 77 *Georgetown Law Journal*, 287 (1988); M.J. Radin, 'Property and Personhood', 34 *Stanford Law Review*, 957 (1982); M. Salter, 'Justifying Private Property Rights: A Message from Hegel's Jurisprudential Writings', 7 *Legal Studies*, 245 (1987). On Hegel's recent influence on legal theory, see D. Cornell, M. Rosenfeld and D.G. Carlson (eds.), *Hegel and Legal Theory* (New York, London, 1991).

10 J. Hughes, 'The Philosophy of Intellectual Property', 77 *Georgetown Law Journal*, 287, 330 (1988).
11 Reeve observes that Hegel's theory is sometimes linked to the Lockean family. See A. Reeve, *Property* (London, 1986), 136–143.
12 G.W.F. Hegel, *Philosophy of Right* (1821; T.M. Knox tr., Oxford at the Clarendon Press 1952, 1st ed., 1967 reprint), [51].
13 Id. [71] and [72].
14 G. Rose, *Hegel Contra Sociology* (London, 1981), 80–81.
15 G.W.F. Hegel, *Philosophy of Right* (1821; T.M. Knox tr., Oxford at the Clarendon Press 1952, 1st ed., 1967 reprint), [5] and [6].
16 Id. [7].
17 Id. [27].
18 Id. [39].
19 Id. [35].
20 Id. [44].
21 Id. [43].
22 Id. [34] and [39].
23 Id. [39].
24 Id. [45].
25 Ibid.
26 See M.B. Foster, *The Political Philosophies of Plato and Hegel* (Oxford at the Clarendon Press, 1935, reprinted 1968), 84.
27 See J. Plamenatz, 'History as the Realization of Freedom' in Z.A. Pelczynski (ed.), *Hegel's Political Philosophy: Problems and Perspectives* (Cambridge, London, 1971), 40-41.
28 G.W.F. Hegel, *Philosophy of Right* (1821; T.M. Knox tr., Oxford at the Clarendon Press, 1952, 1st ed., 1967 reprint), [127].
29 Id., Additions, 252–253.
30 Id. [129].
31 Id. [130].
32 The concept of objective spirit is central in Hegel's philosophy. Reidel identifies a number of meanings for the term, one of which is the supra-individual, transsubjective spirit common to a unified class of subjects. See M. Reidel, *Between Tradition and Revolution* (W. Right tr., Cambridge, 1984), 3. Another way of thinking about it is to say that objective spirit represents the vital practices and institutions in which individuals recognize their community. See C. Taylor, *Hegel and Modern Society* (Cambridge, 1979), 89.
33 G.W.F. Hegel, *Philosophy of Right* (1821; T.M. Knox tr., Oxford at the Clarendon Press, 1952, 1st ed., 1967 reprint), [217].
34 Id. [52].
35 Ibid.
36 Id. [64] and [65].
37 Id. [65].
38 Id. [66].
39 Id. [57].
40 Id. [66].
41 J. Hughes, 'The Philosophy of Intellectual Property', 77 *Georgetown Law Journal*, 287, 340–341 (1988).
42 G.W.F. Hegel, *Philosophy of Right* (1821; T.M. Knox tr., Oxford at the Clarendon Press, 1952, 1st ed., 1967 reprint), [44].
43 Id. [4], [56].
44 These are the words of article 6bis of the Berne Convention. They form the essential core of moral rights. For a discussion of their history and place in the

Convention, see S. Ricketson, *The Berne Convention for the Protection of Literary and Artistic Works: 1886–1986* (London, 1987), 455–76.

45 See S. Strömholm, 'Droit Moral – The International and Comparative Scene from a Scandinavian Viewpoint', 14 *International Review of Industrial Property and Copyright Law*, 1, 11 (1983).

46 See Kant, 'Von der Unrechtmäßigkeit des Büchernachdruckes' cited in Stig Strömholm, 'Droit Moral – The International and Comparative Scene from a Scandinavian Viewpoint', 14 *International Review of Industrial Property and Copyright Law*, 1, 11 (1983). See also I. Kant, *The Metaphysics of Morals* (M.J. Gregor tr., Cambridge, 1991), 106–107 where he discusses the question 'What Is a Book?'

47 For a survey and discussion of some of the European literature, see A.S. Katz, 'The Doctrine of Moral Right and American Copyright Law – A Proposal', 24 *Southern California Law Review*, 1 (1951); E.J. Damich, 'The Right of Personality: A Common-Law Basis for the Protection of the Moral Rights of Authors', 23 *Georgia Law Review*, 1 (1988). See also S. Ricketson, *The Berne Convention for the Protection of Literary and Artistic Works: 1886–1986* (Kluwer, 1987), 456, fn. 435 for a sample of this literature.

48 G.W.F. Hegel, *Philosophy of Right* (1821; T.M. Knox tr., Oxford at the Clarendon Press 1952, 1st ed., 1967 reprint), [68].

49 Ibid.

50 Id. [69].

51 For a clarification of many misconceptions of Hegel's theory of state, see S. Avineri, *Hegel's Theory of the Modern State* (Cambridge at the University Press, 1972).

52 G.W.F. Hegel, *Philosophy of Right* (T.M. Knox tr., Oxford at the Clarendon Press 1952, 1st ed., 1967 reprint), [151].

53 Z.A. Pelczynski, 'The Hegelian Conception of the State' in Z.A. Pelczynski (ed.), *Hegel's Political Philosophy: Problems and Perspectives* (Cambridge, London, 1971), 1–29.

54 Id. 13.

55 C. Taylor, *Hegel and Modern Society* (Cambridge, 1979), 83.

56 Hegel, 'The German Constitution' in *Hegel's Political Writings* (T.M. Knox tr., Oxford at the Clarendon Press, 1964), 153.

57 See the essay, G.W.F. Hegel, 'The Scientific Ways of Treating Natural Law, Its Place in Moral Philosophy, and Its Relation to the Positive Sciences of Law' (1802, 1803; T.M. Knox tr., University of Pennsylvania Press, 1975), 77–80.

58 Id. 79

59 Hegel, 'The English Reform Bill' in *Hegel's Political Writings* (T.M. Knox tr., Oxford at the Clarendon Press, 1964), 297.

60 Z.A. Pelczynski, 'An Introductory Essay' in *Hegel's Political Writings* (T.M. Knox tr., Oxford at the Clarendon Press, 1964), 49, note 2.

61 For an example of the concerns of international business, see *Basic Framework of GATT Provisions on Intellectual Property*, Statement of Views of the European, Japanese and United States Business Communities, June, 1988, The Intellectual Property Committee, Keidanren, UNICE.

62 The story of how this has been done is told in P. Drahos, 'Global Property Rights in Information: The Story of TRIPS at the GATT', 13 *Prometheus*, 6 (1995).

63 G.W.F. Hegel, *Philosophy of Right* (1821; T.M. Knox tr., Oxford at the Clarendon Press 1952, 1st ed., 1967 reprint), [217].

64 Id. [183].

65 Id. [185].

66 Id. [213].

67 Id. [195].

68 Id. [198].

69 Id. [195].

70 Id. [217]
71 Id. [241] and [242].
72 Id. [245] and [246].
73 At the end of his discussion of property Hegel develops a transition which takes him into contract. Id. [71].
74 On the dangers of homogenization for the modern state, see C. Taylor, *Hegel and Modern Society* (Cambridge, 1979), 114–117.
75 For an excellent analysis of the role of work in Hegel's political philosophy, see M. Reidel, *Between Tradition and Revolution* (W. Right tr., Cambridge, 1984), chapter 3.
76 See R.B.M. Cotterrell, *The Sociology of Law*, (London, 1984), chapter 3.
77 Z.A. Pelczynski, 'Hegel's Political Philosophy: Some Thoughts on its Contemporary Relevance' in Z.A. Pelczynski (ed.), *Hegel's Political Philosophy: Problems and Perspectives* (Cambridge, London, 1971), 230, 238.
78 See, for example, T. Parsons, 'An Outline of the Social System', in T. Parsons *et al* (eds.), *Theories of Society* (New York, 1965), 40.

5 Abstract Objects in Productive Life: Marx's Story

Introduction

Marx is typically thought of as one of property's great critics. No one looks to Marx in order to justify rights of property, as they do to Locke and Hegel. And yet, if his scientific and dialectical methodology is to be taken seriously, the goal of Marx's theoretical system is not criticism, but rather to try and provide, amongst other things, an explanation and understanding of the role of property in societal evolution.

Our purpose in looking at Marx is to make use of his distinctive explanatory perspective. We wish in particular to see if it helps us to come to a better understanding of the interconnectedness of intellectual property, especially the connection between intellectual property law and economic change in capitalist systems. Marx is a suitable choice for this purpose because through his dialectical method he sought to comprehend the way in which apparently diverse elements and concepts were related. For both Marx and Engels, dialectics was the key to understanding the processes of the whole.[1] We do not purport, however, in this chapter to reason dialectically. We merely take advantage of the fact that Marx, working dialectically, tried to show the way in which capital, labour, competition, value, property and profit were all organically and dynamically related.

Our central thesis is that intellectual property integrates creative labour into the productive life of capital. The parts of Marx's writings that help to establish this are his analysis of individual capitalists' responses to the pressures of competition, the importance of technology to economic growth, the commodity nature of capitalism and his view of human beings as fundamentally creative.

There are two respects in which Marx's writings do not particularly help in an analysis of intellectual property. First, since Marx was not concerned with trying to gain a juristic understanding of the nature of property, he does not offer a jurisprudential insight into the nature of intellectual property. Second, more than most Marx was focused on the materiality of production. There is no real treatment by him of the role of what we have called abstract objects in the means of production. Although it is not the main point of this chapter, we will see that abstract objects probably cause severe problems for some parts of Marx's economic theory. Amongst other things, it means he cannot treat labour in a homogeneous fashion. We also need to remember that the 19th-century intellectual property landscape was radically different from the one that exists now. While it is true that, during Marx's time in England, (1849 to his death in 1883), copyright and patent law were well established there, other areas, like the trademark registration system and protection of trade secrets, were only just beginning to emerge. The beginnings of the international framework for intellectual property protection in the form of the Paris Convention (1883) and the Berne Convention (1886) came after his death. Intellectual property as we know it today was in its infancy and its profound impact, as shown by such matters as legislation protecting circuit layouts and plant variety rights, could not have been part of Marx's world view. It is clear from Marx's writings that he had more than a passing familiarity with substantive areas of law like property.[2] But it is also almost certainly true that when he wrote of property relations he had in mind physical objects like land and not abstract objects. Ownership for him was ownership of the tangible.

We should also make clear where this chapter stands in relation to the vast literature on Marxian legal theory. Law, we know, did not feature as a principal category of theorizing in Marx. Nevertheless Marx's theory of historical materialism has implications and consequences for the understanding of law, some of which Marx articulated, albeit in a not very systematic way.[3] It is fair to say that both Marx's theory and some of his remarks have, after a slow start, generated a vast body of Marxian legal theory.[4] While much of this would undoubtedly be helpful to an understanding of intellectual property, this chapter focuses on Marx's work rather than on the many interpretations and theories he has inspired in the field of legal theory.

The rest of this chapter is divided up in the following way. The first section identifies some hypotheses which can be generated using Marx's theory of historical materialism in an orthodox fashion. Some problems with these are discussed. The next two sections then articulate the main thesis of the chapter.

Marx on Property: Three Orthodox Views and their Application

There are at least three important ideas which can be found in Marx's work regarding property. The first is that property is a form of alienation. Second, property is a class instrument, which is used by the ruling class to protect its interests. Third is the idea that property (especially private property) is a ruling idea, that is, property is part of ideology.

This list almost certainly does not exhaust other ideas that might be found in Marx concerning property. For instance, in *Grundrisse* Marx admits that property is a precondition to production, although he then goes on to argue that property in this sense means appropriation.[5] A little later he also seems to suggest that law (particularly property) may have important effects on production.[6] Ultimately, though, he does not seem to think that property is an independent institution worthy of analysis in its own right. In a telling remark he suggests that the origin of property lies in the productivity of labour.[7] The idea that property may in various ways increase productivity is not an idea that he really explores. A sympathetic exegesis and interpretation of Marx's works would probably uncover some other views that Marx had of property. This is not undertaken here.

Property as Alienation

The connection between property and alienation is to be found in the *Economic and Philosophic Manuscripts of 1844*.[8] There Marx argues that private property is the outcome of externalized, alienated labour. Alienation was, broadly speaking, a term used by Marx to describe counterproductive relations of separation in capitalism. Workers were alienated from their environment, from the products of their labour and finally from themselves. Alienation was for Marx a brute fact of capitalist production, a fact which led him to formulate a theory of alienation. Property in this theory is a manifestation of alienation rather than a cause. For the moment we will put a discussion of alienated labour to one side and return to it in the next section where we claim that capitalism depends on creative labour.

Class Control over Abstract Objects

The idea that property is an instrument of the powerful is part of Marx's broader thesis about the nature of the connection between law and class. The two principal classes in capitalism, the ruling class (bourgeoisie, capitalists) and the proletariat (workers) are structurally locked in conflict with each other. Law in this struggle belongs, as it were, to the ruling class. It is one of the instruments by which members maintain control over the source of their power, the means of production.[9] The class instrumentalist thesis is connected to Marx's materialist conception of history. The law or laws involved in this conception hold that social life can be divided into a set of economic relations, these economic relations being the real foundation on which a legal and political superstructure is built. There is not much doubt that for Marx law is a systems outcome. That is to say, law is not to be understood as an independent force in social life and history but rather is a consequence of the relations and forces of production, or, to use Marx's phrase, has its 'roots in the material conditions of life'.[10] In a very famous passage, Marx outlines the key ideas that are involved in the materialist theory of history. The following passage is worth setting out:

> In the social production of their life, men enter into definite relations that are indispensable and independent of their will, relations of production which correspond to a definite stage of development of their material productive forces. The sum total of these relations of production constitutes the economic structure of society, the real foundation, on which rises a legal and political superstructure and to which correspond definite forms of social consciousness. The mode of production of material life conditions the social, political and intellectual life process in general. It is not the consciousness of men that determines their being, but, on the contrary, their social being that determines their consciousness. At a certain stage of their development, the material productive forces of society come in conflict with the existing relations of production, or – what is but a legal expression for the same thing – with the property relations within which they have been at work hitherto. From forms of development of the productive forces these relations turn into their fetters. Then begins an epoch of social revolution. With the change of the economic foundation the entire immense superstructure is more or less rapidly transformed.[11]

The materialist concept of history carries with it a kind of algorithmic routine which can be used to analyse any given superstructural phenomenon like, for instance, intellectual property. Essentially, this involves identifying the links between the forces of production and the relations of production in a given historical period and then discovering how the particular superstructural phenomenon comes within the field of operation of the material base. Generally speaking, when this method is applied to law, law emerges as a form of class domination in which the ruling class, that is to say those who own the means of production, use law to protect their economic interests and to further their grip on power. So it is that property and contract law serve to entrench inequality, while the mission of criminal law is to coerce the lower classes. This is not the only Marxist view of law. In fact many working within Marxist legal theory see the class instrumentalist view of law as simplistic.[12] Still, there is little doubt, especially from a reading of *Capital*, that Marx saw class agendas lying at the heart of core areas of law such as property and contract.

One way in which this chapter could proceed, then, would be to adopt the materialist version of history as an article of faith and look for verifying evidence of class interest and exploitation in intellectual property regimes. This would be to treat Marx ideologically rather than philosophically and so we do not take this approach. If, though, we subscribe to methodological tolerance as a value we should not be too hasty in sweeping Marx's theory of history off the table for, like other sharply reductive theories, it remains useful in that it allows one to generate hypotheses for investigation. This is not the time or place to begin to assess historical materialism.[13] One problem with the materialist conception of history is that, on one reading of it, possible contingent social truths are turned into *a priori* truths. The task of the social scientist becomes that of low level verification. The theory in a sense overdirects the empirical work. If, on the other hand, one takes the view that historical materialism is false or inadequate, this does not entail the falsity of the class domination thesis of law in all cases. It remains a contingent possibility that some areas of law are the rigged outcomes of class manoeuvrings. In any case Marx's theoretical framework is one way in which to generate hypotheses about complex phenomena.

The dramatic expansion of intellectual property regimes, both nationally and internationally, in recent decades is in Marx's terms an important superstructural transformation. It may also be evidence of fundamental changes taking place in the productive forces of some major capitalist economies. The creation of legally enforceable international standards of intellectual protection may be evidence that some states (ruling states) are using intellectual property law to maintain their various forms of power as their mode of production undergoes a profound transformation. The march to prominence of intellectual property law suggests that at least some states will largely earn their living through the production and distribution of information.[14]

Historical materialism could also be used to begin an explanation of some other features of intellectual property law. Typically, intellectual property statutes are based on the rights of owners rather than the originators of the relevant piece of intellectual property.[15] Creators will often not be the owners of the intellectual property they generate because of the operation of doctrines of employment law that vest ownership of intellectual property in their employers, or because they have assigned ownership to another. In Marx's terms it is capitalists rather than workers that end up owning most of the intellectual property that is produced within a capitalist economy. Conversely, protection for the interests of performers has tended to be characterized by a minimalist approach.[16]

Given that a standard justification for intellectual property is that it provides individuals with a reason to devote the time and resources to innovation and creation, it is at first instance surprising that intellectual property law is less concerned with the rights and protection of originators of intellectual property than with the rights of others, such as employers or publishers.[17] There would probably be nothing surprising about this pattern for Marx, however. Creative labour (authors, scientists, performers) would in a capitalist economy be 'exploited' labour. Exploitation in Marx's theory is a technical, theoretical term that refers to a social process in which the capitalist acquires labour power. Its essence, though, is simple enough: if a person works for more hours than is required to produce the goods he consumes, that person is being exploited.[18] Unpaid labour is at the heart of Marx's theory of exploitation. Labour power has the peculiar quality of producing *'more value than it has itself'* or, putting it another way, labour produces more value than it exchanges for in a free market.[19] The acquisition of surplus value is the basis of profit within the capitalist economy. Creative workers, that is to say workers who invent, write, paint and so on, would not be in any different position to other workers within capitalism. Out of necessity such workers would offer their creative labour power for sale. For this reason intellectual property laws are not needed to motivate individuals to work creatively. Instead, intellectual property laws would be needed to ensure that ruling interests retained and extended their control over a vital part of the means of production – abstract objects.

Marx in *Capital* clearly assumed that law, and in particular contract and property law, plays a vital role in the workings of the capitalist economy. So, for example, when he discusses the conditions under which labour power can appear as a commodity he stipulates that labour power must be capable of being traded in a free market.[20] Similarly, the market exchange of commodities requires that there be owners who recognize each other's private property rights.[21] The juridical relation between owners remains an expression of 'the real economic relation between the two'.[22] But clearly Marx saw here a facilitative and protective role for property and contract law. Bearing this protective function of law in mind, we can say that another possible role of intellectual property within Marx's theory is that it serves to protect the investment by individual members of the capitalist class in a mode of production based on abstract objects. Intellectual property, in other words, is primarily about the organization and maintenance of production and a set of economic relations rather than an incentive to production by individuals. Intellectual property rights, rather than being a stimulus to creation, form the legal basis upon which one class organizes production by another.

Ideology Theory

Intellectual property for Marx would also have a clear ideological function.[23] A persistent theme in Marx's work is that categories of bourgeois thought, whether they be legal, economic or religious, conceal the true character of capitalist production and its social relations. For Marx the view that intellectual property law functions to motivate and reward the creative proletarian would be an ideological fairy tale designed to hide the systematic exploitation of creative labour in the capitalist mode of production. Intellectual property law, because it turns abstract objects into things of ownership, adds to what Marx called the 'Fetishism of commodities'.[24] Fetishism in Marx's economic theory is a belief by men that commodities and the exchange of commodities are relations that exist independently of their social relations. People's perception of the social world becomes mediated by the seemingly independent world of commodities. People read off truths about the world, not based on a scientific understanding of it, but rather based on the behaviour of commodities. Fluctuations in the price of commodities, for instance, hide the true role of labour in the capitalist economy. Intellectual property, we have said, relates to the ownership of abstract objects. For Marx intellectual property would represent the commodification of the mental life of men and women. In intellectual property commodity fetishism reaches its peak. The mental life of individuals, the very thing which can be most said to belong to a person, becomes externalized (or alienated) and part of the relations between things, part of capitalism's production and exchange mechanisms. One of the consequences of commodity fetishism is that bourgeois economics analyses intellectual property independently of its social relations. Intellectual property, for example, serves to correct the market in information, or is a solution to a free-riding problem or a way to deal with an externality. Nothing is said about the underlying social relations that the production of intellectual property is based on. The fact that people have, in the commodified world of abstract objects, divorced themselves from the social relations to be found in the notion of positive community and the intellectual commons is obscured by the fetishism of commodities.

The use of ideology theory to explain some aspects of intellectual property is worth considering. It may help to cast some light on why individual actors support intellectual property rights when, on the face of it, one might expect that it would be in their rational self-interest not to. We have already observed that many individuals will not be the owners of the intellectual property they produce. Intellectual property enables a price to be put on information. Consumers, generally speaking, will want to pay less rather than more for something and so could be expected to support weaker rather than stronger intellectual property regimes. This is particularly so if it turns out that much of the production of the information for which they are paying was not itself stimulated by intellectual property rights. Individual states which are *net* importers of intellectual property might also be expected to pursue lower rather than higher standards of intellectual property protection.[25] And the costs of enforcing highly protectionist intellectual regimes are likely to be high – and not just in economic terms. Keeping track of who uses what information for pricing and enforcement purposes is likely to involve highly intrusive audit and surveillance procedures. So, in the light of these kinds of problems, what motivates the apparently strong commitment by many individuals in capitalist societies to support the ever-higher levels of intellectual property protection?

Ideology theory is one way in which to account for what at first sight seems a puzzling phenomenon. The direction of the argument would be that intellectual property rights, functioning as ideology, serve to promote beliefs that support one set of interests at the expense of another. One problem with proceeding in this direction is that a theory of ideology that is genuinely explanatory is needed. Marx himself did not pull together all his observations on ideology in one place. His theory of ideology has to be constructed. Moreover, as Elster has observed, it lacks microfoundations.[26] The problem does not lie in accepting the proposition that some knowledge is such that it deludes people about the true nature of the reality that confronts them. Plato's simile of the cave in *The Republic* suggests, in a somewhat clearer fashion, the same possibility. The real difficulty lies in trying to explain how 'ruling ideas' emerge in favour of the ruling class.[27] In Plato's simile all the inhabitants of the cave are equally affected, because all have been made prisoners and forced to look at the wall of the cave opposite them. In Marx's capitalism, it is those who do not own the means of production that are condemned to a life amongst the shadows.

This completes our discussion of what might be termed an orthodox application of Marx to intellectual property. Before moving on we should observe that it is riddled with problems and raises many more questions than it answers. If, for example, one accepts that there is a class pattern which underlies intellectual property regimes then one has to have some general account of how a class (as opposed to individuals, organizations or groups) can be a social force.[28] And there has to be an explanation of how, in the case of intellectual property, this class action is internationally coordinated and furthermore coordinated amongst individual members that have conflicting economic interests (for example, owners of the media having to pay owners of copyright material). The claim that intellectual property is an effect of deeper changes in the economic base also faces a well-known and fundamental problem. Marx made a conceptual distinction between the economic structure of a society and its legal and political superstructure. Having made the distinction, a question naturally arises about the nature of the relationship between these distinct parts of society. On one reading of his theory, Marx is taken to be making a simple causal claim about the nature of the relationship. The economic structure or base causes the superstructure to come into existence; changes in the superstructure are the effects of changes in the economic base. The causal claim is of the kind A ——> B, where B is an effect of A. But using this as a description of the relation between the economic base and the superstructure faces an analytical problem. In describing what constitutes the forces of production and the relations of production (the base) one is dependent upon legal relations and in particular contract and property relations. Law does not just reflect the base but actually helps to constitute it.[29] The existence and exchange of commodities depends on law having a constitutive role. The analytical problem becomes this: if the existence of A is now heavily dependent upon B, can we plausibly continue to assert the simple causal relationship of A ——> B in the case of the relationship between base and superstructure? If B is part of A, are we not asserting that B in some sense is self-causing? The problem is not confined to law. Morality, religion and ideological knowledge can all be made to play a part in the base. This kind of objection to historical materialism is potentially very damaging, for it claims that the driving force of history presupposes for its existence the very thing that it is meant to produce. So it is not surprising that attention has been paid to it and some convincing replies have been made.[30] Rerunning these is not the purpose of this chapter. Here we simply want to illustrate that an orthodox application of Marx's theory to intellectual property is very much the start of an inquiry.

We have seen that historical materialism, with its reductive concentration on the forces of production, does offer the beginnings of a way into the complex, intricate legal structures erected by nation states, world regulatory institutions and transnational corporations as they strive for economic success and domination. In the next section, using parts of Marx's economic theory, we explore the idea that capitalism seeks out creative labour and integrates it into its system of production.

Creative Labour

Marx, unlike some early liberal thinkers, saw labour in positive terms. For instance, he criticizes Adam Smith for his essentially negative portrayal of labour.[31] Marx concedes that certain historically conditioned forms of labour, like slave labour and wage labour, could hardly be described as rewarding. Forms of wage labour such as coal mining or factory work were, for Marx, examples of 'forced labour'.[32] Such labour did not satisfy real human needs but rather provided a means for satisfaction of needs. But Marx did think there was a positive thesis to state concerning labour. Labour could be a creative activity, part of the self-realization of the subject that could lead to real freedom. In Marx's thinking labour ceases to be just an economic variable or category and becomes a philosophical view of what might be in the context of a different set of social relations. He argues that individual labour in essence can in the right social setting and circumstances be simultaneously fulfilling self-expression and an expression of man's universal nature. The connection between self-expression and labour is to be found in earlier thinkers.[33] What is different in Marx's use of it is that private property is not needed to protect that self-expression.

An example which Marx gives of free labour is composing music.[34] For Marx, the fact that free forms of labour such as musical composition, writing, dramatic performance, scientific discovery and so on become commodified and enter the relations of capitalist production would be evidence of intense alienation.

Creative labour does not feature centrally in Marx's analysis of capitalism for the simple reason that most labour which takes place in the capitalist economy is alienated labour.[35] Alienated labour is labour which is external to the worker or, putting it another way, labour with which he has no meaningful connection. By virtue of the relations of production which exist in capitalism it is coerced labour. Alienation takes place in the context of production. Men are separated from both the products of their labour and from themselves. They are also separated from their universal nature, or what Marx calls the species character of man. This fundamental species character is for man free conscious activity. It is just this kind of productive life that capitalism through its commodity-based production form takes away from man.

It is alienated labour rather than creative or free labour that is the paradigmatic form of labour in capitalism, according to Marx. Here we want to suggest that capitalism in its evolution comes to depend on, and actively encourages, creative labour. How does this square with Marx's claim that labour in capitalism is alienated labour? Creative labour in the way it is used here does not refer to the ideal form of unalienated labour that Marx seems to contemplate will come into existence once the social relations of capitalism are replaced by those of communism. We are using creative labour in a more mundane way. Drawing on our discussion of creativity in Chapter 3, creative labour can be said to refer to the type of creativity which is employed in industry and commerce to improve systems, products, methods of production and so forth. It is the creativity which drives competitive capitalism and its processes of innovation. We need to remind ourselves that capitalism, in the way that Marx portrays it, is not a system in restful equilibrium. Apart from recurrent economic crises it is characterized by intense competition and the ceaseless search for new markets.[36] According to Marx, there is within capitalism a 'progressive tendency of the general rate of profit to fall'.[37] This tendency produces a competitive struggle amongst capitalists.[38] And this in turn leads individual capitalists to introduce new methods of production and new products. It follows that innovation turns out to be central to the individual capitalist's survival in the market-place. The future development of capitalism comes in a significant sense to depend on creative labour. Marx does not argue for this last proposition, but it does seem to be a consequence of his theory. To summarize: despite the widespread presence of alienated labour in capitalism, there is also creative labour. It is creative labour which is the source of much-needed innovation within capitalism.

The conclusion we are heading towards in this section is that capitalism seeks out creative labour and integrates such labour into its system of production. The task of integration is achieved through intellectual property law. Before moving to this conclusion we need to digress and make it clear that it does not depend on accepting Marx's theory of surplus value. The theory of surplus value, along with the labour theory of value and his analysis of commodities, forms a central core of his economic theory. The adequacy of Marx's theory of surplus value and his economic theory is a matter of specialist debate amongst Marxist and non-Marxist economists.[39] It is, for example, not clear that his theory of surplus value can form the foundation of a theory of price. Similarly the labour theory of value has to do a lot of work in order to offer a convincing alternative to the concepts of competition and market when it comes to explaining profit and exchange values. For our purposes there is no need to enter the literature on Marx the economist. The reason lies in the fact that Marx's economic theory is located within the broader theoretical framework of historical materialism, which itself is informed by a dialectical methodology. The economic Marx, as the afterword to the second German edition of volume 1 of *Capital* makes clear, never abandons this methodology.[40] Through its use Marx is able to identify the contrary forces that operate beneath the illusory surface phenomena of capitalism and which ultimately make it a system in transition. Similarly the opening parts of *Grundrisse* show that Marx was concerned, not just with the economics of capitalism, but with trying to understand capitalism as a historically distinctive society in which philosophically abstract categories like commodity, labour, capital and value are given a historically unique specification. In *Capital* the emphasis is on the internal organic relations between these categories. Within Marx's broad theoretical framework there are probably a number of theories and arguments that can, if need be, be treated separately. Without defending it here we claim that we can treat Marx's analysis of the internal relations between capitalism's principal categories independently of the surplus theory of value. Marx may still have something to offer on the sources of capitalism's economic growth, even if the theory of surplus value turns out to be a poor microeconomic model.[41] Bearing in mind these observations concerning the theory of surplus value, we can return to our argument.

In bourgeois society capital is the 'all-dominating power'.[42] Marx assumes that individual capitalists are the highly rational pursuers of value (value is converted into profit). According to Marx the 'restless never-ending process of profit-making alone is what he [the capitalist] aims at'.[43] The individual capitalist becomes the representative of a system of production that has for its goal the expansion of value. Value becomes an end in itself. This system of production forces or, putting it another way, makes it rational for, individual capitalists to accumulate capital so that through the introduction of new technology they can extend that capital. A passage from *Capital* illustrates:

> Moreover, the development of capitalist production makes it constantly necessary to keep increasing the amount of the capital laid out in a given industrial undertaking, and competition makes the immanent laws of capitalist production to be felt by each individual capitalist, as external coercive laws. It compels him to keep constantly extending his capital, in order to preserve it, but extend it he cannot, except by means of progressive accumulation.[44]

We can see roughly what Marx has in mind here. Using assumptions that are similar to the model of perfect competition, Marx is suggesting that competition forces the individual capitalist into technological innovation in order to find new sources of value. His ability to do so is conditioned by levels of capital accumulation.

There is an important idea in Marx's discussion of technical change in capitalism. He seems to assume that the demand by individual capitalists for new methods of production will be satisfied. That is to say that the capitalist mode of production seeks machinery that will, at least temporarily, increase profit (in Marx's terms, increase the production of surplus value) and what is more it obtains that machinery. It seems to be part of Marx's theory that technological innovation is at least to some degree endogenous. Technological innovation is a phenomenon that has economic determinants. For Marx the prime, and perhaps only, determinant is the demand for labour-saving technology, although clearly there can be others such as investment rates and industry size. Innovation is not simply the happy outcome of individual inventive inspiration. The supply of innovation in a capitalist market is at least to some degree determined by economic variables.[45]

One clear implication of Marx's discussion of technological innovation is that capitalism needs to foster creative labour and to integrate it into its systems of production. We should make it clear here that this is for us a necessary consequence of Marx's analysis of capitalism. It is not a proposition that he explicitly advances or defends. The same implication occurs in a passage from Engels: 'the ever-increasing perfectibility of modern machinery is, by the anarchy of social production, turned into a compulsory law that forces the individual industrial capitalist always to improve his machinery, always to increase its productive force'.[46] There is simply no way for these technological improvements to occur without the presence of creative labour in the capitalist mode of production.[47] The result is that creative labour comes to find itself in capital's harness. A good example of this general process of the integration of creative labour into the productive forces of capitalism is to be found in some of Marx's remarks on the role of science in capitalism. (Scientific labour is for us an example of creative labour.)

Labour throughout its history undergoes various changes, but the final change in capitalism is the development of the machine and automation. This development is the specific manifestation of capital's tendency to increase labour's productivity.[48] Machines exist as 'objectified labour'.[49] They are the concrete embodiment of society's collective skill and knowledge. What Marx calls direct labour is in later capitalism simply one element in the process of production. Even more importantly the production process has become more scientific in nature. Capital is linked to a definite mode of production which includes science, while simultaneously science helps to bring this mode into being. Once a stage has been reached where industry has significantly progressed, science becomes part of the productive forces of capitalism. It metamorphizes into capital. Two passages from Marx help to illustrate the point:

> The accumulation of knowledge and of skill, of the general productive forces of the social brain, is thus absorbed into capital, as opposed to labour and hence appears as an attribute of capital.[50]

> Invention then becomes a business, and the application of science to direct production itself becomes a prospect which determines and solicits it.[51]

The Tasks of Intellectual Property

We have argued that capitalism comes to depend on creative labour and that, as a result, it integrates such labour into its productive life. How is this done? This section argues that the integration is achieved through intellectual property law.

Marx begins *Capital* with an analysis of commodity. Capitalist wealth presents itself, Marx says, in the form of 'an immense accumulation of commodities'.[52] The emphasis on commodity is both a strength and a weakness in Marx's overall analysis. Boss, in a perceptive analysis of Marx's economic theory, argues that Marx uses a simple factory paradigm to model capitalist economic life.[53] The preoccupation with showing factory workers to be *the* productive force in capitalism leads him into what she terms input–output error. This error occurs where some given labour or activity is thought to be both a necessary intermediate input and an unproductive superfluous output.[54] Marx, Boss argues, commits an input–output error because in his economic universe the producer of commodities is genuinely productive while the provider of services is genuinely parasitic.[55] One colourful example of the kind of error that Boss is talking about is to be found in *Grundrisse*. Marx there says, in relation to the service provided by a woodcutter, 'this performance of a service cannot fall under the category of productive labour. From whore to pope, there is a mass of such rabble.'[56] Marx's analytical objection to classifying the woodcutter's labour as productive is that the capitalist who acquires the service acquires only the *use* value of the service, a use value which is immediately consumed.[57] There is for Marx nothing left to circulate in the economy: the exchange between the capitalist and the woodcutter produces no value.

Marx's analysis of commodity is admittedly complex, for he is seeking to link it to the social relations of production while at the same time explaining the exchange values of commodities. But in some respects his concept of commodity is not so subtle. The problem lies in the fact that Marx is fixated by the materiality of production, with the consequence that the archetypal commodity within the Marxian economic framework is the material object. This preoccupation with material objects, as we have seen, sets limits on what he considers to be productive labour. It also leads him away from exploring the idea that, through law, capitalism engineers new commodity possibilities for itself. In order to support these claims, we need to quote a passage from *Grundrisse*:

> Is it not crazy ... that the piano maker is a *productive* worker, but not the *piano player*, although obviously the piano would be absurd without the piano player? But this is exactly the case. The piano maker reproduces *capital*; the pianist only exchanges his labour for revenue. But doesn't the pianist produce music and satisfy our musical ear, does he not even to a certain extent produce the latter? He does indeed: his labour produces something; but that does not make it *productive labour* in the *economic sense*; no more than the labour of the madman who produces delusions is productive.[58]

Marx's example here is in one sense a contrast between the tangible and intangible. It reveals what is the strong tendency by Marx in both *Grundrisse* and *Capital* to think of productive labour as being linked to the production of material objects.

Earlier, in Chapter 2 it was argued that intellectual property relates to abstract objects and that one view of abstract objects is that they are convenient mental fictions. To say that they are convenient is to understate their value to capitalist production. In fact abstract objects have the effect of qualitatively expanding the commodity production possibilities of capitalism. We can illustrate with the very example which Marx uses to show that services do not amount to productive labour.

Assume that the pianist is playing her own original composition. Generally speaking, copyright statutes create copyright in musical works. The definition of musical works is usually very open-ended or sometimes not defined at all.[59] But once copyright in a musical work exists the pianist has something to own, something to sell or license. The convenient mental fiction (the abstract object) becomes through law a commodity. The pianist is now in the same position as the piano maker, contrary to Marx's assertion. She steps over the economic border that separates the badlands of unproductive workers from the rolling green fields inhabited by productive workers and enters the productive life of capital.

Intellectual property law is critical to her successful passage. It would, however, be a mistake to think that intellectual property law simply creates private property rights in the abstract object and so is no different from property rights in material objects. When he comes to analyse the exchange of commodities, Marx makes it clear that property and contract are necessary juridical phenomena for the exchange of commodities, but these are only reflections of underlying economic relations in the process of exchange.[60] In fact one might go further and observe that what matters for the exchange of commodities is the recognition of rights of control and that these do not necessarily entail the existence of property rights. Commodities can exist and be traded without the existence of formal property rights. Presumably trade can take place in a state of nature. All that is required is some physical control over the goods. For our purposes, the point to observe is that in the case of material commodities the existence of the commodity does not depend on the existence of property rights. But this is not the case for abstract objects. Once copyright in musical works becomes part of law both our pianist and our piano maker can be said to produce commodities. But it is only the pianist who depends on intellectual property for the creation of her commodity. In the absence of an intellectual property right she is left to sell her concert performances (an unproductive service, according to Marx's theory). Without intellectual property there simply would be no abstract object which participants in the market could recognize and make the subject of trade.

The argument we have put can be stated in the following propositions. The existence of physical commodities does not depend on law. The existence of abstract objects does. Commerce in physical commodities and abstract objects depends on a scheme of property rights and contract. Marx's contradiction is that he sees labour as a value-producing commodity and yet does not recognize it as such when it is provided as a service or when it takes the form of an abstract object (in our sense of the term).

Now we are in a better position to see how intellectual property accomplishes the task of integrating creative labour into the capitalist mode of production. Marx more clearly than anyone sees that capitalism is a mode of production in which commodities are amassed on a historically unprecedented scale. Capitalism is not, however, the only mode of production which produces commodities. This is true of earlier forms of production. Where capitalism is distinctive is that it is a system in which the labour power of one class has become a circulating commodity available for purchase by another class, the members of both classes being formally free to buy and sell commodities.[61] It is the condition of being able to readily acquire labour power that gives capitalism its Midas touch in economic production. Our argument has been that capitalism increasingly comes to depend on creative labour. Individual, rational capitalists, subject to competitive pressures, begin to seek out creative labour, for it is creative labour that is the source of much-wanted innovation. We have deliberately steered away from trying to explain this search in terms of the theory of surplus value. Rather our position is this: the search by individual capitalists for creative labour is motivated by the desire for control and ownership of the abstract object so as to gain a competitive edge over a rival. In the next chapter we shall see that the ownership of abstract objects can function to relieve individuals from competitive pressures. This provides another incentive for individual capitalists to chase the ownership of abstract objects. Clearly, if abstract objects exist under conditions of positive inclusive community (that is, they belong to all) the incentives for individual capitalists to pursue them will be considerably reduced. So one task of intellectual property law, from the perspective of the industrialist, is to create conditions of negative community so that the ownership of abstract objects is possible.

Intellectual property, in commodifying universal mental constructs, dramatically increases the commodity horizons of capitalism. Intellectual property is perhaps a sign that the commodity nature of capitalism never stops evolving. Marx thought that the commodity of labour power was the form of commodity that was distinctive to capitalism. Our analysis suggests that understanding the productive powers of capitalism does not stop with the commodification of labour power. Through the creation of abstract objects, intellectual property law provides capitalism with another distinctive commodity form and, potentially at least, another means to its further expansion. By creating abstract objects intellectual property brings creative labour directly into the relations of production. Capitalism can continue its historically spectacular commodity production run because through intellectual property law it has re-engineered the possibilities of commodity production. Not only that, creative labour, through the creation of more efficient means of production, actually diminishes the role of physical labour. The aim of the industrialist is no longer to control physical labour through contract and industrial relations law but to control creative labour through intellectual property law.

One last remark before we close this section. Intellectual property, we have argued, is fundamental to the task of integrating creative labour and abstract objects into capitalism's production processes. This argument does not mean that we abandon Marx's view about the fundamental materiality of production. Much of the literature on post-industrial society or post-capitalist society tends to over-emphasize the role of knowledge in production in order to obtain a convenient and bright dividing line between capitalist and post-capitalist epochs.[62] Drucker offers a typical characterization of this: 'The basic economic resource – "the means of production", to use the economist's term – is no longer capital, nor natural resources (the economist's 'land'), nor 'labour'. *It is and will be knowledge.*'[63] However, our analysis of the role of the abstract object in production, when placed in the context of Marx's overall theory, suggests that perhaps good old-fashioned industrial capitalism has a way to run before it is given its last rites by scholars. Our reasons for thinking this are these. When he comes to discuss the role of physical forces (the laws of nature) Marx says that these cost the capitalist nothing once they are discovered.[64] But in order for these laws to enter the productive life of capital they must be consumed productively and that, for Marx, requires that they be mediated by or be embodied in some item of hardware, some industrial article: 'A water-wheel is necessary to exploit the force of water, and a steam-engine to exploit the elasticity of steam.'[65] Abstract objects cannot just simply step into production.

We now have the makings of a paradox. The greater the role of abstract objects in capitalist production, the greater the production of the hardware of technology there needs to be. Abstract objects propel capitalism into ever-higher levels of industrial production of physical objects. Furthermore it is clear that for Marx each new generation of technologies carries with it greater and greater investment costs. Manual tools are cheap. Machine tools are not – and computer-controlled machine tools, even less so. The rough shape of our paradox is that abstract objects, which once in existence cost nothing or little, when absorbed into capitalist production cost capitalists a great deal in terms of investment. Intangible objects generate ever-higher levels of tangible commodities. It is industrial commodity production that abstract objects help stimulate, with the result that fewer workers are employed in that production directly (because of automation) and more services are required to match the higher levels of production. For the individual capitalist there is no choice about the levels of investment needed to stay in what has become a technological race. Investment is forced upon him by competition.[66] In language not intended to comfort, Marx says, 'one capitalist always kills many'.[67]

The upshot of our remarks is this. We must not make intellectual property reveal more than is there. For post-industrial scholars, the intellectual property phenomenon seems to offer support for their pronouncements of radical social transformation. Our position is a more cautious one. Through intellectual property law, capitalism engineers new production possibilities for itself.[68] Creative labour is brought into the fold of productive labour, but the transformative possibilities of this remain for the time being grounded in a paradigm of commodity accumulation. So-called 'knowledge societies' have, through new communications and information technologies, the opportunity to reorganize the work patterns of their individual citizens in ways that liberate those citizens from conditions of alienated labour. But capitalist knowledge societies, if Marx is right about the commodity nature of capitalism, will not take that opportunity. Abstract objects are absorbed into production as part of a cycle of commodity production. Abstract objects are used to continue capitalism's obsession with, to use modern parlance, the hardware of technology. Inequalities of an apparently new kind (for example, the information-poor versus the information-rich) appear, but in essence they are old forms of inequalities patterned around the ownership of productive forces. 'Knowledge workers' end up more like other workers, for like other wage-labourers they come to find themselves in conditions of alienated labour.

The impact of intellectual property norms upon the activities of the scientific community provides an example of the way in which the positive expressive activity of scientific research and discovery becomes alienated labour. Natural science becomes part of the natural forces of production because individual capitalists realize they cannot survive without constantly 'revolutionising the instruments of production'.[69] Modern industry draws on scientific knowledge to produce a 'science of technology'.[70] This science of technology is derived from many earlier separate forms of production such as trade guilds and craft industries. Modern industry takes the knowledge and know-how which has been locked away in these secretive, almost ritualistic enterprises and applies it to improving production. The modern form of the science of technology as we know it seems to be, for Marx, born out of industry.[71] Once in existence, its utility is apparent to all capitalists who are all constantly seeking to improve their production techniques. Science now finds itself press-ganged into capital's service.

The normative practices of scientists begin to change. Traditionally, scientists organized themselves around the goal of extending knowledge. This goal is served by an ethos of science which consists of four key values: universalism, communism, disinterestedness and organized scepticism.[72] Intellectual property, we have argued, plays a critical role in integrating creative labour into production. Through this process, intellectual property norms come to change the ethos of science.[73] (For Marx the change would only be a symptom of deeper causes.) The ethos of science rewards the sharing of information, the public communication of ideas (the incentives being prizes, scientific immortality, recognition and so on). The existence of an intellectual commons is seen to be crucial to successful individual work. This public domain attitude of science begins to change as intellectual property norms come to govern scientific labour. Open communication and the exchange of ideas are no longer so strongly endorsed by scientists because they might, amongst other things, defeat a proprietary claim to the knowledge.[74] The direction of scientific research becomes increasingly determined by state-based priorities expressed through intellectual property rights. The fact that ideas can in one way or another be owned is itself symbolic of the fact that scientific labour has become alienated labour.

Conclusion

Some of the blunter aspects of Marx's theory such as his class instrumentalism will not take us very far into an understanding of intellectual property. Bringing ideology theory to bear on the expansion of intellectual property will produce some kind of explanatory pay-off. The real benefit of using Marx's theory lies in his analysis of the commodity nature of capitalism, his understanding of individual capitalist behaviour and how this contributes to the growth of economic capitalism. Using these parts of his theory and extrapolating from them we can see that the major task of intellectual property is to integrate abstract objects and creative labour into the commodity life of capitalism. And we have seen that this is not just an economic phenomenon, but a social one. With the dismantling of the intellectual commons comes a change in social relations and community. Capitalist employers and their knowledge workers find themselves living in what we earlier called negative exclusive community. It may be that the integration of abstract objects into production will aid capitalism's growth. This is a matter for economists to determine. But the assumptions of conventional economics also suggest some real dangers in allowing the intellectual commons to be propertized. These dangers are the subject of the next chapter.

Notes

1 For an account of the advantages of dialectics over traditional metaphysical reasoning, see the essay by F. Engels, 'Socialism: Utopian and Scientific' (1880) in Karl Marx and Frederick Engels, *Selected Works* (vol. 3, Moscow, 1970), 95.

2 This is perhaps not surprising given that Marx's father was a lawyer and that Marx studied law at university. For a description of Marx's early life, see the Introduction by Eugene Kamenka in E. Kamenka (ed.), *The Portable Karl Marx* (Harmondsworth, 1983).

3 See the Preface in M. Cain and A. Hunt, *Marx and Engels on Law* (London, New York, San Francisco, 1979).

4 See for example, the essays and the bibliography in C. Varga (ed.), *Marxian Legal Theory* (Aldershot, 1993).

5 Karl Marx, *Grundrisse* (1857–58; M. Nicolaus tr., London, 1973), 87–88.

6 Id., 98.

7 Id., 397.

8 Karl Marx and Frederick Engels, *Collected Works* (London, 1975), vol. 3, 229. (Hereinafter *Collected Works* followed by the relevant volume number.)

9 See M. Cain and A. Hunt, *Marx and Engels on Law* (London, New York, San Francisco, 1979), chapter 3 for readings which support this simplified thesis. As Cain and Hunt point out, in their introduction to the chapter, Marx's work also contains a more nuanced view of law's role in capitalism.

10 Karl Marx, 'Preface to a Contribution to the Critique of Political Economy' (1859) in Karl Marx and Frederick Engels, *Selected Works* (Moscow, 1969), vol. 1, 503.

11 Id., 503–504

12 See, for example, A. Stone, 'The Place of Law in the Marxian Structure-Superstructure Archetype', 19 *Law and Society Review*, 39, 40 (1985).

13 For an excellent discussion beginning with a paper by G.A. Cohen, see J. Roemer (ed.), *Analytical Marxism* (Cambridge, 1986), Part I.

14 Hence the growing discussion of 'information capitalism'. See T. Morris-Suzuki, *Beyond Computopia* (London, New York, 1988); R. Kling (ed.), *Computerization and Controversy: Value Conflicts and Social Choices* (2nd ed., San Diego, forthcoming).

15 The only real exception to this is the authors' rights tradition which was briefly discussed in Chapter 4.

16 See E. Thompson, 'International Protection of Performers' Rights: Some Current Problems', 107 *International Labour Review*, 303 (1973).

17 For a discussion of how socialist law dealt with intellectual property, see W.A. Van Caenegem, 'Inventions in Russia: From Public Good to Private Property', 4 *Australian Journal of Intellectual Property*, 232 (1993).

18 See J. Elster, *Making Sense of Marx* (Cambridge, 1985), 167. There are now sophisticated treatments and developments of the theory of exploitation. See, for example, J.E. Roemer, *A General Theory of Exploitation* (Cambridge, Mass., 1982).

19 Karl Marx, *Capital* I (1867; Moscow, 1959), 193. (Hereinafter the references will be to *Capital* followed by the volume number.) The emphasis is Marx's.

20 *Capital* I, 168.

21 Id., 84.

22 Ibid.

23 Marx discusses ideology in the *Economic and Philosophic Manuscripts of 1844* (Collected Works, volume 3); *The German Ideology* (1845–46) (Collected Works, volume 5); *The Manifesto of the Communist Party* (1848) (Collected Works, volume 6), and *Capital* I. For discussions of Marxist ideology theory, see G.A. Cohen, *Karl Marx's Theory of History* (Oxford, Princeton, 1978), chapter 5; J. Elster, *Making Sense of Marx* (Cambridge, 1985), chapter 8; J. Plamenatz, *Ideology* (London, 1970); M. Seliger, *The Marxist Conception of Ideology: A Critical Essay* (Cambridge, 1977).

24 *Capital* I, 72 and section 4 of Chapter 1.

25 Most countries in the world would be in the position of being *net* importers of intellectual property. The author is not aware of any study that gives net figures on a country basis. However, patent figures show the probable net imbalance that exists for most countries. For example, in Australia in 1992 there were 1066 patents granted to residents (r) and 11 833 to non-residents (nr); Denmark 363 (r), 3410 (nr); Germany 17 833 (r), 28 687 (nr); United States 52 254 (r), 45 189 (nr). Figures are from *Industrial Property Statistics* (WIPO, Geneva, 1992). It is also difficult to get figures on the net effects on countries of trade in copyright. Many countries, like Australia, would have a net deficit in royalty transactions related to copyright. For Australia, in 1993–94, royalty payments to overseas holders of copyright totalled $1,732 million, while royalties earned from overseas amounted to $380 million. See Office of Regulation Review, *An Economic Analysis of Copyright Reform* (Commonwealth of Australia, 1995), 39.

26 J. Elster, *Making Sense of Marx* (Cambridge, 1985), 460.

27 K. Marx and F. Engels, *The German Ideology* (Collected Works, volume 5), 59.

28 For a good discussion of the problem, see B. Hindess, *Politics and Class Analysis* (Oxford, 1987).

29 An example of this line of thought is to be found in H. Collins, *Marxism and Law* (Oxford, 1982).

30 A now classic defence of historical materialism is G.A. Cohen, *Karl Marx's Theory of History* (Oxford, Princeton, 1978). For a criticism of Cohen, see H. Collins, *Marxism and Law* (Oxford, 1982). For Cohen's reply, see G.A. Cohen, 'Base and

Superstructure: A Reply to Hugh Collins', 9 *Oxford Journal of Legal Studies*, 95 (1989).

31 Karl Marx, *Grundrisse* (1857–58; M. Nicolaus tr., London, 1973), 610–614.

32 K. Marx, *Economic and Philosophic Manuscripts of 1844* (*Collected Works*, volume 3), 274.

33 Aristotle, *Nicomachean Ethics*, Book 9, section 7 contains the following striking passage:

> but we exist in activity, i.e. by living and acting, and in his activity the maker is, in a sense, the work produced. He therefore loves his work, because he loves existence. And this lies in the nature of things: what a thing is potentially is revealed in actuality by what it produces.

34 Karl Marx, *Grundrisse* (1857–58; M. Nicolaus tr., London, 1973), 611.

35 The following discussion of alienated labour is based on Marx's analysis of it in *Economic and Philosophic Manuscripts of 1844* (*Collected Works*, volume 3).

36 For a discussion of capitalism's recurrent crises in Marx's economic theory, see M.C. Howard and J.E. King, *The Political Economy of Marx* (2nd ed., London, New York, 1985), chapter 13; P.N. Junankar, *Marx's Economics* (Oxford, 1982), chapter 9; A. Oakley, *Marx's Critique of Political Economy* (London, 1985), vol. 2, 268–277. For a discussion of the role of competition in capitalism, see *Capital* III, 245–261.

37 *Capital* III, 209.

38 Id. 251.

39 A good introduction to the debate is M.C. Howard and J.E. King, *The Political Economy of Marx* (2nd ed., London, New York, 1985).

40 *Capital* I, 19–20.

41 The labour theory of value may well have some problems in accounting for the value of abstract objects which scientific labour produces. Labour for Marx is a value-creating substance. Essentially his labour theory of value holds that the value of any article is determined by 'the amount of labour socially necessary or the labour-time socially necessary for its production' (see *Capital* I, 38–39). Imagine two pairs of scientists employed to analyse the molecular composition of something. Each pair spends the same number of hours at its task. If one pair comes to understand the molecular basis of a perfume while the other pair turns out to be Watson and Crick, there seems to be something wrong in measuring the value of what they have produced exclusively in terms of the amount of labour contained in their discoveries. According to the labour theory of value, one might be led to conclude that there is an equivalent amount of surplus value to be extracted from the work of each pair. Surely the capitalist employer of both teams would be able to extract more surplus value from Watson and Crick's work on DNA. If so, where has this extra surplus value come from? Probably a good Marxist economic theoretician could come up with some replies here. But it does seem that the labour theory of value has some work to do when it comes to explaining this case.

42 Karl Marx, *Grundrisse* (1857–58; M. Nicolaus tr., London, 1973), 107.

43 *Capital* I, 152–153.

44 Id., 592.

45 The debate within neo-classical economics over whether technological change is endogenous or exogenous is comparatively recent. Economists had thought for a long time that technological innovation was more a matter of serendipity than a response to economic factors. However empirical investigation of the patent system in the 1960s began to change this belief. The most well known study here is J. Schmookler, *Invention and Economic Growth* (Cambridge, Mass., 1966). For a good account of this debate as well as a study of the economic causes of invention, see G. Wyatt, *The Economics of Invention* (Brighton, 1986).

46 F. Engels, 'Socialism: Utopian and Scientific' (1880) in Karl Marx and Frederick Engels, *Selected Works* (volume 3, Moscow, 1970), 95, 141.

47 Modern theories which emphasize the role of technological change in economic growth recognize the connection between creative labour and growth. See N. Rosenberg and L.E. Birdzell Jr., *How the West Grew Rich* (New York, 1986); D.C. Mowery and N. Rosenberg, *Technology and the Pursuit of Economic Growth* (Cambridge, 1989); J. Mokyr, *The Lever of Riches* (New York, 1990).

48 Karl Marx, *Grundrisse* (1857–58; M. Nicolaus tr., London, 1973), 693.

49 Ibid.

50 Id. 694.

51 Id. 704.

52 *Capital* I, 35.

53 H. Boss, *Theories of Surplus and Transfer* (Boston, 1990), 96.

54 Id., 7

55 Id., chapter 5.

56 Karl Marx, *Grundrisse* (1857–58; M. Nicolaus tr., London, 1973), 272.

57 For Marx, productive labour is labour that produces commodities that have a use value and value. When discussing commodities, Marx distinguishes between use value, exchange value and value. For a discussion of the role that this plays in his economic theory, see M.C. Howard and J.E. King, *The Political Economy of Marx* (2nd ed., London, New York, 1985), 44–48; P.N. Junankar, *Marx's Economics* (Oxford, 1982), chapter 2.

58 Karl Marx, *Grundrisse* (1857–58; M. Nicolaus tr., London, 1973), 305.

59 *The Copyright Act 1968* (Aust.) does not, for instance, define a musical work. The *Copyright Act 1905* (Aust.) defined musical work in terms of a combination of melody and harmony.

60 *Capital* I, 84.

61 *Capital* I, chapter 6.

62 Bright dividing lines between epochs is something Marx objected to. See *Capital* I, 371.

63 P.F. Drucker, *Post-Capitalist Society* (New York, 1993), 8.

64 *Capital* I, 386.

65 Ibid.

66 *Capital* III, 259.

67 *Capital* I, 763.

68 We are implying by this statement that law has a far more foundational role than the superstructural role which Marx assigns to it. Law, and in particular property law, for us turns out to be crucial to understanding the adaptive strength of the capitalist economy.

69 Marx, citing himself and Engels, from the *Communist Manifesto* in *Capital* I, 486, fn. 2.

70 *Capital* I, 486.

71 Id., 486–487.

72 For a discussion of the normative structure of science, see R.K. Merton, *The Sociology of Science* (Chicago, 1973).

73 For a full discussion, see P. Drahos, 'Intellectual Property Law and Basic Science: Extinguishing Prometheus?', 10 *Law in Context*, 56 (1992).

74 It is standard patent law in many countries that publication of an invention before the registration of a patent application defeats the patent claim on the grounds of a loss of novelty.

6 Property, Opportunity and Self-interest

Introduction

Self-interest is not a total explanation for what drives the self,[1] but as it happens self-interest does explain a lot about the self. And because it does, it makes the use of intellectual property rights by a society costly, to the point where perhaps there should be a presumption against expanding their use. The real-world cost of intellectual property rights remains a complex empirical question. This chapter does not shed any light on those actual costs, but it does provide an argument for thinking that they might be higher than is usually thought.

Intellectual property rights are rights which are created for and exist within market contexts. In such contexts they have a dangerous inner logic. Intellectual property rights create, we shall see, distinctive kinds of opportunities. Rational self-interested actors take those opportunities. By doing so they defeat the social interest that provided the justification for having the rights in the first place. The rational choice theorist's maxim that it is safer to rely on self-interest than on virtue as the foundation for institutions often leads to the adoption of property rights as the institutional design solution.[2] In fact the beneficial effects of the link between property rights and self-interest is, for many, almost a matter of religious faith.[3] This linkage in the case of intellectual property rights runs the real risk of being self-defeating. The problem, we shall see, is that creating property rights in abstract objects invites socially costly levels of opportunistic behaviour. Self-interest makes individuals accept the invitation.

The argument for this claim comes in the following stages. The first section examines the model of perfect competition. Although much criticized, it remains a precise analytical definition of competition. It remains a starting-point in an economic explanation of why in a market some level of property rights in information is needed.[4] Four functions of property in abstract objects are then distinguished:

appropriation, adjustment, self-defence and planning. These functions are linked to two types of generic strategies: rule-changing strategies and preventive strategies. It is the use of specific instances of these generic strategies by individual actors to survive in the market-place that potentially makes the cost of intellectual property rights very high. The proof that these strategies are actually used in the market-place by intellectual property holders is a question of fact. The argument in this chapter suggests that we need more data on the strategic uses of intellectual property by individual firms before we commit resources to a further extension of intellectual property regimes. A final section of the chapter suggests that intellectual property rights are connected to the problem of powerful factions in a society that are prepared to contemplate their extensive use.

To summarize: the basic thrust of the chapter is that property rights in abstract objects offer their holders strategic opportunities within the market-place. These act as a siren call to actors to think about the use and redesign of these rights to suit themselves. The result is that the collective interest and self-interest part ways.

The Rationality of Perfect Competition

The core ideas of the model of perfect competition were given an intuitive expression by Adam Smith. Free competition, he said, required sufficient numbers of individual competitors, knowledge of the market and a ban on conspiracies against the public.[5] These ideas were eventually incorporated into a formal model of perfect competition, based on the following assumptions:[6]

1 there are sufficient buyers and sellers so that no one individual is able to influence price;
2 individuals do not engage in collusive behaviour;
3 traders have near perfect information, including information about production methods;
4 there is mobility of resources so that individual traders can shift resources to every profit opportunity;
5 there are no barriers to entry to prevent resources being shifted to a profit opportunity.

Under these conditions the subjective demands of consumers are matched by the supply of services and goods by an army of traders who have full information about those demands. Costs and prices for each trader in relation to any given good must be the same since any deviation in relation to, say, prices would mean either a loss of profit or a loss of sales. Since traders are rational maximizers the equality of prices implies that output is at a maximum and the equality of costs implies that input is at a minimum. Perfect competition produces this allocation because, amongst other things, sellers are free to move to any part of the market in which there are excess profits and buyers are free to move away from those sectors where prices are too high.

The model is restricted in scope. Its claims are analytical, not empirical. It is basically only concerned with one kind of efficiency: allocative efficiency.[7] It is a tightly knit input–output model in which consumers, through the pricing mechanism, extract from producers the maximum output for a given input. One can view the model as a specific theory of practical rationality – what rational traders would do under conditions specified by the model. This leads to the following question: how should traders, who are rational and self-interested, behave under the conditions of the model when making decisions about investing in the production of new information? There are two obvious possibilities. One is that traders would invest in the creation of new information, for roughly the reasons that Marx gives in explaining technical change. Invention and innovation are a crucial source of profit for the individual capitalist. Competitive pressures and the desire for profit (and survival) make investment in knowledge creation a personal and commercial imperative.

Another answer to our question is that, within the perfectly competitive community, free-riding is the best strategy. Put simply, a free-rider is an economic actor who obtains the benefits of a good without contributing to its cost of production.[8] Free-riding does not necessarily constitute a problem. Amongst other things, it contributes to the diffusion of information and so adds to the productive potential of an economy.[9] However, free-riding is thought to create a problem for the market mechanism when it comes to ensuring that sufficient resources are devoted to the creation of new knowledge. The problem occurs because knowledge is said to have public good qualities. Public goods are individual goods the consumption of which by one individual does not detract from the possibility of consumption of those goods by another individual.[10] Furthermore so-called 'pure' public goods (for example, defence) have the quality of being non-excludable: once in existence it is practically difficult to exclude others from consuming them. If the provision of pure public goods is left to the market, suboptimal amounts of resources are likely to be devoted to their production because free-riders who consume the good, by definition, will not contribute to the cost of production. In a system of perfect competition where information is available free, or at cost, profit opportunities generally do not flow from the creation of information. In much the same way that producers, say, of tomatoes would have less incentive to produce if they knew that a proportion of their crop had to be given away, producers of information have diminished incentives to produce information, the more there is a free-rider problem. Some innovation in information could still be expected under conditions of perfect competition, for it would give traders first market entrant advantages. But the crucial point is that perfect competition would fail to achieve an optimal allocation of resources for the generation of new information. Arrow, in his now classic discussion of this problem, summarizes the position thus:

> To sum up, we expect a free enterprise economy to underinvest in invention and research (as compared with an ideal) because it is risky, because the product can be appropriated only to a limited extent, and because of increasing returns in use. This underinvestment will be greater for more basic research.[11]

There are two standard ways in which to attempt to fix this particular case of market failure. One response is to suggest a greater role for government. The provision of public goods requires collective action. Arrow suggests that in the case of scientific research his analysis leads to this conclusion. By funding research, government provides a public good and compensates for the failure of the market. An alternative is to create property rights in information and allow this reconstructed market to perform the allocative function. Both solutions depend on government intervention. Those who advocate the creation, or expansion, of intellectual property rights to correct market failure in the case of the market in innovation are inviting government regulation.[12] The consequences of this point are not always fully appreciated. It makes theories of government failure potentially relevant to the creation of intellectual property policy and rights.[13]

The economic argument for intellectual property rights is simple and robust but it contains a paradox. Intellectual property rights are rewards, or more accurately opportunities to gain a reward in the market-place. These rewards act as incentives for individuals to produce new information which, provided the information is diffused to others, benefits society. This proviso may not be satisfied or only partially satisfied because holders of intellectual property are given powers to restrict access to the information. This prevents optimal use being made of it. So the very protection which encourages production at the same time thwarts the object of the exercise, namely, the diffusion of knowledge. The rules which stimulate the creation of information do not necessarily help its diffusion. In the words of one writer, there is a 'powerful tension' between such rules.[14] The basic justificatory argument suggests that intellectual property rights have an important role to play in allocating resources to the production of information. But it also suggests that they have to be designed in a way that strikes a balance between the public and private interest. The basic form of economic argument does not assign intellectual property rights an absolute status. For the economist the design of intellectual property rights becomes a matter of complex cost–benefit calculation. In theory at least, the optimal patent term might vary according to the nature of subject-matter of the patent.[15] The types of costs linked to intellectual property rights include the costs of administration and enforcement; the costs of excluding possible free-riders (these include the possible loss of dynamic benefits, since free-riders may well improve a product) and rent-seeking behaviour.[16] There are also the empirically discoverable costs which take the form of various anti-competitive practices that grow up around the use of intellectual property rights.[17] Such practices have both effects within an economy and effects as between national economies. The existence of a patent system in many countries might confer welfare gains on one country but produce an overall net loss in welfare.[18]

The basic *a priori* economic argument we have described can be made problematic in various ways. So, for instance, one might adopt a deconstructionist approach in order to show the socially constructed and contingent nature of the categories of the theory.[19] Alternatively, one might show that information has many more qualities than just its public good qualities that matter to an economic theory and understanding of the role of intellectual property in an information society.[20] Our approach will be different. We will read the model of perfect competition as a specific model of practical rationality in which individual actors possess a strongly maximizing rationality. To this we will add another behavioural assumption: actors are assumed to be mildly opportunistic. Transaction cost theory assumes opportunism, defined as 'self-interest seeking with guile'.[21] This includes lying, stealing and worse. Our mildly opportunistic actors are of the bad but not rotten kind. The mildly opportunistic athlete will not poison a fellow competitor, but will try and disadvantage that competitor by making it difficult for that competitor to get access to the training ground, for instance. Mild opportunism correlates with the kind of capitalist rationality that Marx assumes in *Capital*. It is a rationality which involves the individual in maximizing while at the same time thinking strategically about disadvantaging others in order to maximize. Bearing these assumptions in mind, we will revisit perfect competition.

Property rights under perfect competition function in two obvious ways. They provide the basis on which actors control resources and they allow the appropriation of value to take place. The introduction of property rights in abstract objects conflicts with the assumptions of the model in at least two ways. Perfect competition posits perfect information. All actors within the market are assumed to have information about market opportunities and technological production possibilities. But some areas of intellectual property, such as trade secret protection, prevent the flow of information altogether. A producer who has knowledge of a process that lowers production costs may rely on trade secret protection indefinitely to protect that information and experience higher profit margins as a result. Perfect competition also assumes that there are no barriers to entry so that producers can switch to the production of those goods or services where there is a profit to be made. But as the work by Bain shows, intellectual property rights are one major kind of barrier to entry.[22]

When the model of perfect competition and intellectual property rights are juxtaposed in this fashion, one conclusion which suggests itself is that an important source of competitive advantage in imperfectly competitive economies is various informational asymmetries. Stock markets and insider trading are one example where this is true, but informational asymmetries are endemic throughout economic life. It is how speculators and middlemen of all kinds make their living. The broader connection between information asymmetries and economic advantage is a matter for economic theory, but it is clear that intellectual property rights offer actors new opportunities for managing uncertainty and interdependencies within the economy. The model of perfect competition and imperfect markets have one thing in common. They are both examples of interdependent decision making. What one trader does affects another and that decision is itself affected by what that other trader does and so on. Under conditions of perfect competition traders have full knowledge and because of this their decisions are deterministically driven. The net effect of the interdependencies is to drive production and profit in one way – towards allocative efficiency. Intellectual property, however, in the imperfect economy offers traders the opportunity to introduce information asymmetries. Trade secret law, for example, can be used to keep one's economic opponent in a state of ignorance about which compounds make the strongest plastic chairs. Patent law can be used to weave a web of patents around a particular technology and deter a competitor from carrying out R&D in that area.

Apart from the fact that intellectual property rights allow traders the possibility of creating and maintaining informational asymmetries, they also allow individual actors to benefit from high transaction costs. Transaction cost theory seeks to explain organizational relations on the basis that individuals seek to minimize transaction cost.[23] And this approach has had considerable explanatory force. It is also clear that property rights can only have positive economic effects where transaction costs exist. In the absence of transaction costs, the initial property distribution we know, *pace* Coase, does not affect allocative outcomes.[24] Property rights in abstract objects create transaction costs (costs of enforcement and contracting). These costs are high for many reasons. Unlike the case of tangible objects, abstract objects have no natural boundaries, so there is the cost of identifying the object. There is also the problem of enhanced opportunities for free-riding because of the nature of abstract objects. Nevertheless, in the case of abstract objects, some mildly opportunistic actors may favour high transaction costs. A large multinational, for instance, may favour the high transaction costs of the patent system because it means that small R&D competitors may not be able to take advantage of the system.[25] Moreover the creation of property rights in abstract objects, when combined with a strategy of deliberately maintaining the option of high transaction costs in relation to such rights, would allow large players the free-riding option while denying it to small players. Large companies could infringe the intellectual property entitlements of small companies knowing that only a small percentage of actions against them would be brought, let alone succeed. This kind of free-riding strategy by powerful, mildly opportunistic actors is, to some extent, safeguarded by high transaction costs to which intellectual property rights contribute.

As Coase observes, factors of production can be thought of as rights rather than physical objects.[26] Rights are unusual factors of production. As social artefacts they can be radically redesigned. Once mildly opportunistic actors realize that intellectual property rights have a clear strategic value in helping them to steer their way through the freedom-restricting interdependencies of perfect competition, those actors become interested in the rights themselves and their further redesign.

The value of intellectual property to rational actors depends on four functions of intellectual property. Identifying these is the task of the next section. Later we argue that these functions ground certain kinds of strategies that tend to defeat the welfare gains that intellectual property rights are meant to bring.

Four Functions of Property

The Appropriation Function

Property is for the economist an instrumental institution. It is a means for solving problems of resource distribution and use. A fundamental reason for economists preferring private property rights over collective ownership is that they define and protect individual entitlement. This entitlement can then be subjectively valued by its owner and traded for other entitlements.[27] Property rights are a secure means by which individuals can appropriate value (the appropriation function). For these reasons they form powerful incentives for individuals. They help to motivate and frame trading activity. For economists private property rights are perhaps the most important device that a society has at its disposal. Typically it has been assumed that much the same things that can be said in favour of property rights can also be said in favour of intellectual property rights.[28]

The Adjustive Function

The appropriation function of property is not the only function. Within capitalist systems property rights are adjustive mechanisms which distribute benefits and burdens. Individuals use property law either to gain advantages for themselves or to shift burdens onto others. This process works under a legal regime in which individuals, now legal subjects, are said to have formal equality and freedom of contract.[29]

The broad adjustive function that property performs in social systems is recognized within that part of economic theory that deals with externalities. Within economics there are arguments over how to define externalities.[30] The idea behind an externality is that an individual takes an action which has consequences (negative or positive) for another and there is no economic mechanism by which that other can influence the decision that leads to that action. Property rights may internalize externalities by bringing the effect of the decision to bear on all the interacting persons. Demsetz, in an important attempt to articulate an economic theory of property rights, argues that, within a given society experiencing change in knowledge and technology, new sets of harmful and beneficial effects arise, and therefore new sets of externalities.[31] Moving towards that border where economics and sociology meet, he claims that 'property rights develop to internalize externalities when the gains of internalization become larger than the cost of internalization'.[32] Demsetz uses some anthropological work dealing with the fur trade of an Indian tribe (the Montagnes) to illustrate the thesis. Hunting within the commons is a good example of an externality. The decision to hunt has costs for other hunters, but given the lack of control in the commons over hunting there is no incentive for any given individual to take these costs into account. The arrival of a commercial fur trade raises the stakes. Furs rise in value and more hunting takes place. The problem of externalities is intensified, with the real danger that the fate of the fur trade will be that of the animals, namely, extinction. The development of private property rights in land makes it feasible to encourage the preservation of game. The cost of future hunts is made internal to individual property holders.

The Self-defence Function

The claim that property rights are a societal response to the problem of externalities is an empirical one. It is an empirical claim because the key to explaining the emergence of property rights is said to lie in the cost of adjusting to new harms and benefits. But the example is also suggestive of another feature of property. Why did the Montagnes not continue hunting under their traditional arrangement? It would not have been the first time that a natural resource in the commons had been depleted. One plausible conjecture here is that they were particularly concerned to maintain a way of life within their lands and the instrument of private property was a suitable means to that end. The decision to adopt the mechanism of private property was motivated by an emotional commitment to customs and traditions which the externality problem threatened. Private property rights in this case functioned as a kind of self-defence mechanism for a group struggling to preserve their ways. Property seems so obviously connected with reason and self-interest that we are apt to neglect its connections with the passions. Focusing on the Montagnes' predicament exclusively as an externality problem tends to play down the non-economic motivations which would have been significant in this situation, just as it obscures the important defensive function that property has for actors.

Another example of property in its role as a mechanism of defence comes from copyright history. The invention of the printing press, it is generally thought, constituted an important stimulus to the development of copyright. One explanation for the creation of printing privileges might be that copyright emerges to deal with a positive externality: free-riding on the efforts of established publishers. This seems to be a straightforward case of property rights emerging to adjust externalities. Equally, though, it could be argued that printing rights functioned as a form of self-defence in this case. The prime motivation for the English Crown to create privileges in relation to printing was to try to prevent the spread of heretical and seditious ideas. The dangers of the new technology were for the Crown primarily political. Political self-preservation, at least at this point in history, rather than the economic costs of externalities seems a better way in which to explain the emergence of copyright privileges.

The Planning Function

So far three functions of property that matter to rational actors have been identified: appropriation, adjustment and defence. Property rights are critical to rational actors in a fourth way – they are vital to planning. Rational actors plan. The plans can be good or bad, long-term or short-term, well thought out or not, but whatever their range or worth they are an inescapable part of social and economic life. Planning is an activity of the present that relates to the future. One way to think about norms, a functionalist way, is to see them as a way of reading the expectations of others.[33] Planning is made possible by norms. Clearly norms have to be stabilized across time if they are to be of any use in planning. This becomes the role of institutions, most especially contract and property.

We know, according to Parsons and Luhmann, that law is an expectational structure.[34] It is the capacity of institutionalized law to act across time that conditions the possibility of planning. Law has to create in the minds of individuals the belief that the future to a large extent will be a consequence of the past and present and that their present fragile expectations will not be harmed or disappointed too much by an uncertain future. The role of property law in planning and the transmission of expectations over time is crucial. My property claim in my house is not just a signal of my expectations to others in the present, but acts, so I think and hope, as a command to others in the future. This claim that we make about the centrality of property law in planning links up with our discussion of Hegel. Property for Hegel was crucial to the establishment of personality in the world and, now we can also say, the passage of personality over time.

Property comes to the aid of rational planners in different ways, depending on the nature of the property right and its context. Our interest is in intellectual property in the context of markets. There are two questions which we need to address. What is the nature of planning in modern markets? How might rational actors utilize intellectual property rights to help meet their planning needs? A famous passage from the *Wealth of Nations* provides the answer to the first question: 'People of the same trade seldom meet together, even for merriment and diversion, but the conversation ends in a conspiracy against the public, or in some contrivance to raise prices.'[35] Smith saw clearly that traders were disposed to plan against the market. In modern times this theme of traders planning against the force of the market has been pursued by Galbraith. He argues that the nature of modern production in the industrial system requires planning to overcome the uncertainties that a consumer-driven competitive market economy generates.[36] Modern industrial systems are characterized by the presence of large corporate traders investing and using large amounts of capital over time. Above all such traders seek to minimize risk and uncertainty. They do so by spending much of their time planning against the uncertainties that the market might impose on them.

The second question was how intellectual property might help to service the planning needs of rational actors in modern markets. These needs we have broadly characterized in terms of a need to manage uncertainty. The question we are asking involves a change in perspective. In Arrow's discussion of the problem of an optimal resource allocation for invention, the question is asked from the perspective of the competitive market. Our vantage point is that of the individual firm in a situation where the property rights have been introduced in order to help the competitive market reach some allocative optimum for invention. Such a firm is both a rational planner and a manager of uncertainty. It has a new institutional tool at its disposal to help it manage uncertainty: intellectual property. To what uses might it put this tool? A standard answer we have seen is appropriation of economic value. But this does not exhaust the possibilities.

There are basically three sources of uncertainty to consider in relation to the creation of information. First, there is the state of nature itself. Investigating a scientific problem does not mean that it will be solved. Intellectual property rights do not change the complexity of a scientific problem, although they may help towards its solution if they encourage more resources to be thrown at it.[37] A second source of uncertainty stems from the complex nature of social systems. Who knows what markets or governments will be doing ten or twenty years from now? As Keynes put it: 'About these matters there is no scientific basis on which to form any calculable probability whatever. We simply do not know.'[38] Intellectual property rights probably have no role to play in dealing with this kind of uncertain knowledge.[39]

There is a third source of uncertainty in relation to the production of information under conditions of competition: the presence of competitors. Competitors contribute to uncertainty in various ways when it comes to the production of information under conditions of competition. They may free-ride. Intellectual property rights are one way to tackle this problem. Even assuming that intellectual property rights solve this problem (which is doubtful), competitors contribute to uncertainty in other ways. They may be the first ones to solve the scientific problem. Patent systems operate on a 'first past the post' principle. The first company to invent (or register) obtains all the rewards for a period. Companies having to make decisions about the amount of R&D to undertake are, on the face of it, only partly helped by patent rights. Elster offers a clear picture of the uncertainty that still faces individual firms.[40] The amount of R&D which a firm is prepared to invest depends on the probability of a successful outcome. Even in the absence of competitors the outcome is inherently uncertain. In the presence of competitors the uncertainty is worse. If it invests large sums of money the individual firm may still lose the patent race and thus the money. If the competitors do not make large investments then the firm may be justified in doing so. But all firms are making these calculations and hence a circularity is produced. When lots of firms decide to invest it is rational for an individual firm not to. But since all firms are making the same individual calculation it becomes rational for individual firms to invest. The upshot, says Elster, is that there 'is no basis here for rational belief formation, and hence no firm basis for action'.[41]

Elster may or may not be right about this. Let us assume that he is. Even if actors cannot come to a rational belief about a given situation they may nevertheless start to develop strategies for the management of this problem. The brute empirical fact is that firms do invest in research. In the absence of probabilistic knowledge that might serve as the basis of a rational belief, firms might nevertheless engage in some kind of management or coping strategy for dealing with investment uncertainties. The same rationality that leads one into the circle of uncertainty that Elster depicts can also lead one out. One route we shall see in the next section is through property. But it is not necessarily the only one. Another solution is that one firm might hire the Mafia to scare off the other firms, but actually there is less need to hire the Mafia, we shall suggest, when one has intellectual property rights.

The Property in Pay-offs

The preceding discussion suggested that in addition to the appropriation function there were three additional functions of property: the adjustive function, the self-defence function and the planning function. In this section we want to show how these functions in the case of intellectual property combine to enable individual actors to manage the uncertainties of generating new knowledge under market conditions.

One way in which intellectual property is clearly vital to interacting individuals is that it can be used to change pay-offs.[42] Assume that two firms are competing in a market where they have the same costs and profit. Either firm can lower its costs through research and development but neither can prevent the other from copying. This is a standard free-rider problem. The pay-off matrix under these assumptions is that both firms earn the same returns if both do the research, but each does best if it free-rides while the other does the research. But a firm doing its own research is still better off when compared with doing no research. Under these conditions the cautious firm does its own research.

In Telser's discussion of this problem property rights are silent operators.[43] There must obviously be some ordinary property rights so that firms can appropriate returns on the goods they sell, but no enforceable property rights in the research results, otherwise the pay-off matrix could not be what it is. It is actually the definition of property rights that conditions the form of the pay-off matrix.

Imagine that a firm's R&D efforts become appropriable through property rights. The pay-off matrix changes. Where neither firm does the research, returns to both remain at zero. Where one firm does the research the other cannot appropriate. There is a return to the firm doing the R&D. The critical question is the size of the return. The answer to this depends again on the definition of the property right. The property right may prevent the appropriation of another firm's R&D, but may not prevent the independent discovery of the same research (copyright is an example of such a right – software companies could independently engineer the same software and have property rights in that software). The second firm would have to follow the first in doing the research or face a competition on price it could not win. If both do the research then returns are equal, but if only one does then the other has zero returns. Most importantly, if the intellectual property regime is changed, or 'stronger' intellectual property rights can be employed, the firm which invests in R&D does even better. So, for example, where the nature of the property right is such that one firm is prohibited from independently making commercial use of the research once the other has (patents) then it follows that the firm doing the research makes all the returns while the firm not doing the R&D or failing to do it first makes zero returns.

This example shows that in the interaction between the two firms the presence and content of property rights shape the pay-off matrix. The result could equally be applied to two countries having to make decisions about R&D expenditure. Another claim that seems hardly controversial is that firms engaged in R&D can be said to be engaged in a search for the most favourable pay-off matrix. Actors could be expected continually to seek ways in which to renegotiate or redevelop prevailing property norms. Once private individuals have some limited set of property rights that turn knowledge into a private good, one eminently rational strategy is to work on the further favourable redevelopment of those rights. An abstract way of putting this is to say that rational actors within the market seek to make use of property law's alterability in time.[44] Our argument points to a feedback effect of property rights within the market system. Intellectual property rights are created to stimulate individual interests in the supply of inventiveness and creativity. The extent to which they do this is not really known. But these rights do one thing: they stimulate the rational agent's interest in the property rights themselves. And rational agents become particularly keen on such rights once they realize that they can escape the unfavourable constraints of a fixed-rule game by switching to another more favourable game through the strategy of redefining the rules of the game by redefining the property right. They begin to focus more clearly on the rule mutability of games.

Games, generally speaking, are what we might term fixed-rule games. This simply means that they have a number of set rules all of which potential players know or can learn beforehand so that they know what actions are permissible under any given circumstances. When von Neumann and Morgenstern introduced the formal theory of games they did so on the assumption that the rules of any game remained fixed. Within a given game, players could pursue strategies, but the one strategy not available to players was to seek a modification of the rules of the game, for these functioned like 'absolute commands'.[45] Breaking the rules of the game meant that by definition one was no longer transacting in the same game. Since these beginnings it has become customary to distinguish between cooperative games and non-cooperative games.[46] In the former players can negotiate and make enforceable agreements, while in the latter players simply choose between strategies without communicating and obtain rewards the shape of which are determined by the combined effects of their choices. Both cooperative and non-cooperative games are fixed rule games.

The rules of games need not always be fixed. One can imagine a game in which the rules were changed by the players as the game progressed. Games might in other words be rule mutable. Children and adults sometimes play rule mutable games where one of the players, usually the child, introduces a rule change. Young children do this because either they are not winning the game under the existing set of rules or they see an opportunity to win if they make the rule change. Adults will sometimes allow this, for a variety of reasons. They may want to help the child's confidence, make the child happy, avoid a tantrum and so on. Rule mutable games, then, are games in which players secure changes to the rules during the course of the game in order to secure a win. The means of securing these changes can vary from bargaining and negotiation to coercion of one party by the other. The idea of the rule mutable game draws attention to the fact that rational actors are just as likely to think strategically about the structural elements of the game as they are about the options that they have under a set of rules that define a pay-off matrix, possible moves and communication possibilities. At a given moment we can use the formal theory of games to give us an analytical snapshot, as it were, of the consequences for the players of their various interdependent decisions. Our earlier discussion of the two competing firms investing in R&D is an example of that. But at the same time those players may be running strategies outside the game itself to change the constraints which the game imposes on them. Much of economic life, we suggest, is a complex mixture of fixed-rule and rule mutable games in which the actors are trying to shift the constraints that operate on them and increase the opportunities available to them. Property rights are fundamental to this process.

Property rights feature in both rule mutable and fixed-rule games. If we model investment in R&D as a fixed-rule game then one clear function of property rights is to fix the pay-offs. But property rights also become targets for rational actors within the context of rule mutable games. Firms may begin the search for information under one kind of pay-off matrix, but because the game they are playing is a rule mutable one the possibility of obtaining a more favourable matrix remains. Given that it is property rights that are an important factor in determining the pay-off matrix, a natural and parallel strategy for any firm doing R&D is to seek through some means (litigation and lobbying are two examples) either individually or as part of an organized group, a redefinition of the relevant property rights in order to obtain a more favourable pay off matrix. The extent to which this kind of strategic use is made of intellectual property rights is an empirical matter, but it does seem a natural strategy for at least some actors to pursue.

Preventive Strategies

The previous section discussed reasons why intellectual property rights become the object of strategic thinking for rational actors. This section considers a kind of generic strategy that holders of intellectual property might employ. The strategy is based on the idea of preventing others from acting. In order to make sense of this we need to draw a distinction between the effects of exclusion and the effects of prevention. Exclusion and prevention sometimes amount to the same thing. Assume that I am disbarred from medical practice. I am simultaneously formally excluded and formally prevented from undertaking the activity of practising medicine, although I may choose to flout the law. But there are cases where I might be excluded from an activity, but not prevented from undertaking it. Clubs, for example, exclude people for all sorts of reasons. A tennis club might exclude a person on the grounds of race, religion or dress code. Those excluded are not necessarily prevented from the activity of playing tennis provided they can find somewhere else to play. Excluding somebody from a particular activity does not necessarily entail that the person is prevented from undertaking that same activity. To exclude is not necessarily to stop. This distinction, as we shall see, has some important ramifications.

Exclusion is very often thought to be the dominant signifier of a property relation. Exclusion is clearly crucial in the case of intellectual property rights, for it allows the act of appropriation to take place in relation to information. Exclusion, appropriation, markets and competition all connect strongly. Individuals competing against each other in a given market are involved in a process of checks and balances in which no one individual has the total power to determine price. The incentive to engage in this unpleasant process is that property rights allow individuals to appropriate the outcome of individual investment. Appropriation relates neatly to the view of property which sees it as being fundamentally about exclusion.

Intellectual property has another dominant signifier, that of prevention. Prevention is an extra dimension of intellectual property law. The following example can be used to illustrate the claim. Imagine a farmer growing cherries on a five-acre plot for sale at the market. The farmer's property right in the land and the cherries does not of itself prevent others from acquiring similar plots of land and growing cherries. If there are profits to be had from doing so, all other things being equal, the cherry farmer can expect competition. Others will enter the market. Property rights in this example function in their standard fashion. Now imagine that the cherries are genetically engineered with the effect that they are bigger, tastier, redder and that the farmer has a patent right over them. This does not mean the end of competition if it is the fruit market which we define as the relevant market.[47] The patent right does have one very important effect here, though. Unless the farmer chooses to license, others are prevented from doing as he does. Others cannot supply the market with the bigger, redder, tastier cherries. We can contrast this with our first example, where the farmer has rights of property over the physical objects (the land and the cherries), but not the abstract object (the DNA code of the cherries). In that first case others are in a position to imitate the farmer, to do as he does. In the second case others are not at liberty to imitate the farmer and can only do so if he grants them permission. This feature of intellectual property rights is better conceptualized in terms of prevention rather than exclusion.[48] All intellectual property rights are concerned with stopping the imitative conduct of others. Copyright and trademarks are both concerned with stopping the imitative behaviour of others rather than the exclusion of others from physical objects. Doing the latter does not stop the abstract object from being reproduced. Preventing others from imitating is an additional feature of intellectual property rights, a feature which the exclusion function of property does not fully pick up.

For traders experiencing competition the preventive function of intellectual property has great appeal. This is so because competition is a process in which traders risk injury. As two judges have put it, 'Competition by its very nature is deliberate and ruthless. Competitors jockey for sales, the more effective competitors injuring the less effective by taking sales away. Competitors must always try to "injure" each other in this way.'[49]

Competition does not just involve the risk of injury. It is also a fundamentally imitative process. Competitors, at the same time as they are trying to distinguish their products and services from that of others in the market-place, are also engaged in providing the same kind of service or product. Competition is a process which begins when others begin to imitate someone's good idea. The person who first thought of dial-a-pizza had a good idea which very soon attracted lots of imitators. No doubt that person would have liked to have some means of preventing that imitation. Competitive markets are centrally to do with encouraging traders to imitate one another, while intellectual property rights are centrally concerned with preventing imitation. The tension between wanting to encourage imitative conduct and wishing to prevent it leads in turn to a fundamental tension between markets and intellectual property.[50]

The appeal that intellectual property rights hold for rational self-interested traders can now be seen more clearly. Such rights offer the possibility of appropriation. Traders can also use them to shield themselves from the competitive process. Intellectual property rights offer individual traders the possibility of developing preventive strategies to protect their interests within markets. The kinds of preventive strategies intellectual property rights give rise to is an empirical matter, as are the costs and benefits those strategies generate. Here we have been concerned to show the conceptual link between prevention and intellectual property. Without pursuing the matter in detail we can make some observations about the kinds of preventive strategies that intellectual property holders might pursue. There seem to be two basic types. The first we might call a rights-expanding strategy. Intellectual property rights can be expanded through the creation of new rights (for example, *sui generis* protection for semiconductor chips, data bases and plant varieties)[51] or a redefinition of existing rights (for example, bringing computer software under copyright protection,[52] recognizing the possibility of subconscious copying[53] and expanding the meaning of copying by taking an unrestricted view of what constitutes indirect copying).[54] The second type of strategy involves using the rights as bargaining chips in order to make other traders do something they would otherwise not choose to do. The first kind of strategy, the rights-expanding strategy, relies in part on the fact that abstract objects do not have obvious boundaries, at least not in the way that physical objects have. Their very abstractness means that it is possible for their owners to assert relations of equivalence, isomorphism, identity, similarity or sameness between two physical objects in an attempt to expand the boundary of the abstract object which they own. The opportunity to alter the boundary of the property right is an option that has to be taken seriously by private actors within the market-place because that alteration carries with it the possibility of preventing others from becoming direct competitors. The essential idea here is that, as the scope of the abstract object expands, it sets limits on the substitution possibilities that competitors can offer in the market-place. In other words the degree of permissible imitation shrinks.

The second type of preventive strategy we mentioned was the use of intellectual property rights as a lever within the market-place. A rich source of these kinds of strategies is to be found in the intersection between the licensing of intellectual property and competition law. Licensing essentially is simply a conditional permission by the intellectual property holder which gives somebody else access to the intellectual property. Jurisdictions that have both intellectual property and competition statutes have to make some decisions about the ways in which they will permit intellectual property owners to make use of the monopoly provided by their intellectual property and where, for reasons of competition policy, they will draw the line.[55] In the analytical terms of this chapter competition policy has to distinguish between permissible and impermissible preventive strategies.[56]

So far we have seen that intellectual property rights offer self-interested actors within market contexts certain strategic possibilities which are based on the adjustive, defensive and planning functions of property. The possibilities include using property to change the pay-off matrix to suit oneself and developing preventive strategies to stop one's opponent in the market-place. These strategies do not exhaust the possibilities, but they do constitute examples of the way in which the collective interest which intellectual property is meant to serve can be defeated. It remains an empirical matter as to what strategic uses manifest themselves in relation to the use of intellectual property rights. Our task in the next section is to make good our claim that intellectual property rights have a dangerous inner logic.

Intellectual Property Factions

That intellectual property rights have a dangerous inner logic has in part been shown, for we have provided reasons why rational actors might use them to plan against the market. In this section we want to go further and suggest that this planning against markets is more likely to be carried out by powerful factions. We use 'faction' here in the way that Madison does in *The Federalist Papers* to convey the idea of a group of individuals organized on the basis of some common interest that is 'adverse to the rights of other citizens, or to the permanent and aggregate interests of the community'.[57] We begin our argument with a claim made by Madison that property is the source of factions within a society:

> But the most common and durable source of factions has been the various and unequal distribution of property. Those who hold and those who are without property have ever formed distinct interests in society. Those who are creditors, and those who are debtors, fall under a like discrimination. A landed interest, a manufacturing interest, a mercantile interest, a moneyed interest, with many lesser interests, grow up of necessity in civilized nations, and divide them into different classes, actuated by different sentiments and views.[58]

Madison's claim is a historical generalization but it is a plausible one. Human beings probably have been more inclined to organize to protect their property interests than they have been to free slaves or protect whales. Economic interests, generally speaking, have proved to be powerful motivators of human conduct. There is, as we indicated at the outset, much more to say about motives and human nature than just this, and in fact *The Federalist Papers* present a more nuanced picture of human motivation.[59] But our purpose is not to show this, but rather to show that economic self-interest, because it is a powerful motivator of conduct, makes intellectual property a dangerous institution for a society to rely on too extensively.

Our question is: why should intellectual property owners organize into factions? The obvious answer is that they would do so in order to protect their interests. Madison suggests that men are more likely to divide into factions on the basis of their interests and passions than to cooperate for the common good. But in one respect this is an incomplete answer, for not all groups that have interests organize. What reasons do we have for thinking that intellectual property owners will organize? The answer lies in the logic of collective action.[60]

Olson's analysis of collective action problems begins uncontroversially by claiming that organizations serve to further the common interests of the group they represent. When groups achieve a common goal they in effect provide a public or collective good for that group. When it comes to the provision of public goods, not all groups behave in the same way. Small groups can produce collective goods for their members without relying on coercion or extra incentives because at least some of the members of the small group would be better off by having the public good and so are prepared to bear the cost of providing it.[61] The problem facing large groups is that the cost of organization exceeds the benefits to any one individual. This is not to say that large groups do not get organized.[62] They do, trade unions and environmental groups being examples. The logic which Olson identifies suggests reasons for large groups being less likely to organize.

The logic of collective action operates at its strongest when the gains of the small group are economic. For example, pharmaceutical companies chasing drug patents all have a common interest in seeing that the drug patents which they obtain are enforced or that the patent term is as long as possible, to cover the costs of development. When a drug company successfully sues an infringer or a pharmaceutical lobby group manages to gain a more favourable deal on the patent term it provides a public good for members of the group. Because the pharmaceutical market is global and worth billions of dollars, private players have enormous economic incentives individually to defend their interests as well as to organize collectively. The diffuse interests of large groups are also present in the intellectual property arena. All members of society could be said to have an interest in an inclusive intellectual commons of the kind we described in our discussion of Locke. But one would expect that organizations supporting the maintenance of an intellectual commons would be in short supply, for the kinds of reasons that Olson gives. Amongst other things, the costs of organizing such a large amorphous group would act as a massive disincentive.

So far we have suggested reasons why intellectual property holders are likely to be factions. The logic of collective action provides us with one reason, but it is a reason which is not inherent to property. One possibility that seems implicit in Madison's observation about property being the most persistent cause of factions is that property has a distinctive inner logic that promotes factionalism. A way into this issue is to consider the role that property rights play in determining opportunity sets of individuals in the market. The notion of opportunity set refers to that set of actions from which an individual may actually choose.[63] The choices that individuals can make vary from being more or less unconstrained to fully constrained. One constraint which individuals face is the property rights of others. But property rights are not just constraints on choice: they are also constraint-shifting, for they confer opportunities on their holders to control resources. Property rights operate both to set constraints and to confer opportunities. Clearly when property rights shift constraints they do so at the expense of reducing the opportunity sets of other individuals. This, from a market perspective, is not a problem providing that constraints set by property are part of an 'invisible hand' process. In other words, the constraint-setting nature of property will operate in favour of the collective interest for as long as no one individual has the total power to set constraints for others within the market. The power to set constraints is itself a function of the ownership of property rights. (This does not entail, however, that property rights are the exclusive source of power.) When it comes to intellectual property rights the constraint-setting possibilities that owners have increase dramatically. The constraint-setting process operates in relation to abstract objects which have no natural boundaries. This offers, as we shall see in Chapter 7, the promise of enormous power to individuals, for now it becomes possible for a few to own a form of capital on which there is a global dependence. Property rights in abstract objects push the invisible hand away; self-interest is released in ways that threaten the negative liberties of others.

Perhaps one reason why property and factions have such an intimate connection is that property provides the power to shift constraints in the market and this kind of power is the best form of power to have in the market. Factions form naturally around property because it sustains their power and way of life. Intellectual property, because it offers the possibility of preventive strategies in such a strong way, could be expected, if we are right, to have strong factions promoting its extension.

Conclusion

Adam Smith presented an argument explaining why property rights, opportunity and self-interest combined to produce beneficial social outcomes. His invisible hand mechanism provides powerful reasons for relying on property rights and markets. The effectiveness of this mechanism depends on the existence of clearly defined property rights. The four functions of property identified in this chapter are all aided when property rights provide their holders with an expectation of security concerning their possession of goods. However when property rights take the form of privileges in abstract objects the invisible hand mechanism may cease to be a reliable guide to the collective good. In the market players are intent on winning. As rational, opportunistic actors they seek winning strategies. Changing the pay-off matrix by changing the nature of the privilege that they have been granted is one generic strategy. The preventive function of intellectual property rights also grounds such strategies. Powerful factions are more likely to promote such strategies. These strategies, we have suggested, operate against markets. They are part of the cost of intellectual property rights. It is a cost the dimensions of which are yet to be fully realized. And it is a cost which will continue to grow as more and more of economic life becomes entangled in privileges over abstract objects. Perhaps, somewhat ironically, this entanglement will produce less security of possession for, as we argued in Chapter 2, through the ownership of abstract objects many more material objects can be reached.

Our argument is one to which Smith might have been receptive. He would have been no more sympathetic to private sovereigns interfering in the market-place than he was to public sovereigns. The connection between power and intellectual property which has been suggested in the last section of this chapter is the subject-matter of the next.

Notes

1 For some reasons as to why not, see A.K. Sen, 'Rational Fools: A Critique of the Behavioral Foundations of Economic Theory', 6 *Philosophy and Public Affairs*, 317 (1977). For criticisms from another perspective, see J.A. Nelson and M.A. Ferber (eds.), *Beyond Economic Man: Feminist Theory and Economics* (Chicago, 1993).

2 G. Brennan and J.M. Buchanan, *The Reason of Rules: Constitutional Political Economy* (Cambridge, 1985).

3 'The truth is as simple as fundamental: that private property and private property rights, and only private property, is an indisputably valid, absolute principle of ethics and the basis for continuous "optimal" progress ...'. See H. Hoppe, *The Economics and Ethics of Private Property* (Boston, 1993), 227.

4 See K.J. Arrow, 'Economic Welfare and the Allocation of Resources for Invention' in *The Rate and Direction of Inventive Activity: Economic and Social Factors* (a Report of the National Bureau of Economic Research, Princeton, 1962), 609.

5 For a historical discussion of the model, see G.J. Stigler, 'Perfect Competition, Historically Contemplated', LXV *Journal of Political Economy*', 1 (1957).

6 C.A. Tisdell, *Microeconomics of Markets* (Brisbane, 1982), 182–83.

7 Economists generally distinguish between allocative efficiency, Pareto optimality, Pareto superiority and Kaldor-Hicks efficiency. See J.L. Coleman, *Markets, Morals and the Law* (Cambridge, New York, 1988), 68. The capacity of markets to stimulate invention is captured by the idea of dynamic efficiency.

8 For a survey of the different approaches to the free-rider problem, see J. McMillan, 'The Free-Rider Problem: A Survey', 55 *Economic Record*, 95 (1979).

9 For a general discussion of the benefits of diffusion, see P. Stoneman and P. Diederen, 'Technology Diffusion and Public Policy', 104 *The Economic Journal*, 918 (1994). For a nuanced discussion of the role of law in innovation, see C. Arup, *Innovation, Policy, and Law* (Cambridge, 1993).

10 In the USA the seminal work on public goods is by Samuelson (what he refers to as collective consumption goods). See P.A. Samuelson, 'The Pure Theory of Public Expenditure', 36 *The Review of Economics and Statistics*, 387 (1954); P.A. Samuelson, 'Diagrammatic Exposition of a Theory of Public Expenditure', 37 *The Review of Economics and Statistics*, 350 (1955); P.A. Samuelson, 'Aspects of Public Expenditure Theories', 40 *The Review of Economics and Statistics*, 332 (1958). Since then there has been a lot of water under the bridge. See R. Cornes and T. Sandler, *The Theory of Externalities, Public Goods, and Club Goods* (Cambridge, New York, 1986); A. de Jasay, *Social Contract, Free Ride: A Study of the Public Goods Problem* (Oxford, New York, 1989).

11 See K.J. Arrow, 'Economic Welfare and the Allocation of Resources for Invention' in *The Rate and Direction of Inventive Activity: Economic and Social Factors* (a Report of the National Bureau of Economic Research, Princeton, 1962), 609, 619. See also R.R. Nelson, 'The Simple Economics of Basic Scientific Research', 67 *Journal of Political Economy*, 297 (1959).

12 All property rights are a form of government intervention in that their initial creation involves a collective decision of some kind. See G. Calabresi and A.D. Melamed, 'Property Rules, Liability Rules, and Inalienability: One View of the Cathedral', 85 *Harvard Law Review*, 1089, 1092 (1972).

13 For such theories, see C. Wolf Jr., 'Market and Non-Market Failures: Comparison and Assessment', 7 *Journal of Public Policy*, 43 (1987).

14 F.H. Easterbrook, 'Insider Trading, Secret Agents, Evidentiary Privileges, and the Production of Information', *The Supreme Court Review* 309, 313 (1981).

15 So, for example, the length of the patent term is ultimately a matter of cost-benefit calculation. See F.M. Scherer, 'Nordhaus' Theory of Optimal Patent Life: A Geometric Reinterpretation', 62 *American Economic Review*, 422 (1972); W.D. Nordhaus, 'The Optimum Life of a Patent: Reply', 62 *American Economic Review*, 428 (1972).

16 See W.M. Landes and R.A. Posner, 'Trademark Law: An Economic Perspective', 30 *Journal of Law and Economics*, 265 (1987).

17 The classic study of the costs of patents is F. Machlup, *An Economic Review of the Patent System* (Study No. 15 of the Subcommittee on Patents, Trademarks, and Copyrights of the Committee on the Judiciary, U.S. Senate, 85th Congress, Washington, D.C., 1958). See also F. Scherer, *Industrial Market Structure and Economic Performance* (2nd ed., Chicago, 1980), chapter 16.

18 For critical discussions of the impact of the patent system internationally, see C.V. Vaitos, *Intercountry Income Distribution and Transnational Enterprises* (Oxford, 1974), 76–79; E. Penrose, 'International Patenting and the Less-Developed Countries', 83 *Economic Journal*, 766 (1973); S. Lall, 'The Patent System and the Transfer of Technology to Less-Developed Countries', 10 *Journal of World Trade Law*, 1 (1976); A.S. Oddi, 'The International Patent System and Third World Development: Reality or Myth?', *Duke Law Journal*, 831 (1987).

19 For a good example, see J. Boyle, 'A Theory of Law and Information: Copyright, Spleens, Blackmail, and Insider Trading', 80 *California Law Review*, 1413 (1992).

20 See D.M. Lamberton, 'Innovation and Intellectual Property' in M. Dodgson and R. Rothwell (eds.), *The Handbook of Industrial Innovation* (Cheltenham, UK, 1994), 301; D.M. Lamberton, 'The Economics of Information and Organization' in M.E. Williams (ed.), *Annual Review of Information Science and Technology* (American Society for Information Science and Technology, White Plains, NY, 1984), 3.

21 O.E. Williamson, *The Economic Institutions of Capitalism* (New York, London, 1985), 47.

22 J.S. Bain, *Barriers to New Competition* (Cambridge, Mass., 1956).

23 O.E. Williamson, *The Economic Institutions of Capitalism* (New York, London, 1985), chapter 1.

24 R.H. Coase, 'The Problem of Social Cost', 3 *Journal of Law and Economics*, 1 (1960).

25 This strategy runs into a problem if the multinational comes up against an equally well resourced opponent. The solution is for such opponents to agree to a cheaper dispute resolution procedure (like mediation) that has lower transaction costs.

26 R.H. Coase, 'The Problem of Social Cost', 3 *Journal of Law and Economics*, 1, 44 (1960).

27 For general discussions of property rights, see G. Calabresi and A.D. Melamed, 'Property Rules, Liability Rules, and Inalienability: One View of the Cathedral', 85 *Harvard Law Review*, 1089 (1972); B.A. Ackerman (ed.), *Economic Foundations of Property Law* (Boston, 1975); R.A. Posner, *Economic Analysis of Law* (4th ed., Boston, 1992).

28 For example, see M. Lehmann, 'Property and Intellectual Property – Property Rights as Restrictions on Competition in Furtherance of Competition', 20 *International Review of Industrial Property and Copyright Law*, 1 (1989).

29 E.B. Pashukanis, *Law and Marxism: A General Theory* (C. Arthur ed., B. Einhorn tr., London, 1978).
30 R. Cornes and T. Sandler, *The Theory of Externalities, Public Goods, and Club Goods* (Cambridge, New York, 1986), 29–30.
31 H. Demsetz, 'Toward a Theory of Property Rights', 57 *American Economic Review*, 347, 348 (1967).
32 Id., 350.
33 As Parsons and others point out, this becomes the expectations of expectations. See T. Parsons and E.A. Shils (eds.), *Toward a General Theory of Action* (New York, 1951).
34 N. Luhmann, *A Sociological Theory of Law* (M. Albrow ed., E. King and M. Albrow trs., London, 1985). For Parsons' specific views on law, see T. Parsons, 'Law as an Intellectual Stepchild' in H.M. Johnson (ed.), *Social System and Legal Process* (San Francisco and London, 1978), 11.
35 A. Smith, *An Inquiry into the Nature and Causes of the Wealth of Nations* (1776; Glasgow ed., Indianapolis, 1981), 145.
36 See J.K. Galbraith, *The New Industrial State* (Harmondsworth, 1967), chapter 3.
37 If we model research as a fishing process, then we might say that the more fishermen there are working a particular ground, the more likely it is that a particular fish will be caught. Intellectual property rights might have the effect of causing more fishermen to work a particular ground. See G. Wyatt, *The Economics of Invention* (Brighton, 1986), 122–123.
38 J.M. Keynes, 'The General Theory of Employment', 51 *The Quarterly Journal of Economics*, 209, 214 (1937).
39 The reason for being slightly cautious is that one can imagine circumstances in which knowledge of the ownership arrangements for particular kinds of important information might help one to come to some probabilistic assessment of the likelihood of a given institutional scenario coming to pass. An example would be if the patent system were used to lock up all the genetic pool.
40 J. Elster, *Nuts and Bolts for the Social Sciences* (Cambridge, 1989), 33–34.
41 Id., 34.
42 The term as used here comes from game theory. Game theory is the study of decisions by rational agents under conditions of interdependency. See R.D. Luce and H. Raiffa, *Games and Decisions* (New York, 1958).
43 A discussion of this model can be found in L.G. Telser, *A Theory of Efficient Cooperation and Competition* (Cambridge, NY, 1987), 205–210.
44 This is a feature of law in general and not just property law. For a discussion, see N. Luhmann, *A Sociological Theory of Law* (M. Albrow ed., E. King and M. Albrow trs., London, 1985), 159–166.
45 See the discussion of the simplified concept of a game by J. Von Neumann and O. Morgenstern, *Theory of Games and Economic Behaviour* (3rd ed., Princeton, 1953), 49.
46 See J.C. Harsanyi, 'A New General Solutions Concept for Both Cooperative and Non-cooperative Games', in J.C. Harsanyi, *Papers in Game Theory* (Dordrecht, Holland, 1982), 211–212.
47 Market definition issues lie at the centre of competition law. See M. Brunt, '"Market Definition" Issues in Australian and New Zealand Trade Practices Litigation', 18 *Australian Business Law Review*, 86 (1990).
48 A striking example of what amounts (in our terms) to the preventive nature of intellectual property is to be found in the Australian case of *Davis* v. *The Commonwealth* (1988) 166 C.L.R. 79. In that case the Australian Bicentennial Authority was given the power to regulate the uses of expressions like '200 years', 'Bicentenary' 'Founding' 'Sydney' etc. The Court took the view that the *Australian Bicentennial*

Authority Act 1980 had simply gone too far, for it was an 'extraordinary intrusion into freedom of expression' (at 100).

49 *Queensland Wire Industries Pty. Ltd.* v. *BHP Ltd.* (1988–89) 167 C.L.R., 177, 191 *per* Mason CJ and Wilson J.

50 There are different points of view about the existence of this tension. Some argue that intellectual property rights are pro-competitive because they promote the dynamic efficiency of an economy by encouraging innovation. See, for example, OECD, *Competition Policy and Intellectual Property Rights* (Paris, 1989), 11–12. The form of this kind of argument is misleading. There may sometimes be welfare gains from intellectual property if it does produce innovation, but the price of these welfare gains is an interference in the processes of competition. Once it is seen that intellectual property is about preventing imitative conduct and that competition is about a process that permits imitative conduct to take place, there is no escaping this conclusion.

51 Examples of *sui generis* protection are the *Semiconductor Chip Protection Act 1984* (US); European Commission, *Amended Proposal for a Council Directive on the Legal Protection of Databases*, OJ 1993 C308/1 15 November 1993; *Plant Breeder's Rights Act 1994* (Aus.).

52 In the USA copyright protection for computer programs was 'firmly established after the 1980 amendment to the Copyright Act'. See *Williams Electronics, Inc.*, v. *Artic Intern., Inc.*, 685 F.2d 870, 875 (3d Cir. 1982). In Australia the *Copyright Act 1968* was amended in 1984 to include 'computer program' in the definition of literary work.

53 *Francis Day & Hunter Ltd* v. *Bron* [1963] Ch 587 (United Kingdom Court of Appeal).

54 See, for example, *Frank M Winstone (Merchants) Ltd* v. *Plix Products Ltd* (1985) 5 IPR 156 (Court of Appeal of New Zealand). For a discussion of the appropriate limits to the meaning of indirect copying, see Lord Griffiths in *British Leyland Motor Corporation Ltd* v. *Armstrong Patents Company Ltd* [1986] 1 All E.R. 850, 876–884 (House of Lords).

55 In Australia the intersection between intellectual property and competition is governed by section 51 of the *Trade Practices Act 1974*. For the Trade Practices Commission's view on the balance to be struck between the two areas of policy, see Trade Practices Commission, *Application of the Trade Practices Act to Intellectual Property* (Commonwealth of Australia, July 1991). In Europe the Treaty Establishing the European Economic Community (Treaty of Rome – renamed the European Community Treaty in 1992) contained rules on competition (articles 85–86) and the free movement of goods (articles 30–36). These articles have given rise to a jurisprudence surrounding the relationship between intellectual property and competition policy. For a discussion, see V. Rose (ed.), Bellamy and Child, *Common Market Law of Competition* (4th ed., London, 1993), chapter 8. Similarly in the United States the Supreme Court, through an interpretation of its antitrust laws (beginning with the Sherman Act of 1890 and the Clayton Act of 1914), has worked out principles of coexistence for competition and intellectual property policy. For a discussion, see A.D. Neale and D.G. Goyder, *The Antitrust Laws of the USA* (3rd ed., Cambridge, 1980). See also S.W. Waller and N.J. Byrne, 'Changing View of Intellectual Property and Competition Law in the European Community and the United States of America', XX *Brooklyn Journal of International Law*, 1 (1993).

56 One example of a preventive strategy that has sometimes run into trouble with the courts in the United States has been the practice of patent pooling ('if you can't beat them join them' strategy). This involves two or more patent owners agreeing to cross-license (pool) their patents, the aim very often being to achieve monopoly power in a market. See *United States* v. *Krasnov* 143 F. Supp 184 (E.D. Pa. 1956), *aff'd per curiam*, 355 U.S. 5 (1957).

57 *The Federalist Papers* (1788 ed., I. Kramnick ed., Harmondsworth, 1987), Number X, 123.
58 Id., 124.
59 For a discussion, see M. White, *Philosophy, the Federalist, and the Constitution* (New York, Oxford, 1987).
60 M. Olson, *The Logic of Collective Action* (Cambridge, Mass., 1965).
61 Id., chapter 1.
62 See Id., chapter 6 for reasons why.
63 See A.K. Dragun, 'Externalities, Property Rights, and Power', XVII *Journal of Economic Issues*, 667, 668 (1983); Jon Elster, *Nuts and Bolts for the Social Sciences* (Cambridge, 1989), 13.

7 The Power of Abstract Objects

Introduction

A discussion of the link between power and intellectual property could easily turn into a discussion about the nature of the links between intellectual property rights, monopoly and market power. Intellectual property rights are sometimes said to be monopoly rights.[1] To be described as a monopolist sometimes involves more than just description. It can also be a condemnation. The reasons for the pejorative use of monopoly probably have something to do with early Church teaching. The Church condemned monopolists because their opportunistic behaviour (the sin of avarice) did not fit the model of a good Christian and monopolies seemed to cause real damage to Christian communities by driving up prices over essential items like food.[2]

Economic thinking about monopolies in the 20th century is more nuanced than outright condemnation. It may be that monopolies have a vital dynamic role to play in the evolutionary growth of capitalism.[3] Likewise economies in a given phase of technological development and economic differentiation may find that some monopolies are 'natural'.[4] Neo-classical economic theory describes and evaluates monopolistic behaviour on the basis of its impact on efficiency. Monopoly is not a moral evil, but there are economic grounds for not encouraging its development. The standard economic objection to it is that it causes a dead weight loss.[5] In the case of the perfectly competitive market there is no unmet consumer demand. In the monopoly market the one producer sets price at a level which means there will be unmet consumer demand. The monopolist producer has some choice about setting price and so sets it at a level that maximizes the wealth transfer to him from the consumers. The wealth transfer is not an economic problem (although clearly there may be a problem in terms of some distributivist theory of justice). The economic problem with monopolies is that the unmet consumer demand is not compensated for (in terms of a static analysis) by a gain to producers and so the total benefit of the monopoly market is less than the total benefit of the competitive market.

One way in which to proceed to attack intellectual property rights is to insist that they are monopolies. This way of proceeding leads into a debate over who really is a monopolist and who is not. It is a debate which the pro-patent and anti-patent forces have been having for a long time.[6] The pro-patent forces greet the charge of monopoly with the claim that a patent does not necessarily translate into market power. I may have a patent on a mousetrap, but I still have to face competition from killer cats. A legal monopoly does not necessarily translate into an economic monopoly.

Another way of thinking about the issue of intellectual property and monopoly is to concede that intellectual property owners are monopolists *as are all other property owners*. A monopolist is one seller in a market. If I own a block of land I am the one seller of that block of land.[7] The fact that there are other sellers of *other* blocks of land does not change my monopoly status as the one seller of that block of land. Clearly the presence of other land holders does affect the amount of power I have in the market. Roughly speaking the degree of power of monopolists is a function of two variables – the demand (or dependence) for the product (or service) and the extent to which consumers are prepared to accept substitutes or the extent to which substitutes are feasible. An extreme example of extreme market power is a world in which there was one supplier of air. If in this world consumers depended on air and there were no feasible substitutes, then the concentration of market power in the one producer would be very great.

The purpose of the discussion so far is not to set the stage for a discussion of intellectual property and market power since this is very much a matter of economic theory.[8] Rather the conclusion which we draw from the preceding discussion is that not much is to be gained by deciding whether or not intellectual property rights are monopolies. So far as we are concerned, all property rights confer monopolies. Here we want to investigate a different kind of relationship, that between intellectual property and power, that is power broadly conceived. Bertrand Russell suggested that power is like energy: it has many forms.[9] The focus of analysis in this chapter is on intellectual property as a distinctive form of power and the effects of that power on areas of social life. The remainder of the chapter is organized in the following way. The next section develops the claim that property is a form of private sovereignty. Intellectual property, we have seen in preceding chapters, relates to abstract objects. It follows that intellectual property is a form of sovereignty over abstract objects. The nature of abstract objects is the topic of the third section. This section is followed by a discussion of the connections between abstract objects, the mechanism of property, dependency relationships and the threat power that arises in the context of such relationships.

Property and Private Sovereignty

In an important treatment of the property concept that pays little heed to the public–private distinction, Morris Cohen argued that private property was a form of sovereignty over others.[10] The argument has a disruptive quality because sovereignty is a public law concept while property usually features as part of private law.[11] Cohen's analytical argument rests on the now accepted view that property consists of a relation between persons in respect of an object rather than a relation between a person and an object. The link between *dominium* and *imperium* is accomplished by arguing, quite plausibly, that the dominant feature of property is the right to exclude others. The capacity to exclude others from things where those things are important or necessities gives the property owner considerable or even great power over others. Hence Cohen's conclusion that '*dominium* over things is also *imperium* over our fellow human beings'.[12]

What are we to make of this argument? One might choose to bypass it by rigidly adhering to a definition of sovereignty in which the sovereign is an originator of law and the property holder a holder of legal rights. Austin's definition of a sovereign – as somebody in relation to whom a pattern of habitual obedience has emerged – might serve this purpose.[13] But this is to treat Cohen's argument too hastily. His deeper message about the connection between property and sovereignty can best be captured through the application of some analytical jurisprudence. Analytical jurisprudence has had a central role to play in the construction of a rights analysis of property. Although radical critiques have tried to shift rights talk from its position of prominence, it remains true to say that rights, especially when linked to an analysis of property, form a master discourse.[14] Within this rights-based approach to thinking about property, the intimate connections which power and property enjoy have not been dissolved. One influential analysis of rights that forms part of the analytical tradition has been Hohfeld's.[15] We shall use it here.

The goal of Hohfeld's theory is entirely practical: it is to reduce open ended jural interests and concepts like property, contract, trust and so on to a set of basic or fundamental legal concepts so that it becomes easier to solve practical legal problems. The pairs right/duty, privilege/no-right, power/liability and immunity/disability are jural correlatives in Hohfeld's scheme. Jural opposites consist of the pairs right/no-right, privilege/duty, power/disability, immunity/liability. Our interest here is in the way the scheme relates to the property concept.

Right, for Hohfeld, was a chronically ambiguous generic term. Its potential referents included power, immunity and privilege. Hohfeld proposed that its meaning be confined to a claim for which there was a correlative duty. The link between rights proper or claim rights and duty is axiomatic; such rights necessarily have correlative duties.[16] The correlativity thesis has its critics, but for present purposes their criticisms do not matter.[17] Property relations are perhaps core examples of the right/duty correlativity thesis and in fact many of Hohfeld's examples of the thesis are property examples: 'if X has a right against Y that he shall stay off the former's land, the correlative (and equivalent) is that Y is under a duty toward X to stay off the place'.[18] When correlativity is linked to property the claim that property is a form of sovereignty begins to gain some credence since sovereigns can be said to stand in relations of right and duty towards their citizens. A feature of analytical models of law such as Bentham's, Austin's and Hohfeld's is that the definitional differences between sovereign and property owner do not manifest themselves in anything like so strong a fashion when the logical structure that belongs to the functions of these concepts is analysed. Sovereigns have the function of making law within a jurisdiction. The analysis of law varies from model to model but command and prohibition are canonical forms of law common to all, with some, like Bentham's, adding other forms such as permission.[19] These forms, like command, prohibition and permission, have the function of directing the action of others. The capacity of property owners to direct conduct in a manner analogous to that of sovereigns comes into view when the logical structure of the general concept of property right is identified. Hohfeld's jural scheme neatly reveals this structure. One of its aspects is that the property owner has a claim right as against other individuals who have correlative duties. Apart from a claim right, property owners also have privileges (the privilege to enter land), powers (for example, to pass title, possession) and immunities (the inability of others to alienate). Hohfeld's scheme shows how property can be decomposed into a 'bundle of rights', the bundle giving the property owner considerable capacity to direct action. The rights, powers, privileges and immunities of the property holder can be thought of as being in microcosm the structural analogue of the sovereign's power to regulate conduct through commands, prohibitions and permissions.

Enough has been said to strengthen Cohen's claim that property is a form of sovereignty. Establishing this is important because it leads us away from linking private property to private power. Private property is a form of both private and public power. The private nature of this power comes into focus in Hohfeld's scheme when he presents the property relation in terms of a single place relation between the right holder and the duty bearer. The public power of property is also captured by Hohfeld's analysis, for property rights are within his scheme a class of similar rights held by an individual and used against an indefinite number of persons – the right to exclude the world, as property lawyers like to say. Property rights are, in effect, a kind of institutionalized open-ended contractual relation into which an indefinite number of people can enter with the property owner, but which remains a relation between the right holder and the duty bearer.

By linking property rights to sovereignty we seem in our analysis of intellectual property and power to be heading down a path which, Foucault has suggested, gives a very incomplete view of power. It is a classic juridical view in which power and its exercise are linked to the idea of possessing a kind of magical legal token on the basis of which the holder of the token can act negatively: prohibit, restrict, obstruct and so on.[20] By contrast, Foucault's methodological approach is to treat power in terms of flow and network concepts. Power circulates, it is 'exercised through a net-like organisation' and individuals 'are always in the position of simultaneously undergoing and exercising this power'.[21]

Treating power in terms of network flows is a profoundly important contribution to the analysis of power. However, under this approach, an important question remains to be answered: how do agents within the relevant network harness power flows? Clearly, individual agents have to harness power in order to exercise it. Foucault's own analysis suggests that the answer to this question has to be given in terms of mechanisms that allow the individual agent (A) to concentrate to some degree the flow of power so that A can affect B in a manner contrary to B's interests.[22]

Our purpose here is not to give a general description of the mechanisms that can be utilized to harness power. Rather the purpose is to show that property is one such mechanism, what we might call a sovereignty mechanism. This mechanism is obviously dependent upon the law. Here our analysis converges nicely with Foucault's, for law for him is an instrument of power, albeit a more complex and partial one than traditional analyses would have it.[23] Property for us is a law-dependent mechanism of power. It is a mechanism of power that all individual property holders are, in Foucault's words, simultaneously undergoing and exercising.[24] This is true because property is a *single*-place relationship between X, the property holder, and a non-holder of property. The fact that X may enter into many such relations does not make the right itself a many-place relation.[25] In any society, but especially one in which all individuals own some private property, there will be a very large number of single-place relations in which the individual is either the property holder or the non-holder. When property is analysed in this way it appears to be a mechanism that in formal terms creates a pattern of relations in which power is diffused and dispersed amongst all the individual holders of property. The social geometry of property is based on an individual standing in a multiplicity of single-place relationships, with a multiplicity of other individuals, each of whom in turn stands in a multiplicity of single-place relationships with other individuals, and so on. Power, which is based on property, does appear to be something which is 'exercised from innumerable points'.[26]

The analytical shift to conceiving of power as a polycentric phenomenon has still to confront and explain how individuals harness power. It still has to explain power imbalances between individual actors and how those imbalances are maintained. Here our analysis parts ways with Foucault's, for he is seeking to replace the juridical–political theory of sovereignty which has formed the traditional basis of analysis of power with an approach that is focused on the mechanisms, tactics and strategies of domination.[27] The approach being advocated here adopts Foucault's emphasis on mechanisms of power, but retains the link to sovereignty. It does so because it wants to argue that the mechanisms of power, and in particular property, lead to new forms of sovereignty and thus new kinds of domination. The mechanism of property in other words plays a crucial role in displacing one kind of traditional, and therefore easily recognizable, form of public sovereignty for a private form of sovereignty. Thus we should not follow Foucault when he suggests that we should 'eschew the model of Leviathan in the study of power'.[28] Instead we need to recognize that, through mechanisms of power, Leviathan changes its shape and produces progeny, which ultimately come to threaten its supremacy.

To this point our argument has been that property is a mechanism of power. This mechanism does not necessarily produce one specific pattern of the distribution of power. The pattern which is produced is a contingent matter depending upon, among other things, the initial set of social conditions. Under certain conditions the property mechanism concentrates power to produce imbalances in the relations of power between individual actors. Property has, as it were, a sovereignty effect. In the remainder of this chapter we will argue that intellectual property has this sovereignty effect because it relates to abstract objects. Property quite clearly, is, not the only mechanism which is relevant to an analysis of power, but it is an important one, perhaps the most important. Likewise the link between abstract objects and the sovereignty effect of property is not an exclusive link. There are other sources of power which can cause the property mechanism to have this effect. We will confine our discussion to abstract objects. Abstract objects are only one kind of base of power or power resource.[29] Similarly property is only one mechanism for drawing on this particular power resource.

The following section sets out to give a more complete answer to the question of what are abstract objects for the purposes of intellectual property law. Once an answer to this question is in place we can move on to consider how intellectual property achieves its sovereignty effect.

Abstract Objects

What are abstract objects? The beginning of one answer to this question was given in Chapter 2 when it was suggested that abstract objects are subsistent entities or, putting it another way, convenient mental constructs. By postulating the existence of abstract objects, the law may simply be engaging in a legal fiction, a fiction on which, as it happens, much real power rests.

While the purpose of this section is not to provide a treatment of abstract objects outside the intellectual property context, it is worthwhile considering briefly their general philosophical treatment. Doing this shows that thinking about abstract objects as fictional but useful entities is a coherent and defensible option, albeit one that has many philosophical critics.

Within metaphysics abstract objects are a possible category of existence. Moving from this starting-point to a more precise definition turns out to be difficult. Abstract objects are very often defined in terms of lists of examples (for example, the property of being x, relations and structures) and negative properties.[30] The negative features of abstract objects include things like not being tangible, not being in space time, not being agents of causal change, and so on.[31] In the words of one philosopher, the meaning of the term 'may not be entirely clear, but one thing that does seem clear is that such alleged entities as numbers, functions and sets are abstract – that is, they would be abstract if they existed'.[32] The last part of this statement highlights what has been a major philosophical issue concerning abstract objects, the question of whether or not they exist. Denying the existence of abstract objects leads to some form of nominalism. The challenge for nominalists has been to show how, in the absence of abstract objects, we can have an account of certain kinds of truths like mathematical truth. To what do mathematical propositions refer if not abstract objects?[33] Realists admit to the existence of abstract objects but in doing so have to provide an account of the way these objects connect with the world of human action and knowledge.[34] The difficulty which realists have to face is that, if abstract objects do exist, they do so apparently outside the spatiotemporal bounds that concrete objects inhabit. How is it possible for such entities to be knowable?

This specialized metaphysical and ontological debate between nominalists and realists within modern philosophy does not connect the existential concerns over abstract objects to questions about the nature and basis of power, but it is important to remind ourselves that this was not always so. One of the virtues of Plato's *Republic* is the unity of his metaphysical and political theory. The fundamental part of his metaphysical theory is the theory of Forms. The theory holds that there exists an ideal and eternal world of perfect Forms of which the physical world is but an imperfect imitation. The reason that the philosopher is ruler in the Republic is that she or he has unique access to this transcendental world of abstract objects. Knowledge of these abstract objects is, by definition, perfect knowledge and it is this perfect knowledge that qualifies philosophers who can gain access to this knowledge to be rulers of the Republic.

The sovereign power of the rulers of the Republic is based on the fact that it is they, and they alone, who have access to the world of Forms. The exercise of this power, which is based on abstract objects (for that is what Plato's Forms are) is not abused. Plato's Republic is an ideal state, a perfect society. In it the power of its philosopher rulers is applied with wisdom. Plato's philosopher kings gain power because they have exclusive access to abstract objects, but they do not use this power to further their power over others. Rather they use their knowledge of abstract objects to develop a craft of just rule. It seems to be a consequence of Plato's theory that the private knowledge of its philosopher rulers is, through a process of statecraft, diffused throughout the population and therefore becomes, at least to some extent, a shared public knowledge.

The conclusion which follows from Plato's use of ideal theory stands in stark contrast to the argument of the previous chapter. The argument in that chapter proceeded on the assumption that actors in the market-place would act opportunistically and that they would use intellectual property rights in ways that defeated the collective interest. Put shortly, that chapter suggested that in an imperfect society individuals who gained power on the basis of being able to restrict access to abstract objects would use that power to gain more power. In imperfect societies, creating a link between the mechanism of property and abstract objects turns out to be a risky institutional design strategy.

Having shown that there is at least one philosophical precedent for connecting power and abstract objects we can return to the main task of this section which is to provide a clearer account of the nature of abstract objects as they relate to intellectual property. Before doing so it is crucial to observe that the use of the term 'abstract object' in the context of intellectual property is not meant to imply an ontic commitment to the existence of such objects. A belief in the existence of abstract objects may simply turn out to be false. But for legal purposes this is irrelevant. The intellectual property system may reject the ontological reality of abstract objects but still retain the category as a convenient fiction to be used in making decisions about relations between actors.

The important feature of abstract objects which we want to concentrate on here is the role they play in *legal* judgements of identity. Before describing this role we need to make clear our focus. We are not here interested in the role that abstract objects play in a general philosophical theory of identity.[35] One way in which to begin an answer to the question of what makes object x and object y identical or similar is to propose that they are so if they share exactly the same properties or some properties.[36] But this is not a beginning that is relevant for our purposes. We have opted for the view that abstract objects are fictional entities, albeit highly useful ones. Our question is, what role do these entities play in the concentration of power? Our answer will be that within law they form the basis of identity judgements, judgements that ultimately determine who has access to vital capital resources. The fact that these judgements are made using fictional entities suggests that the judgements are themselves pragmatic and based on conventions.

To reiterate, the following discussion of abstract objects is not part of a general philosophical theory of identity, but rather an inductive account of the role that abstract objects play in legal judgements concerning, in particular, the infringement of intellectual property rights.

The term 'abstract object' refers to a putative category of being. It is not a term of legal art. We saw in Chapter 2 that intellectual property rights are classified legally as incorporeal rights. The objects to which these rights relate and over which relations between individual actors are formed are abstract objects. Juristically, physical objects are not the objects of intellectual property. However the identity of the abstract object becomes known by the law through the physical object. At some point before property rights attach to the abstract object the various different regimes of intellectual property law require some kind of 'corporealization' of the abstract object.[37] A given abstract object is not, however, just the ethereal mirror image of its concrete physical counterpart. The book or the invention is not, at least within the legal universe, to be exclusively identified with its abstract, intangible twin. If the abstract object is not identical with its concrete counterpart, what is it? An answer is that the abstract object is that core structure that is integral to the identity of the concrete object. This core structure forms the basis upon which an observer makes an identity judgement between two particular physical objects. It is the criterion by which the 'sameness' of objects is assessed. Abstract objects are those core structures that are used by legal actors in the process of making a decision about whether disparate physical objects are the same or similar, or resemble each other.

As a rule, the law relating to infringement in the different areas of intellectual property recognizes that infringement will occur in those cases where something less than the whole abstract object is taken.[38] Naturally the law relating to infringement of a given intellectual property right varies from jurisdiction to jurisdiction. And even in the same jurisdiction, some domains of intellectual property are thought to offer less protection for abstract objects than others.[39] But, despite this variation between different jurisdictions and separate fields of intellectual property, it is a basic proposition that intellectual property law protects abstract objects in the form of core structures rather than abstract objects that are identical with their material counterparts.[40]

Judgements of identity and recognition lie at the heart of infringement issues in intellectual property. Whether a judge has to decide an issue of copyright, patent, design or trademark, the basic process involves a comparison of two physical objects or processes and deciding whether or not one is an impermissible imitation of the other. Judges see the answer to this question as being a matter of fact. But this conclusion of fact is underpinned by a complex dynamic of social, psychological and ideological factors. In order to make the decision, judges are necessarily involved in a process of abstraction in which they, as it were, create the abstract object that then forms the basis of their identity judgement.[41] This process is deeply problematic because the abstractness of abstract objects is a matter of variation rather than being an all or nothing matter. Abstractness comes in degrees. Imagine, for example, stories based on the idea of the last three of something left in the world, whether these be nations, people or dinosaurs. The concrete expression of these stories is likely to be very different. Yet at a sufficient level of abstraction they might be thought to be equivalent. At the most abstract level it might be claimed these are stories which are a concretization of a three-point geometry in which it is assumed that there are no more than three points, no more than two points form a line and there is always a point not on a line. In the stories the lines and points are given an interpretation and definition such that, for example, the points and lines become respectively actors and possible alliances. The reduction of stories to geometric structures is probably a level of abstraction that no judge would choose. But some level must be chosen so that the identity judgement which has to be made in the case of an infringement matter can be made. Clearly, if judges choose high levels of abstractness for the core structures upon which they base their judgements of identity then the more likely it is that isomorphisms, equivalences of all kinds, will be 'seen' which in turn will lead to an increase in the findings of infringement.

So far the analysis of abstract objects reveals that they have two distinct roles: first, they form the object of relations in intellectual property; second, they form the basis for identity judgements in the context of infringement actions in intellectual property. The degree of discretion that judges have in the construction of abstract objects has two sources. The first we have already mentioned. There are many degrees of abstractness. The second stems from the fact that the conventional task of drawing boundaries in relation to abstract objects is far more difficult than in the case of physical objects. Real property has boundaries. Boundary is a conventional concept.[42] Boundaries are socially, politically or militarily created, but because they relate to a real-world physical object the boundaries of physical property, once decided, can be maintained with some precision.[43] The intangible abstract objects of intellectual property rights cannot be marked with boundaries in the manner of physical objects. The result is that an abstract object can be used to group very different physical objects. Under copyright law, for example, a film can be said to reproduce or be a copy of a literary work, and a three-dimensional work can be a reproduction of a two-dimensional work. Very different physical objects, in other words, can be said to share the same identity in intellectual property law because they all imitate the same abstract object. Such judgements of identity are dependent upon the existence of a core structure that provides the conditions of identity for the relevant judgement. This core structure, we have suggested, is itself a matter of judicial composition. Constitutive judgements about core structures are judgements of convention. Once in place they determine the extensional reach of a given property right into the material world.

A well known example where this conventional judgement has proved difficult to make is in the field of copyright and computer software. It is a feature of computer programs that the functions of a program can be captured in detail by a program written in a different computer language. Protection for the literal expression of a program or a substantial part of it does not help to protect the functions of that program. A now famous judicial solution in the United States was to begin talking about protection for the structure and sequence of a program.[44] This approach basically amounted to increasing the abstractness of the abstract object so that identity judgements concerning computer software could include their non-literal elements.[45] The protection of computer software raises in a stark fashion a problem that had always been there in other parts of copyright and in other regions of intellectual property.[46] This is the problem of identifying and determining the boundaries of the core structures that form the basis of identity judgements in intellectual property.

The Power of Abstract Objects

The previous section offered an account of the role of abstract objects in intellectual property. We can now return to our earlier concern, which was how intellectual property rights allow holders of such rights to achieve a sovereignty effect. We already have the outline of an answer to this question because property rights are, as we have already argued, a form of sovereignty. But this is only a formal characteristic of property which is not necessarily linked to a specific pattern or distribution of power. We are also interested in how intellectual property can function to produce power imbalances between individual actors. Intellectual property not only is a sovereignty mechanism but it has a sovereignty effect in social systems. The remainder of this chapter expands and defends this claim.

When sources of power are listed, wealth or capital is typically among them.[47] Abstract objects are not. Capital, it can hardly be disputed, is an important source of power. The extent of its distribution is one factor to take into account when assessing where economic and other forms of power in a society are concentrated. It is one (but only one) measure of power.[48] Non-human capital is usually identified with the tools and equipment of production.[49] From our analysis it follows that standing behind many capital goods, the processes of production and the products (including services) themselves are abstract objects and these can through intellectual property law be the subject of separate ownership and control. Abstract objects are themselves capital goods that can be traded within the market-place.

The proposal, then, is that abstract objects are a form of capital.[50] Intellectual property both constitutes the existence of this type of capital and determines its ownership. We can view this proposal as an extension of Schumpeter's conceptualization of capital. Schumpeter argues that capital is not identical with concrete goods but rather is a lever that the entrepreneur uses to obtain control over the concrete goods he needs in order to develop new production possibilities – what Schumpeter terms 'new combinations'.[51] This definition is advanced by him in the course of developing the idea that capital must allow entrepreneurs control over production goods so that they can redirect those goods in new ways. Capital, in Schumpeter's words, is a 'fund of purchasing power'.[52] This can be modified to accommodate abstract objects by saying that capital is a fund of controlling power over productive means. Abstract objects also exert control over the product, not just the means of production.[53] Ideally the entrepreneur ties up both. Within modern economies this fund increasingly consists of abstract objects. Intellectual property law determines rights of ownership over parts of this fund and who has access to the fund. The controlling power over the fund is given by the property mechanism.

The claim that the abstract objects which are constituted by intellectual property are a form of capital contains the following elements. Abstract objects function as gateways to valuable physical objects. These physical objects may be capital items important in the processes of production, or they may be the end result of such processes – products like penicillin, a genetically modified organism, seeds and so on – products that cannot be imitated. Abstract objects are also capital entities in their own right and can be used and traded as such.[54]

The idea that the abstract object is a form of capital and that therefore it is a source of power is an idea which in part is to be found in Veblen's theory of the nature of the business enterprise. Veblen proposes that the 'substantial foundation of the industrial corporation is its immaterial assets'.[55] One thought behind this proposal is that crucial to the success of a business is some element of monopoly.[56] One source of monopoly is 'custom and prestige (goodwill)'.[57] These kinds of monopolies, described by Veblen as less definite in character, are linked to advertising. It is through advertising that traders achieve levels of product differentiation between articles such as bars of soap, which at first glance seem more or less the same.[58] Intellectual property law is indispensable to modern marketing.[59] Without trademark law, for instance, advertising could not create the high degree of product differentiation that exists in many markets. At the heart of modern marketing is the creation of an image that aims to persuade the consumer to choose the product of which has a value in itself for the consumer. Abstract objects like trademarks form convenient tags for such images. The trademark in the modern consumer society no longer just informs.[60]

The importance of the abstract object to business survival resurfaces in Veblen's discussion of capital and capitalization. Rejecting a definition of capital which is tied to the material objects of production, he suggests that within the corporate sector the basis of capitalization is 'the earning-capacity of the corporation as a going concern'.[61] This earning capacity is in turn fixed by goodwill, which Veblen stipulates to include business reputation, franchises, trademarks, patents, copyrights and trade secrets.[62] Absolutely crucial to the life of a corporation, argues Veblen, is the acquisition of intangible property, for it is intangible property, that confers differential advantages on its owners.[63]

The argument so far has been this. Property is a sovereignty mechanism. This sovereignty mechanism in the case of intellectual property applies to abstract objects. Abstract objects are core structures that are essential to legal identity judgements. They are a form of capital and as such function as a source of power. The mechanism for the utilization of this source of power is property. But how does this mechanism, when applied to abstract objects, come to have a sovereignty effect? That is to say, how is it that property in abstract objects promotes the concentration of power amongst individuals within a society rather than its diffusion?

Part of the answer lies in our discussion of the nature of abstract objects. One of their distinguishing features is that they are fuzzy, indeterminate objects. Their boundaries depend on the identity judgements of a legal elite. These judgements are judgements of fragile convention that may easily break down or be influenced by specific interest groups, with the consequence that they cease to serve the broader, more diffuse societal interests to which they are meant to be directed. The fact that these abstract objects are gateways to many other kinds of capital resources provides a strong motivation for individual actors to accumulate those abstract objects. Moreover the fuzzy nature of these objects provides an incentive for financially well-endowed actors to change conventional judgements about the identity of these objects in ways that suit them. Such actors may be able, by exploiting the fuzziness of abstract objects, to gain capital transfers for themselves because they manage to change conventional legal judgements about the reach of the relevant abstract object. They acquire a stronger capital asset.

Each time the law constitutes new abstract objects by, for instance, increasing the scope of patentable subject-matter or legislatively creating new forms of abstract objects such as plant variety rights, the law in effect creates capital. But this kind of capital has the danger that it can act as an enormous power resource for a select few. Not all abstract objects have a power-creating effect. Producing an artistic work or a poem which is protected by copyright is probably unlikely to increase the power base of the author. But there are other kinds of abstract objects that relate to resources upon which there is considerable or universal dependence. Once the law creates abstract objects in relation to resources like genes, seeds, chemical compounds or forms of medical treatment it opens the way to the private ownership of resources upon which there is some level of collective dependence. For the economist, creating abstract objects in these kinds of resources is justifiable if there are real dynamic efficiency gains to be had that outweigh the costs of such rights. But there is a broader consequence to consider here, one that is harder to measure in terms of some economic metric, and this is the potential effect of abstract objects upon the distribution of power within a given social system.

There are some resources, like the ones we have just mentioned, upon which many people depend. Once abstract objects come to govern access to these resources we have added to the resource-dependent relationship a formal, legally constituted person-dependent relationship. A farmer, in order to plant crops, is dependent upon having seeds to plant. This we might term an object-dependent relationship. If those seeds are now the subject of a patent or plant variety right the farmer is dependent upon the permission of the owner of the abstract object for access to those seeds. A person-dependent relationship has been added to the object-dependent relationship. A relationship of dependence between persons we can broadly characterize in the following way. B is dependent upon A if B believes that he cannot give up that relationship because doing so would affect one or more of B's interests in a way that B does not want.

Relationships of dependency between persons can arise in many ways. Where a dependency relationship exists between A and B, one possible consequence is that B may face a coercion claim from A. Coercion claims in their most general form are cases where A is said to coerce B to do x. Theories of coercion attempt to specify the conditions under which such a claim can be said to be true.[64] One proposition in coercion theory which has substantial assent is that threats are coercive. There is much more debate over whether offers can be regarded as coercive as well as the right kind of test to use for separating threats from offers.[65] Pursuing this debate is not necessary for present purposes. Here we simply want to make the intuitively plausible claim that relationships of dependence create the conditions necessary for the making of credible threats. A clear-cut example of where a threat is being made in the context of a dependency relationship is if B is dependent upon A, her doctor, for treatment, treatment which A is obliged to provide and which A proposes to withdraw unless B does x (for example, pays A more money).[66] Whether or not an attempt by A to get B to do x in the context of a dependency relationship amounts to a coercion claim will be affected by the position one takes on offers, since one may take the view that offers, or at least some offers, are not coercive. But clearly coercion claims include at least threats. To summarize: dependency relationships make coercion claims feasible. They create conditions that allow A to make use of 'threat power' against B.[67] For A to be able to harness this power, A has to make use of some mechanism, property being an example of such a mechanism.

Property rights of all kinds, potentially at least, create person-dependent relationships. Clearly much depends on the object of the property right. When those objects are abstract objects and the resources to which they relate are the subject of considerable or universal object dependency, there are two consequences for the distribution of power. The first is that new kinds of threat power come into being. This happens because, as we have seen, the creation of a property of abstract objects creates relationships of person dependency and those relationships create an essential condition necessary for the exercise of threat power by the owners of those abstract objects.[68] Where those abstract objects relate to resources upon which many people rely, the scope of that threat power can be said to be extensive.[69] The range of power based on abstract objects is potentially global. It is certainly a power that can cross territorial boundaries. When in 1984 Australia was considering its position in the international patent system, the main cost it took into account of withdrawing from that system was the threat power it would face, as a technology importer.[70]

The second consequence which the creation of a property of abstract objects has for threat power within a social system is that this kind of extensive power is likely to be unevenly distributed within the social system and to become increasingly so. This is not an analytical consequence, but an empirically probable consequence of the nature of modern economic production. The reasons for thinking it to be empirically probable go back to our discussion of Marx and abstract objects. There we saw that Marx believed that each new generation of technology carried with it greater and greater investment costs. Scientific production, Marx correctly foresaw, would become more important and more costly. Under the pressure of competition, capitalists would be forced to meet this investment cost. A good example comes from the making of metals. Making iron and steel was for centuries a process of trial and error, with progress depending on enough combinations of materials being tried.[71] Once the chemical processes behind the techniques being used were understood, the techniques could be applied to produce better and better products. As science proved itself commercially and militarily useful, industry began to make an increasing and systematic use of scientists, this use taking the form of industrial laboratories.[72] The chemical and steel industries were among the early recruiters of scientific expertise.

> For the period 1916–45 it has been shown that the number of patents granted annually grew much more rapidly in classes dependent upon

> the application of knowledge from scientific disciplines such as chemistry and physics, whereas the growth in classes dependent upon empirical or practical knowledge and mechanical ingenuity has been much slower.[73]

This example illustrates that the ownership of some kinds of abstract objects requires both high-level scientific capability and large capital investment. In certain exotic areas of science it may be that the ownership of the relevant abstract object is open to only a handful of well-resourced players. And where those abstract objects are gateways to universally important resources it follows that proprietors of those objects acquire vast threat power. The owner of a block of land and the pharmaceutical company which owns the patent on a lifesaving drug both have a sovereignty mechanism at their disposal (the property right). Formally both are in single-place relations with relevant others, but the person-dependent relationship that is created through the recognition of the abstract object (the patent over the drug) means that the pharmaceutical company can harness much more threat power. It is only in the case of the pharmaceutical company that the sovereignty mechanism of property has a sovereignty effect. The declaration of property rights in certain kinds of abstract objects leads to the concentration of vast threat power in their owners.

The morality of threat power based on abstract objects is not something that this chapter has tried to address. Its main goal has been to show that the price of a property of abstract objects is a sovereignty effect. That is to say that extensive, possibly global, power will probably be concentrated in the hands of those who, through their scientific/technological capabilities and superior capital resources, are able to capture, through the property mechanism for abstract objects, resources upon which there is a universal reliance.

Reactions to increasing the threat power of some agents in this way will differ. How much of a problem it will be will obviously be influenced by the kind of political tradition to which one belongs. Some republican traditions would be worried by the concentration of global threat power in the hands of an elite. Such power would make it harder for a society to achieve the republican ideal of liberty, an ideal in which citizens are part of a free society and have their interests safeguarded by the rule of law.[74] Since, for republicans, the ideal of negative liberty is rooted in groups, any mechanism that created extreme discrepancies in the distribution of threat power in groups would be critically viewed. Some libertarians may be more sanguine about the presence of threat power based upon abstract objects, or perhaps not even see it as threat power. Nozick, in his discussion of the Lockean proviso, suggests that the person who finds and appropriates the total supply of some medically beneficial substance does not worsen the situation of others because no other would have found the substance.[75] He makes a similar point about the effect of patents. Patents do not deprive others of access to the patented object since that object only comes into existence because of the patentee's efforts.[76]

Assume now that A (a pharmaceutical company or perhaps two or three companies) proposes that if B (a developing country or countries) does not do x (pay more for some life-saving drug such as penicillin) it will do t (revoke patent licences, cut B off from technological information, know-how or something of that kind).[77] In terms of our earlier analysis this is a dependency situation and a coercion claim is certainly feasible in such a situation. But perhaps some libertarians would want to say that there is no threat power being exercised by A. Implicit in such a view would have to be an assumption of negative community. The substances in question are open to all to own, including A. And property rights for roughly Lockean reasons (or rather an interpretation of Locke's labour theory) would have a high degree of inviolability about them. This, combined with the view that patents do not offend the Lockean proviso, because they do not deprive anyone of the relevant thing, might allow A in this case to satisfy the morality test for distinguishing between threats and offers. The morality test simply states that whether or not A is making an offer or threat depends on what A is morally obliged to do.[78] If A is not morally obliged to provide the drugs to B then A is making an offer. (Of course, some offers may be argued to be coercive, but that is not something that matters for the purposes of this illustration.) A libertarian might argue that under conditions of negative community A is entitled to the drugs it discovers and is under no obligation to B with respect to price since property rights enjoy some kind of lexical ascendancy over other kinds of rights. Our claim is not that all libertarians would reason this case in this way or see the threat power of abstract objects in this way. Rather, it is to show that the connections and inferences that are made concerning abstract objects, property and threat power depend on deeper assumptions such as the nature of community. Clearly those libertarians that subscribed to some kind of moral proprietarianism would be less likely to see activity based on the exercise of those property rights as coercive.

Threat power based on the ownership of abstract objects is a form of power that is law-dependent. It is law, as we have pointed out, that constitutes the abstract object. This, in one sense, makes it a fragile form of power, for it relies on the acceptance of legal norms and on the efficacy of the enforcement mechanisms that support those norms. But it is precisely because threat power is law-dependent that it may be hard to recognize as a form of threat power. Threat power which is so inextricably linked to law is perhaps the most dangerous kind of power for a society to contemplate creating and facilitating because it derives legitimacy from the law itself. The dangers of doing this are made worse because threat power based on abstract objects is linked to the property mechanism. Again, because of the central importance of property rights in liberal ideology, the likelihood that this kind of threat power will be largely uncritically accepted, seen as natural, or even not seen as threat power increases. The authority of law masks, as it were, this kind of threat power.

When threat power based on abstract objects is placed in the hands of opportunistic actors, it is likely to give rise to all kinds of economic and social dangers. During his defence of liberalism, Hayek distinguishes liberal economies from collectivist economies by saying that the former are committed to the presence of competition.[79] The principal virtue of competition for Hayek is that it limits the extent to which any one individual can hold power in society. Collectivist economic planning is dangerous because of the amount of power it gives to planners: 'whoever controls all economic activity controls the means for all our ends, and must therefore decide which are to be satisfied and which are not. This is really the crux of the matter.'[80] Much the same can be said about planning by global private sovereigns.[81] States that enact property forms that enable private sovereigns to harness enormous threat power embark on a dangerous strategy, for they increase the capacity of those private sovereigns to discipline markets and to plan against competition. Private sovereigns, like their collectivist counterparts, are likely to plan against competition rather than for it.[82]

Conclusion

Within liberalism the possibility that individuals through the acquisition of large property holdings may also acquire power and be a danger to others remains muted. When a society creates property rights in abstract objects, it faces the prospect of an extensive threat power being concentrated in the hands of a few. The route to this conclusion has been to argue that property is a sovereignty mechanism. When this sovereignty mechanism operates in relation to abstract objects, threat power within a social system increases dramatically. This occurs because abstract objects are both a form of capital and a gateway to other kinds of capital, capital upon which others depend. The property mechanism allows property owners to make use of the threat power that arises because of the dependency relationships that occur around this kind of capital.

The suggestion that abstract objects are one type of capital and that they are linked to the formation and exercise of threat power leads to a question about the distribution of such capital. Because this form of capital is constituted through law, the state and its law makers play a crucial role in its distribution. What arrangements should be set in place for the distribution of such objects? The next chapter explores one possible answer to this question.

Notes

1 In Australia, see Mason J in *Parkdale Custom Built Furniture Pty Ltd* v. *Puxu Pty Ltd* (1981–82) 149 C.L.R. 191, 206–207. In the USA, see *Hartford-Empire Co* v. *United States* 323 U.S., 386, 452 (1944).

2 The evil of monopolies was something that religious opponents could agree on. 'Of combinations I ought really to say much, but the matter is endless and bottomless, full of mere greed and wrong. ... Who is so stupid as not to see that combinations are mere outright monopolies, which even heathen civil laws – I will say nothing of divine right and Christian law – condemn as a plainly harmful thing in all the world?' Martin Luther, *Von Kaufshandlung und Wucher* quoted in R.H. Tawney, *Religion and the Rise of Capitalism* (West Drayton, Middlesex, 1938 ed.), 104–105.

3 Schumpeter thought that monopolies of some kind played a vital role in economic development: J.A. Schumpeter, *The Theory of Economic Development* (Cambridge, Mass. 1949); J. Schumpeter, *Capitalism, Socialism and Democracy* (5th ed., London, 1976).

4 W.W. Sharkey, *The Theory of Natural Monopoly* (Cambridge, 1982).

5 R.A. Posner, 'The Social Costs of Monopoly and Regulation', 83 *Journal of Political Economy*, 807 (1975).

6 See J.T. McCarthy, 'Intellectual Property and Trade Practices Policy: Coexistence or Conflict? The American Experience', 13 *Australian Business Law Review* 198 (1985). The tide seems to have turned in favour of those who do not see intellectual property rights as necessarily leading to monopolies. See the discussion of this by F.H. Easterbrook, 'Intellectual Property Is Still Property', 13 *Harvard Journal of Law and Public Policy* 108 (1990).

7 M. Friedman, *Capitalism and Freedom* (Chicago, London, 1962) 127.

8 Posner and Landes say that a simple economic definition of market power is 'the ability to set price above marginal cost'. See W.M. Landes and R.A. Posner, 'Market Power in Antitrust Cases', 94 *Harvard Law Review*, 937, 939 (1981).

9 B. Russell, *Power: A New Social Analysis* (London, 1938), 10.

10 M.R. Cohen, 'Property and Sovereignty', 13 *Cornell Law Quarterly*, 8 (1927). Cohen's analysis also converges with the arguments made by Robert Hale. See R.L. Hale, 'Coercion and Distribution in a Supposedly Non-Coercive State', 38 *Political Science Quarterly*, 470 (1923); R.L. Hale, 'Bargaining, Duress, and Economic Liberty', 43 *Columbia Law Review*, 603 (1943).

11 Cohen observes that, while the distinction between property and sovereignty is based on the Roman property concept of *dominium* and the political concept of *imperium*, the distinction was not recognized in tribal law; nor was it particularly clear within feudal law where personal services were directly linked to property. Id., at 8–11.

12 Id., 13.

13 J. Austin, *Lectures on Jurisprudence* (5th ed., London, 1885), Lecture VI.

14 See, for example, C. Smart, *Feminism and the Power of Law* (London, New York, 1989); M. Tushnet, 'An Essay on Rights', 62 *Texas Law Review*, 1363 (1984).

15 W.N. Hohfeld, *Fundamental Legal Conceptions* (W.W. Cook ed., Westport, Connecticut, 1919, reprinted 1978).

16 Hohfeld was not the first to advance the correlativity thesis. He derives the thesis from the language of case law. Austin also argues that all laws conferring rights impose a duty. See J. Austin, *Lectures on Jurisprudence* (5th ed., London, 1885), Lecture I. Likewise Bentham sees a logical link between laws creating obligations and rights. For a discussion of Bentham's theory, see L. Lindahl, *Position and Change* (Dordrecht, Holland, 1977), 4–21. Whatever the merits and demerits of the correlativity thesis, it forms part of the deep structure of liberal thinking about law.

17 See N. MacCormick, *Legal Right and Social Democracy* (Oxford, 1982), chapter 8; A.R. White, *Rights* (Oxford, 1984), chapter 5. One of the reasons why the criticisms do not matter is that the correlativity thesis is best understood as a rule of inference within Hohfeld's system. The fact that it is possible to think of counter examples to the correlativity thesis only amounts to saying that another system can have a different inference rule. While this is undoubtedly true, Hohfeld's system might nevertheless deliver sufficient analytical power for us not to be troubled by the limits of one of its rules of inference.

18 W.N. Hohfeld, *Fundamental Legal Conceptions* (W.W. Cook ed., Westport, Connecticut, 1919, reprinted 1978), 38.

19 See D. Lyons, 'Logic and Coercion in Bentham's Theory of Law', 57 *Cornell Law Review*, 335 (1972).

20 See M. Foucault, *Power/Knowledge* (C. Gordon ed., Brighton, 1980), 88, 139–140

21 Id., 98.

22 A's capacity to act in this way is fundamental, Lukes argues, to different approaches to power. See S. Lukes, *Power: A Radical View* (London, Basingstoke, 1974), 27.

23 M. Foucault, *Power/Knowledge* (C. Gordon ed., Brighton, 1980), 141.

24 Id., 98.

25 On this crucial point see L. Lindahl, *Position and Change* (Dordrecht, Holland, 1977), 37.

26 M. Foucault, *The History of Sexuality* (R. Hurley tr., New York, 1980), vol. 1, 94.

27 M. Foucault, *Power/Knowledge* (C. Gordon ed., Brighton, 1980), Lecture 2, 92–108.

28 Id., 102.

29 These terms come from H.D. Lasswell and A. Kaplan, *Power and Society* (New Haven, 1950), 83–86.

30 This list is by no means exhaustive. See P. Simons, 'What is Abstraction & What is it Good For?' in A.D. Irvine (ed.), *Physicalism in Mathematics* (Dordrecht, Boston, London, 1990), 17, 18 for more examples. For an extended discussion of what is an abstract object in philosophy, see W.K. Künne, 'Criteria of Abstractness' in B. Smith (ed.), *Parts and Moments* (Munchen, Wien, 1982), 401.

31 B. Hale, *Abstract Objects* (Oxford, 1987), 46–50.

32 H.H. Field, *Science Without Numbers* (Oxford, 1980), 1.

33 For a good discussion of the issues, see the papers in A.D. Irvine (ed.), *Physicalism in Mathematics* (Dordrecht, Boston, London, 1990).

34 For an example of a modern defence of a version of platonism, see B. Hale, *Abstract Objects* (Oxford, 1987).

35 Identity is a large topic. See the collection of papers in H. Noonan (ed.), *Identity* (Aldershot, 1993).

36 A. Brennan, *Conditions of Identity* (Oxford, 1988), 6. See also S. Shoemaker, 'Identity, Properties and Causality' in H. Noonan (ed.), *Identity* (Aldershot, 1993), chapter 7.

37 Copyright statutes, for example, typically insist on the requirement that works must be in material form before copyright subsists. In the case of patents there is usually a requirement that the invention is fully described before a patent can be granted. In the case of designs and trademarks there is normally an obligation on the applicant to represent graphically the design or mark. Trade secret protection in a sense also involves a requirement of materiality. It is because trade secrets exist in some materially accessible form that owners want legal protection.

38 The English common law early on took the position that something less than identical copying could amount to copyright infringement. See, for example, *D'Almaine* v. *Boosey* (1835) 1 Y. & C. EX. 288; 160 E.R. 117. In the case of patent infringement, the common law developed the 'pith and substance' test. See *Clark* v. *Adie* (1875) L.R. 10 Ch. App. 667. The requirement that only a substantial part of a copyright work need be taken is now legislatively entrenched in most copyright statutes. See, for example, section 14 of the *Copyright Act 1968* (Aus.). The degree of similarity required between the original work and the copied work does seem to have changed. On the more relaxed social attitudes of Elizabethan times to copying, see B. Kaplan, *An Unhurried View of Copyright* (New York, London, 1967), 23–24.

39 An example in Australia is to be found in designs law. The Australian Law Reform Commission, in its reference on designs, reported that there was a widespread perception that Australian courts 'have narrowly construed the infringement provisions so that registered design owners are protected only against virtually exact copies'. See Australian Law Reform Commission, *Designs* (DP 58, Australia, 1994), 94.

40 There are some useful judicial illustrations of this proposition. In *Francis Day & Hunter Ltd.* v. *Bron* [1963] Ch. 587, the court had to decide whether one song infringed another. The court approved the proposition by Astbury J, in *Austin* v. *Columbia Gramophone Co. Ltd.* (1923) Macg.C.C. (1917–1923) 398 at 415, that 'Infringement of copyright in music is not a question of note for note comparison'. Diplock LJ in the *Francis Day* case (at 627) observed that one element of copyright, infringement was that the original and infringing works be objectively similar, but this did not mean that they had to be identical. Speaking in the context of copyright, Lord Shand in *Franz Hanfstaengl* v. *H R Baines & Co Ltd* [1895] A.C. 20 at 31 said, 'All that can I think be said is that the question of infringement of the right depends on the degree of resemblance'. Similarly in the patent field the Australian courts have made it clear that patent protection extends to the 'substantial idea' behind the patent. See Dixon J in *Radiation Ltd* v. *Galliers & Klaerr Pty Ltd* (1938) 60 C.L.R. 36 at 51; *Minnesota Mining & Manufacturing Co and 3M Australia Pty Ltd* v. *Beiersdorf (Aust.) Ltd* (1980) 29 ALR 29.

41 For examples of creative definition and definition by abstraction in the case of mathematical objects, see H. Weyl, *Philosophy of Mathematics and Natural Science* (Princeton, 1949), 8–13.

42 For a conceptual discussion of boundaries in real property, see T. Steinberg, 'God's Terminus: Boundaries, Nature, and Property on the Michigan Shore', XXXVII *The American Journal of Legal History*, 65 (1993).

43 For example, it is a requirement of the Torrens system that land should be properly surveyed.

44 *Whelan Associates, Inc.* v. *Jaslow Dental Laboratory Inc.*, 797 F. 2d 1222 (3rd Cir. 1986).

45 Since the Whelan case, US courts have tried to develop tests that narrow the boundary of the abstract objects that relate to software. See *Computer Associates International, Inc* v. *Altai, Inc.*, 982 F.2d 693 (2d Cir. 1992).

46 Dramatic works have posed similar kinds of problems. See J. Lahore, *Copyright Law* (Service; Sydney, 1988), para 9.20.215.
47 See D.H. Wrong, *Power* (Chicago, 1988), 124–125.
48 On the difficulties of measuring power, see D.A. Baldwin, *Paradoxes of Power* (New York, Oxford, 1989), 24–30.
49 A.A. Alchian and W.R. Allen, *Exchange and Production* (3rd ed., Belmont, California, 1983), 173.
50 The idea that abstract objects are a form of capital resembles the assumption of modern growth theory that knowledge is the basic form of capital. See P.M. Romer, 'Increasing Returns and Long-Run Growth', 94 *Journal of Political Economy*, 1002, 1003 (1986).
51 J.A. Schumpeter, *The Theory of Economic Development* (Cambridge, Mass., 1949) 116.
52 Id., 120.
53 This control by the owner of the abstract object over the physical product can include some acts of distribution. So, for instance, under section 37 of the *Copyright Act 1968* (Aus.) it may be an infringement of copyright to import a work into Australia without the permission of the copyright owner. The parallel importation provisions have been the subject of much discussion in Australia. For example, Copyright Law Review Committee, *The Importation Provisions of the Copyright Act 1968* (Canberra, 1988). See also note 82 for the work done by the Prices Surveillance Authority. Academic discussions include M.J. Davison, 'The Market for Books: Open or Closed?', 18 *Australian Business Law Review*, 179 (1990); A. Fels and J. Walker, 'The Market for Books and the Importation Provisions of the Copyright Act 1968', 17 *Melbourne University Law Review*, 566 (1990); C. Turner, 'Copyright and Parallel Importation: The Australian Experience and Recent Initiatives', 7 *Intellectual Property Journal*, 149 (1992). The right to prevent importation is also to be found in patent law. See W.A. Rothnie, *Parallel Imports* (London, 1993), chapter 3. For a discussion of the importation right in the context of US copyright, see *BMG Music* v. *Perez*, 952 F.2d 318 (9th Cir.), *cert denied*, 112 S. Ct. 2997 (1992). See also R.H. Stern, 'Some Reflections on Parallel Importation of Copyrighted Products into the United States and the Relation of the Exhaustion Doctrine to the Doctrine of Implied Licence', 4 *European Intellectual Property Review*, 119 [1989]. For a discussion of parallel importation in general, see W.A. Rothnie, *Parallel Imports* (London, 1993).
54 The conclusion that propertized abstract objects are tradeable entities in themselves follows from their classification as a form of personal property that may be assigned. For an example of a typical statutory provision, see section 196 of the *Copyright Act 1968* (Aus.). See also note 34, chapter 2. Intellectual property plays an increasingly important role in the modern economy as a form of security. Intellectual property may be the subject of a mortgage or charge. See M. Henry, 'Mortgages of Intellectual Property in the United Kingdom', 5 *European Intellectual Property Review*, 158 [1992]; S.M. Pollard, 'Aspects of Lenders' Security Over Computer Software', 6 *Australian Intellectual Property Journal*, 80 (1995). Even trademarks, which in the past were not recognized as commodities that could be traded in their own right, are coming to be recognized as such. For a judicial discussion of English history on the prohibition on trafficking in trademarks, see Lord Brightman's judgement in Re 12 *Applications by American Greetings Corporation to Register the Trade Mark 'Holly Hobbie'* (1984) 1 IPR 486.
55 T. Veblen, *The Theory of Business Enterprise* (1904, reprinted New York, 1965), 143.
56 Id., 54. Monopoly is not used by Veblen in the strict economic sense of exclusive control over supply, but something less than that. See note 2 at 54.
57 Id., 55.
58 Bain concludes that the most important barrier facing new traders wishing

to enter a given market is product differentiation: J.S. Bain, *Barriers to New Competition* (Cambridge, Mass., 1956), 216.

59 Veblen saw that it was advertising and salesmanship that would take 'first place' in manufacturing. See T. Veblen, *Absentee Ownership* (London, 1924), chapter XI. The general neglect of marketing and the role of intellectual property within economic theory are nicely brought out in W. Kingston, *The Political Economy of Innovation*, (The Hague, Boston, Lancaster, 1984), chapters I and II.

60 See the discussion of trademarks in the section entitled 'Proprietarianism in Action' in Chapter 9. Trademarks are not the only form of abstract object important in the marketing of products. The use of famous personalities, whether real or fictional, to advertise products has become a routine way to generate and capture consumer allegiances and preferences. The law relating to the commercial use of personality has undergone significant development in Anglo-American jurisdictions. Once again lying at the heart of the legal issues has been the question of ownership of the abstract object, namely the public personality that has the much sought-after promotional power. For a discussion of English and Australian developments, see S.K. Murumba, *Commercial Exploitation of Personality* (Sydney, 1986). In the US, see M. Madow, 'Private Ownership of Public Image: Popular Culture and Publicity Rights', 81 *California Law Review* 127 (1993); S.R. Barnett, 'At a Crossroads: The Right of Publicity in the United States', 160 *Revue Internationale du Droit d'Auteur*, 5 (1994).

61 T. Veblen, *The Theory of Business Enterprise* (1904, reprinted New York, 1965), 137.

62 Id., 139.

63 Id., 139–143.

64 See A. Wertheimer, *Coercion* (Princeton, New Jersey, 1987), 5.

65 Id., chapter 12.

66 See Id., 207–208 for a discussion of occasions when similar cases can be said to contain an offer.

67 K.E. Boulding, *Three Faces of Power* (Newbury Park, London, New Delhi, 1989), 25.

68 The exercise of this power is dependent upon the existence of a social system that recognizes, at the very least, the rule of law and private property rights. Power based on abstract objects is a form of power that is heavily rule-based and structure-dependent. There is a debate between those who support structuralist or individualist accounts of power. See K.M. Dowding, *Rational Choice and Political Power* (Aldershot, 1991), 5–8. The position we take here, without offering a defence for it, is that setting up a dichotomy between structuralist and individualist approaches to power does not seem a useful way to proceed. Structures are critical to the creation, definition and maintenance of some types of power. Power runs through these structures. Individuals operating within these structures do not so much have power as the facility, through various social mechanisms, to harness power.

69 Extensiveness being a feature of power. See B. De Jouvenel, 'Authority: The Efficient Imperative', in C.J. Friedrich (ed.), *Authority* (Cambridge, Mass., 1958), 159.

70 *Patents, Innovation and Competition in Australia* (Industrial Property Advisory Committee, Australia, 1984), 17.

71 N. Rosenberg, *Technology and American Economic Growth* (New York, 1972), 120.

72 N. Rosenberg and L.E. Birdzell Jr., *How the West Grew Rich* (New York, 1986), 247.

73 N. Rosenberg, *Technology and American Economic Growth* (New York, 1972), 118.

74 For a discussion of the republican ideal, see J. Braithwaite and P. Pettit, *Not Just Deserts* (Oxford, 1990), chapter 5.

75 R. Nozick, *Anarchy, State, and Utopia* (Oxford, 1974), 181.

76 Id., 182.

77 For the use of patents as conspiratorial devices by pharmaceutical companies on an international scale, see P.M. Costello, 'The Tetracycline Conspiracy: Structure, Conduct and Performance in the Drug Industry', 1 *Antitrust Law and Economics Review*, 13 (1968).

78 Nozick has an important discussion of this test in R. Nozick, 'Coercion' in S. Morgenbesser *et al.* (eds.), *Philosophy, Science, and Method* (New York, 1969), 440.

79 F.A. Hayek, *The Road to Serfdom* (London, 1944).

80 Ibid., at 68.

81 Institutional economists have made the idea of a private form of centralized planning in the capitalist economy a major theme of their work. Simplifying, institutionalists are not happy with neo-classical models that locate power within markets and portray power as an outcome of market structures. For institutionalists a much more realistic picture of the economy is obtained once the market is seen as an outcome of those groups that hold power, especially those in the corporate sector of the economy. See J.R. Commons, *Institutional Economics* (New York, 1934); W.J. Samuels (ed.), *The Economy as a System of Power* (New Brunswick, New Jersey, 1979); M.R. Tool and W.J. Samuels (eds.), *State, Society and Corporate Power* (2nd ed., New Brunswick, Oxford, 1989).

82 Using abstract objects to discipline or order the market has many forms. Prohibiting parallel imports is one form of 'orderly marketing'. In Australia the economic consequences of this are well documented. See Prices Surveillance Authority, *Inquiry into Book Prices: Final Report* (Canberra, December 1989); Prices Surveillance Authority, *Inquiry into the Prices of Sound Recordings* (Canberra, December 1990); Prices Surveillance Authority, *Inquiry into Prices of Computer Software: Final Report* (Canberra, December 1992).

8 The Justice of Information

Informational Justice

Information is a primary good. It may be, perhaps, the most important primary good we can imagine when we consider its role in the economy, the development of knowledge and culture and, as we saw in the last chapter, its impact on power in a society. How should this primary good be distributed? This chapter devotes itself to developing an answer to this question.

Before proceeding we need to clarify quickly our terminological shift. In this chapter we will talk mainly about information. We use this broader generic term to include abstract objects and knowledge of various kinds. The term 'abstract objects' has the specialized meaning assigned to it in the last chapter. Abstract objects are a species of information. When it comes to talking about justice and intellectual property it is better to cast the net widely and use a generic term like 'information'. Information is the daily lifeblood of human agents as communicating beings. Talking about information rather than abstract objects captures the pervasive effect that intellectual property rights in information can have on the daily lives of people.

Discussions of justice proceed under certain conditions, one of the most common being that of relative or moderate scarcity. This, for example, is a condition that Rawls stresses as part of the objective circumstances of justice.[1] This condition does not hold for information. There can be a scarcity of information about a particular subject. People may be ignorant, or they may be restricted from having access to information by social norms or encryption technology. But, once in existence, information is not a scarce resource. The supply of information to one person does not diminish the amount available for supply to another person. Information has, in the language of economics, the property of being non-rivalrous in consumption. There is another contingent feature of information that matters for present purposes and that is its natural tendency to spread. Humans are information gatherers and exchangers. In a world full of digital technology and pathways the capacity of humans to spread information is greatly enhanced. The idea of a global electronic village increasingly approximates to reality.

Most discussions of justice choose some level of group life as their setting. Typically this group life is linked to the state. Part of the present discussion concentrates on justice between states; inter-state as opposed to intra-state justice. Global justice remains a critical long-term issue within international politics. The poorer states of the world seek to obtain the kind of economic riches that developed states have acquired. Because the developmental path has proved rocky and because, as is becoming increasingly clear in the environmental area, rich states have often developed at the expense of poor states, the normativity of justice has been utilized in an attempt to increase the developmental prospects of poorer countries. Much of the work by the United Nations on the new International Economic Order is redolent of this utilization of the normativity of justice.[2]

In thinking about the problem of distributive justice there are a number of frameworks to choose from. Within traditional philosophy there is a choice to be made between contractarian approaches to justice and utilitarian or consequentialist accounts of justice.[3] And there is also the natural rights-inspired entitlement theory of Nozick.[4] These traditional offerings face competition from feminist and postmodernist frameworks.[5]

All theories have their critics. In choosing a theory in which to work up a normative argument concerning the distribution of information we will automatically acquire some opposition. Defending our chosen theory against its critics is not something that occupies any space in this chapter. That is not the point of this chapter. Our purpose is to think critically about the impact of intellectual property arrangements on the distribution of information. This is important to do, for intellectual property rights, by their very nature, create artificial conditions of scarcity for information, which should not be scarce. To this end we will choose Rawls' theory of justice. There are several reasons for this. The theory is centrally dependent on the intersubjective agreement of persons and this, in metaphysical terms, is much less problematic than natural rights. His theory also has a strong *a priori* normative edge to it. For present purposes this is a strength rather than a weakness. We want a theory against which the distributive effects of intellectual property can be clearly judged. Unlike the case of utilitarianism, there is no dependence upon a complex summing procedure, which in any case is frequently impossible to do. Finally, because of its impeccable liberal pedigree, Rawls' theory is not predisposed to be hostile to property rights. There is probably no other theory of justice in which intellectual property rights are likely to receive a fairer hearing.

We can now offer a more detailed statement of what we are seeking to achieve. Essentially, it is to try and outline what the relations between property and information ought to be through the lenses of a theory of contractarian justice. There are obviously very many factors that go to affect the distribution of information in the world: technology and its distribution, culture, language, social and economic networks, individual capacities and communicative skills are some examples. Institutional arrangements or organizations are undoubtedly important factors in this distribution and intellectual property systems are important aspects of institutional design that affect the spread of information.

Questions of institutional design or organization are of interest to the theorist of justice in that a general theory of justice has implications for the structure and organization of societal institutions. Rawls, for instance, argues that the institutions of constitutional democracy satisfy his principles of justice. Our purpose is to trace the implications of Rawls' theory for the distribution of information and the role of property in affecting that distribution. By linking justice and property we are following Hume, who argues that the ideas of justice and property arise together to make conventions of non-interference in the possessions of others work properly on a societal scale.[6] Since Hume, discussions of distributive justice have moved away from a concern with property to range widely over the distribution of all kinds of benefits and burdens.[7] The object of distribution being discussed here is information and so it might be said that it is informational justice with which we are concerned.

Information as a Primary Good

Our way into informational justice begins with the claim that information is a primary good. Primary goods can be natural or social.[8] For Rawls, the chief social primary goods are rights, liberties, powers, opportunities, income and wealth. These things are primary goods in the sense that every rational person is presumed to want them because they have such a crucial role in the implementation of one's life projects, whatever they may be. Except in relation to self-respect,[9] Rawls does not offer much in the way of argument to defend this list of primary goods. Instead he relies on the dangerous strategy of an appeal to self-evidence. This is dangerous because matters taken to be self-evident may turn out to be only evident to one's self. Information is too important to be left off the list of primary goods. Just as individuals can be assumed to want rights, liberties, income, wealth, self-respect and so on, we are suggesting that they want and need information. It is possible to push the argument for information being a primary good beyond an appeal to self-evidence.

One reason for thinking that information is a primary good is its crucial role in human planning. The idea of planning plays an important part in Rawls' theory of the good. Persons in the original position are assumed to have a specific conception of the good.[10] This means that they have life plans that form the basis for the judgements of value they make. Rawls' theory of the good claims that 'the good is the satisfaction of rational desire'.[11] Rational desire is itself determined by a life plan devised through a process of deliberative rationality. Equipped with this conception of the good it is plausible to argue, as Rawls does, that rational persons in the original position would want a scheme of justice which delivered more of those primary goods which are necessary for the implementation of the good, rather than less.

The psychological premise that humans are creatures who live according to plans is defensible provided planning is thought of in the loose terms of individuals thinking about a way of proceeding to some goal or the satisfaction of some desire.[12] It should not be taken to imply some notion of masterly long-term design. Having argued that the good for a person is tied to the existence of a rational plan for that person, Rawls argues that primary goods are those things that have a general utility in the execution of any life plan.[13] Things which for Rawls are self-evidently primary goods are liberty, opportunity, income, wealth and self-respect. Why should information be added to this list? One reason is that individuals in the original position are rational life planners. While they do not know the specifics of their plan or anybody else's, they do know that they will live in a society in which they will be in the business of planning. Given that individuals know that they will be the rational formulators of plans, it is also likely that they will want some basic level of information and access to information as one of their primary goods. After all, the act of planning requires information. Plans take their shape according to the information available to the planners. The more information they have about the world to which their desires, purposes and goals relate, the more specific their plans can be. The less information individuals have, the more general their plans have to be. In a world where the amount of information available for planning was ever diminishing, a point would be reached where planning could not take place.

The importance of information as a primary good can be better appreciated when one focuses on the consequences of its imperfect distribution. Prejudices of various kinds are examples of imperfect information. The belief that because someone is of a certain skin colour they are therefore lazy, incompetent, less intelligent and so on is, in the dispassionate language of economics, an example of imperfect information. Imperfect information has both economic and social consequences. From an economic perspective the presence of stereotypes means that individuals will not attain their optimum marginal productivity, that is, some skilled and talented people will not be hired.[14]

Rawls' theory requires a basic social structure in which citizens have equal rights to basic liberties. Our point is that more than this is needed. Citizens pursuing their equal rights need access to information so that they can make plans and correct decisions. Social institutions themselves have to treat information in ways that minimize distortions of their functions. At a general level this means trying to disseminate relevant and accurate information. Information is the primary good which citizens need in order to be able to make the abstract infrastructural principles of justice work in a concrete way in their daily lives.

Ironically it is information that participants in the original position are largely denied. This lack of information is designed to encourage the moral point of view. Self-interested planning becomes a risky proposition. While those in the original position are information-poor planners, it is more than likely that, while they were still in the original position, they would agree to a set of institutions that would allow them to be information-rich planners in their ultimate social world.

Before shifting to the next stage of our argument we can bed down the claim that information is a primary good by looking at the various definitional cloaks it wears. If one thing is clear, there is no one view of information that enjoys a transdisciplinary validity. The diversity of approaches to information suggests that information itself has a number of functions or roles.[15] One approach sees it as a resource. This view of information gains some limited implicit recognition in Rawls' list of basic liberties, some of which, like political liberty and freedom of speech, presuppose for their meaningful exercise access to and use of information. Likewise commodity-based perspectives of information draw attention to the fundamental wealth-creating role of information in society. Yet other definitional approaches to information emphasize the idea that information is itself a constitutive force in society. Here the idea is that information and information flows act, via various social feedback mechanisms, like the legal system and the market-place, to alter social structures. Naturally the various definitional approaches can be debated, but when taken together they have a cumulative impact which suggests that information is a primary good that is foundational for some of the other kinds of primary goods that Rawls lists. It is, therefore, the kind of primary good that most rational individuals can be taken to want.

Distributing Information

We can now make some suggestions about how information stands in relation to Rawls' two principles of justice. These principles are the ones which Rawls claims would be chosen by participants in the original position: a hypothetical position of ignorance in which individuals do not know enough about their particular place in their social world to choose principles that maximize the benefits going to their place. These principles are widely known but, for the sake of convenience, we restate them. The first principle asserts that each person is to have an equal right to the most extensive basic liberty consistent with a similar liberty for others and the second claims that social and economic inequalities are to be ordered so that they 'are both (a) to the greatest benefit of the least advantaged and (b) attached to offices and positions open to all under conditions of fair equality of opportunity'.[16]

Each principle has a separate sphere of operation. The first operates in what might be termed the political–social sphere, while the second governs what might be termed civil society. Civil society in its narrow sense refers to that part of the basic social structure that deals with those economic relations that surround production and distribution within a society. Thus the first principle regulates the distribution of basic citizenship rights such as the right to vote, freedom of speech and assembly, right to hold property and so on. The second operates on the distribution of wealth, income and questions of institutional design. The first principle has priority over the second. It follows that, for Rawls, individuals cannot trade up to a position of economic advantage by disposing of or compromising their rights of equality of citizenship and opportunity.

Rawls' neat division of the social system into the two independent parts of the political and the civil comes under strain when we look at information. Initially one might think that information is a primary social good which, like income and wealth, would naturally vary in its distribution. But in some ways information shows the artificiality of the division which Rawls relies on. Information may be the kind of primary good that can be thought of in terms of a basic liberty. To Rawls' classical list of political freedoms we might add the freedom of information. This, like other basic liberties, it might be argued, should be equally distributed in a society. The kinds of goals or interests that freedom of information serves overlap, at least to some extent, with those served by freedom of speech, a primary good explicitly mentioned by Rawls. One classical defence of freedom of speech has been to argue that truth is more likely to emerge from an ungoverned than from a governed market-place of ideas.[17] A similar argument could be used to justify freedom of information. In fact, for the reductively minded, it might be possible to take the line that the free speech principle is a social convention designed to help facilitate the more important goal of information access and exchange, which in social and biological terms is critical to whatever joint enterprises humans undertake. Pursuing this line of thought is not something that needs to be done here. The important point is that information is a primary good that has a place in both political and civil society, that is in both of Rawls' principles.

Information, once created, finds its optimal use when it is made available to all. This is an economic claim about information which, as it happens, converges with Rawls' theory of distributive justice, when applying that theory to information. Within Rawls' general conception of justice, primary goods are distributed equally. Equal distribution is the hypothetical distribution by which improvements are judged. Positive economics justifies the unequal distribution of information in terms of its incentive effect. (Although appropriation is the preferred way of thinking about the problem, it amounts to unequal distribution). By allowing some individuals to control or own information and denying access to others, the belief is that more socially useful forms of information will be produced. This economic prescription for the production of socially valuable resources can be easily accommodated under Rawls' difference principle (the second principle of justice). That principle allows inequalities provided that these work to improve the lot of the least advantaged. One can imagine cases where the unequal distribution of some socially useful information through, say, the patents mechanism would satisfy the difference principle and be therefore a permissible inequality. If it were really true, for example, that certain kinds of beneficial drug inventions would only have taken place because of the patent system then the temporary inequalities that the patent system creates in terms of access to information could be accommodated under the difference principle. This accommodation is made easier in the case of intellectual property rights since most of those rights have a fixed period.[18] Formally at least, they create only temporary inequalities. One implication of the difference principle for intellectual property rights, however, is that we should be wary of increasing terms of protection. By doing so we are formally increasing the period for which one important primary good is unequally distributed in society. Unless there are some very clear-cut gains to the least advantaged the difference principle cuts across increasing temporal bars to information.

A fundamental feature of Rawls' two principles is that they have a lexical order. The first has priority over the second. Put shortly, this has the consequence that political liberties cannot be exchanged for economic gains. For our purposes, one consequence of this lexical ordering means that certain instrumental uses of property are prohibited. The right to hold personal property remains one of the basic political liberties of the citizen. However, when the background institutions that are to fit the two principles of justice are being formed, it necessarily follows from the lexical priority of the first principle that these institutions cannot adjust or create property rights in such a way as to subvert basic political liberties. An example will make this point more concrete. Copyright creates property in expression and property in expression clearly stands in tension with freedom of expression.[19] Governments who own the copyright in politically sensitive documents or films can rely on copyright to prevent their circulation.[20] One can imagine a society in which it was decided that the economic gains from having rights of property in expression outweighed freedom of expression and so freedom of expression suffered accordingly. It is just this kind of calculation which Rawls' distributive theory rules out. From the point of view of his theory, the growth of property forms is not to occur at the expense of basic political liberties.

The instrumental nature of property in Rawls' scheme reveals itself in his section on the background institutions of government where the functions of government, such as allocation and distribution, are mediated through changes in the definition of property rights.[21] Although Rawls does not argue the case, he assumes, with some plausibility, that the continuous adjustments in rights of property are necessary 'to correct the distribution of wealth and to prevent concentrations of power' detrimental to fundamental political liberties.[22] The wide dispersal of property is a necessary condition for maintaining the value of these liberties. Property rights do not, in Rawls' theory, have the iron-clad guarantees of safety which, for example, Nozick gives to such rights in his theory. Rather than a primary protected status, they have a secondary instrumental status. Thus, in thinking through the design of major social institutions, the Rawlsian designer would use property rights as a tool to preserve political liberties and maximize access to, and the distribution of, primary goods such as information. It is hard to see how a massive propertization of information is, in terms of the design of the basic social structure, consistent with the distributive requirements of the theory. Rawls' theory does not, of course, rule out private property rights or suggest that there is no scope for intellectual property rights. Rather, in abstract terms, it implies that an evolutionary institutional trajectory that favoured the massive propertization of information would be contrary to the distributive principles that the theory establishes for the purposes of just institutional design.

The sceptical, instrumental approach to intellectual property rights, which flows out of contractarian theory employing a Rawlsian procedural rationality, can be better seen once we focus on the idea of information and organization as capital. Abstract objects, the last chapter argued, are an important form of capital.[23] How might the parties in the original position deal with this knowledge? Putting the argument concisely, it seems reasonable to think that, since other kinds of capital resources such as minerals, land, talent, money and so on would be distributed unequally and known to be so, the contractors in the original position would opt for a societal scheme which distributed at least one form of capital, information, as widely as possible. Monopoly rights over information, it would probably be agreed by those in the original position, should be severely limited. Why this position is a likely outcome can be seen more clearly if we look at the concept of human capital and how this intersects with intellectual property. The parties in the original position would know about the concept of human capital since there are no restrictions on knowledge of general laws and theories.[24]

Human capital has a disarmingly simple economic definition: 'knowledge embodied in people'.[25] Human capital theory begins with the assumption that human beings have a personal base of knowledge, skills and habits which they further through forms of education and training. The decision whether to increase this base or not is a matter of individual cost–benefit calculation.[26] Roughly the chain of causation thought to hold true is that human capital as embodied knowledge and skills is the springboard for technological and scientific development which, in turn, is an important (or perhaps *the*) condition of economic growth. Human capital, in short, turns out to be foundational for economic development. So, by way of illustration, one important suggestion has been that in the United States, perhaps the biggest user of capital in the world the contribution of education to economic growth up to 1956 probably exceeded that of physical capital.[27]

How does intellectual property link up with human capital? This is rather a big question and nothing like an answer can be given here. The first thing to observe is that there is a clear overlap between the two. Human capital is embodied knowledge and skills. Intellectual property rights are, via the mechanism of the abstract object, rights to knowledge. The way in which intellectual property rules are designed makes a difference to things like the rates of return on human capital investment and the formation of human capital. Pinning down precise relations between human capital and intellectual property is a major empirical and analytical project. Here is one possible relation. Intellectual property rights allow a price to be charged for knowledge and skills. An individual's decision to add to her stock of knowledge and skills will clearly be affected by the price she has to pay for that knowledge or skill. As the scope and duration of intellectual property increases (more kinds of knowledge can be charged for over longer periods) there might be possible adverse outcomes for human capital accumulation. Raising the price of knowledge may mean that fewer people are prepared to invest in increasing their own stock of knowledge. Here is another possible outcome. The more people are encouraged through a general intellectual property consciousness to play the 'let's price our knowledge' game, the more likely they are to hang on to that knowledge. After all, why diffuse any of it free of charge if you can make money out of it? But this also reduces the opportunity for others to build on their existing stock of human capital. The capacity of any one individual or organization to exploit fully *all* the relational aspects of a body of knowledge is limited. Yet through the pricing of knowledge individuals may be encouraged to cling to knowledge that they do not have the resources to exploit fully or at all. A society with a highly developed intellectual property consciousness may find it is encouraging the underexploitation of its knowledge and human capital. One final example of the way human capital may be affected by intellectual property: copyright law regulates who may print books, who may import books and the scope of free access to books (fair dealing). The way that copyright law is designed has a profound impact on the supply of books and other copyright material to different groups in the community. The education sector, which is a major producer of human capital, is, quite naturally, a major user of books. The supply of books to this sector is critical to the performance of its task. It is for this reason that copyright regimes generally contain statutory licence schemes that allow educational institutions to make use of books on terms more favourable than those given to private individuals. Compulsory licence schemes for the education sector can be thought of as a way in which the goal of building up human capital is maintained while allowing the private copyright owner a reward for his efforts. If the education sector were not given more liberal access to works under copyright then one consequence might be that the social returns from the investment in education would be lower. Property rules that limited the diffusion of knowledge within the education sector, or limited the access of that sector to knowledge, would mean, amongst other things, that there were inefficiencies in the use of existing human capital stock. Putting it another way, fewer people might be trained, or they might not be trained as well.

The preceding argument based on human capital only suggests some possibilities. It does not demonstrate them. It does, however, give rational actors in the original position another reason for treading cautiously in the design of intellectual property rights. It gives parties in the original position a reason for preferring minimal rather than maximal forms of these rights. Just how sceptically and cautiously intellectual property rights are to be treated under a contractarian theory of justice becomes clear when we transfer our attention to justice and relations between states.

Global Informational Justice

The move to inter-state relations forces some observations about the relationship between Rawls' principles and international distributive justice. Some theorists have suggested that Rawls' failure to globalize his theory of justice is a shortcoming.[28] Beitz, for example, has argued that Rawls' principles should not be confined to nation states because these states are not in fact the closed systems which Rawls assumes them to be. Rawls limits the conception of justice to a given individual nation state in the belief that once a sound theory is developed at this level other problems of justice, like those of international justice, will become more 'tractable'. The nation state is for Rawls a convenient political identification of those individuals who participate in a society which is governed by rules that make that society a 'cooperative venture for mutual advantage'.[29] It is this cooperative scheme in relation to which some guiding principles for the division of advantages must be formulated.

If there were in some sense a world society with a scheme of cooperation that generated advantages and disadvantages then this would on Rawls' approach allow one to generate principles that could be applied globally rather than nationally. Beitz tries to build the case for global distributive justice by pointing out that states are interdependent through their participation in international trade and financial systems. The argument involves recognizing that various international regimes which relate to free trade, investment and monetary stability produce 'a pattern of global interdependence'.[30] This in turn generates advantages and disadvantages. The advantages lie in economic growth and productive efficiency. The disadvantages have to do with increasing the unequal distribution of wealth and the loss of sovereignty. The existence of an interdependent system with advantages and disadvantages leads Beitz to argue that there exists a global scheme of social cooperation which has to have global principles of social justice. Citizens of Rawls' original position have now to think about their place in the world rather than the state. This modification does not change the choice of principles (according to Beitz and others).[31]

One possibility in the present context is to go along with an argument like Beitz's for the global application of Rawls' principles and then argue that societies or groups which are wealthy in terms of information, particularly technological information and human capital, are under distributive obligations towards poorer societies or groups. The precise content of these obligations would be a matter for argument. One would expect that there would be, at the very least, negative duties on information-rich groups not to restrict access to information. If there were a distributive theory of justice that could be applied internationally it could be used to evaluate critically the distributive effects of intellectual property within the world economy. For example, every time the international standard of protection for patent or copyright is raised, the cost of the information protected by those rights also rises. Clearly this has distributive implications for states within the global economy. (It also has, as our discussion of abstract objects and person dependency suggests, important consequences for power relations.) A global theory of justice could, then, help point the way to some set of morally desirable international property arrangements for the distribution of information and in particular abstract objects.

The problem, though, with using a theory of international justice to develop an argument concerning the distribution of informational capital is that it may be difficult to establish such a theory in the first place. Take, for example, an argument for global justice based on interdependence.[32] It is undoubtedly true that, since Beitz proposed such an argument, states have become much more interdependent. The integration of financial markets, international standard setting, the increased scope of multilateral trading instruments to include services and intellectual property, the emergence of strong regional blocs like the European Union and the North American Free Trade Agreement, a consensus on the fundamentals of macroeconomic policy and its implementation through supranational regulatory institutions like the International Monetary Fund and the World Bank are just some aspects and examples of this greater interdependence.[33] Interdependence is a brute empirical fact about the modern world. The fact that there are trade and other economic interdependencies between states does not mean, though, that there is a scheme of mutual cooperation between those states in the social sense. The fact of interdependence does not necessarily entail the presence of the deeper social connections that characterize social groups. More seems to be involved in the mutual cooperation which is characteristic of a society, including shared values, norms, culture and some notion of group identity. It is plausible to say that mutual cooperation implies some degree of interdependence of an economic or non-economic kind, but relations of interdependence do not necessarily entail the presence of a scheme of mutual cooperation. A leap from interdependence to a global cooperative scheme with its implications of a superordinate group seems too great a leap to make. At a psychological level it is not clear that the extent to which individuals form social groups depends on the degree to which they are mutually dependent upon one another for the satisfaction of various needs and desires. Another explanation for group formation suggests that the crucial causal factor is an act of self-categorization rather than the existence of interdependence amongst individuals.[34] On this view group formation seems to precede interdependence.

There are other ways in which one might argue for global distributive principles. Bietz himself has suggested that a preferable route to demonstrating that the principles of justice apply to the world lies in focusing on the requirements for membership of the original position. For Rawls persons in the original position are equal moral persons who have the capacity to formulate a conception of their good and are 'capable of a sense of justice'.[35] For Beitz it is at least possible that such persons would choose to globalize the principles of justice irrespective of whether there was some international social cooperation.[36] Whether or not such principles could be implemented in some practical way would depend on the existence of some international set of institutions or social scheme. The crucial point for Beitz is that the existence of global principles of justice is no longer dependent upon some international scheme of mutual cooperation.

Perhaps, though, we should consider the possibility that there is no satisfactory route to principles of world justice. Justice is a group phenomenon. It is when groups of individuals have to find ways of distributing resources or righting wrongs that justice is invoked as a value. To some extent the choice of group in relation to which the principles of justice are to have a functional role is arbitrary. We know, sociologically speaking, that individuals participate in many groups, both primary and secondary. There is no reason in principle why these groups could not choose conceptions of justice. Rawls' own open-ended description of society as a self-sufficient association of persons subscribing to a set of rules means that society is not necessarily equivalent to the group which is circumscribed by the boundaries of the nation state. Why, then, might we not have principles of world justice applicable to all persons in the world? There is nothing logically incoherent in this idea. The problem it meets with is the sheer heterogeneity in the world. The diverse patterns of beliefs, moral codes, cultural practices and conduct that exist in the world suggest that there is no world group or society to which the principles of global justice could be meaningfully extended. Groups do form and interact across traditional territorial borders, especially with modern communications technology, but the existence of international groups does not ground the existence of a world group to which global principles of justice might apply.

The evidence of heterogeneity makes one wonder whether persons in the original position would in fact seek to globalize the principles which they choose for their group. One cannot simply assume this as a matter of ideal theory. In the way such theory is practised by Rawls, original participants know about human nature and psychology, as well as the existence of cultural and moral diversity. They know that they will live in a world where there will be differences of culture, taste, temperament, religion and ideologies.[37] The presence of this knowledge lends Rawls' ideal theory a degree of plausibility. It means that the deductive powers of those in the original position are exercised in the light of some real-world facts. Without the input of those facts ideal theory would run the risk of becoming fantasy.

Working out whether the persons in the original position would globalize the principles of justice is not, as Rawls says of his whole project, an exercise in moral geometry, but is rather a more conjectural affair. There are some reasons why the original citizens might not be prepared to tread the path to global justice. The evidence of difference and heterogeneity might make them wonder about the feasibility of institutionalizing a global theory of justice.[38] Perhaps the original participants confronted by such evidence might conclude that a global theory of justice might not, for psychological reasons, be a salient normative concept for all the different groups in the world. Then world justice, with its connotations of order and objectivity, might become the banner under which the intolerant and the imperialistic crusade to remake the world. What reason would there be for thinking that those charged with interpreting a charter of global justice would do so in a way that was sensitive to local conditions and customs? The desire for group sovereignty may well see the original citizens choosing to tie the principles of justice to some entity smaller than the world. Using some territorial unit like nation state to limit the application of a conception of justice is perhaps more anthropologically faithful to what the evidence tells us about humans, their natures and the cultures they invent.

Thus far we have given some reasons why a global theory of justice is going to be hard to deliver, at least in the context of Rawls' theory. Nothing we have said rules out such a theory,[39] but there are enough problems with it to suggest that for present purposes we should not pursue it. Nevertheless, working within the confines of a domestic rather than a global view of justice, it is possible to show that states would, under a contractarian theory of distributive justice, be committed to a sceptical instrumental approach to intellectual property rights.[40] Such a theory of justice would require one or more states to avoid, under most circumstances, globalizing a set of property standards for all states. It is time to make good this claim.

We begin with a brief description of the way in which Rawls handles the choice of principles to regulate relations between states, or what he subsequently comes to call the law of peoples.[41] The law of peoples is simply Rawls' distinctive term for those principles of right, justice and the common good that give a liberal conception of international justice its content. His discussion of justice between states in *A Theory of Justice* arises not out of concern for issues of resource distribution but rather the relation between civil disobedience and foreign policy.[42] This does not matter, for it is his specification of parameters for his initial situation in which we are interested. Not surprisingly the procedure for developing principles to regulate international relations is similar to that chosen for the nation state.[43]

Having chosen principles for the nation state, representatives of the state come together in a conference of nations to determine the principles of justice between states. Once again these principles are chosen under conditions of imperfect information. Representatives know that they are binding their state to some regulatory principles but they do not know whether their state is at the centre of trade or on the periphery, whether it is resource-rich or poor, the size of its territory and so on. The principles derived under such assumptions are, according to Rawls, basically the ones that form part of existing international law. They include principles of freedom and independence of peoples and their governments, equality of peoples, the right to self-defence and a commitment to the principle of human rights.[44]

The bulk of Rawls' analysis of the law of peoples takes place in the context of ideal theory. Essentially this means that agents are assumed to be faithful to the agreements and principles they devise. Rawls devotes little attention to non-ideal theory in the context of the law of peoples. Non-ideal theory recognizes that the actual world is an imperfect place, full of inequalities and abuses of power. No longer is everyone presumed to act justly. The existence of brutal regimes like those of Pol Pot and Hitler are recognized. The object of non-ideal theory is to provide some answers as to how an ideal liberal conception of justice for an international society of peoples might best be implemented.[45] Of interest here are Rawls' brief remarks about the operation of non-ideal theory under unfavourable conditions. Basically, for Rawls the problem of underdeveloped and unstable societies stems from a failure of political culture and social organization rather than a lack of natural resources or capital.[46] A solution to this problem has its beginnings in the recognition that some simple act on the part of rich states to redistribute wealth to the poor states will probably not solve the problems of such states. Rawls says nothing beyond this about the application of non-ideal theory to international relations, relations in which weak or helpless states and hegemonic states often figure.

Rawls, it is fair to say, makes a somewhat sparing use of his procedure when he discusses principles of international justice. He really only uses the first stage of his original position to identify the key principles of justice for peoples. But there are in his theory of domestic justice three other stages in which the original position is modified so that a constitution can be chosen and social and economic policies can be developed and applied through law.[47] These same stages could not be applied to principles of international justice. Amongst other things, the representatives of states in the original international position would not be meeting to decide the powers of a constitutional world government. It is not world government but rather cooperative association that the representatives of states would be seeking to achieve.[48] This seems a plausible assumption. On the other hand, representatives at this international justice conference would be interested in choosing some basic international structures and institutions that made cooperative life between their respective states possible. Naturally these would have to be consistent with the law of peoples which they had worked out in the original position. Rawls' emphasis at the domestic level is on describing a basic structure (essentially that of constitutional democracy) that is consistent with the principles of justice. Our use of his method has a different purpose in mind. We want to argue that certain international arrangements for intellectual property would be inconsistent with those principles that were chosen to underwrite international law. We are, in other words, suggesting that the contractarian theory of justice, when extended to international relations, excludes as unjust certain basic arrangements for intellectual property. This claim is supported by the following line of reasoning.

Participants in the international original position, we have noted, would be interested in coming to some accord concerning the basic institutions and structures that might economically and politically affect their respective nation states. At the very least, financial and trade interdependencies would provide them with a reason for thinking about the kinds of international regimes they would want to implement. After all, the original parties are rational planners and so would want any scheme of justice for peoples to be capable of meaningful implementation in an interdependent world. More particularly, these original planners of justice would want to ensure that the principles of justice which governed international relations did not jeopardize the viability and operation of the conception of justice they had chosen at the national level. One outcome of Rawls' method, if repeated with different groups, might be the creation of more than one version of justice. This is a possibility because, even after participants in the original position have been stripped down to their rational frames, they might still retain the cultural and social traces of the state or territory of which they are representatives and which in a deep sense form part of the common understanding of that group of people.[49] Rawls' method, if repeated amongst different peoples, might lead to the construction of local variants of justice as fairness. One issue which would then face participants in the international conference would be to think of ways in which local conceptions of justice could survive in an economically interdependent world. Solutions to this problem would not be easy to find. One possibility is that participants would seek ways in which to institutionalize conditions of non-interference in their affairs. The condition of non-interference, hardly surprisingly, is strongly present in Rawls' list of core principles for the law of peoples. Peoples are free and independent and they have a duty of non-intervention.[50] It is at this point that we can return to thinking about how the participants at this justice conference would plan the fate of intellectual property.

International arrangements for property would be high on the agenda for parties in the international original position. Why so? We need to remind ourselves of some of our earlier discussion. In the previous chapter we argued that property is a form of sovereignty and that intellectual property, under certain conditions, gives rise to enormous levels of threat power. Clearly this has implications for the condition of non-interference. Depending on their form, international arrangements for intellectual property could easily contravene this condition and so would be an important subject for discussion by participants. Related to this, participants would have to think very carefully about the relationship between the territoriality of property and the impact of any international arrangement on that territoriality. We need to clarify this crucial point.

Property (including intellectual property) has been for most of its institutional life a highly territorial institution. Legally speaking, this has meant that the rules which govern property rights have been determined by a sovereign who has jurisdiction over a particular physical area. Territoriality, like property, is a notion that is linked to sovereignty and the state. One aspect of the definition of sovereignty is the power of the state over territory.[51] Territory is also intimately related to foundational concepts within political philosophy. Locke, for instance, at various points in the *Second Treatise* links territory to government, community and citizenship.[52] Roughly the picture one gets in the *Second Treatise* concerning property and territory is that government is under an obligation to act in a way which is consistent with the property interests of a group of individual property holders, that group having at the very least a territorial identity. It is also clear from our discussion in Chapter 3 that for Locke the property rights of an individual within the state can be adjusted by the state. Governments have the power to regulate property. This power has to be exercised in a way that is consistent with the goals of natural law. But governments have, when it comes to making regulatory decisions concerning property rights, leeways of choice:

> For it would be a direct Contradiction, for any one, to enter into Society with others for the securing of and regulating of Property: And yet to suppose his Land, whose Property is to be regulated by the Laws of the Society, should be exempt from the Jurisdiction of that Government, to which he himself the Proprietor of the Land, is a Subject.[53]

It is hardly surprising that Locke should think this. The importance to governments of being able to adjust property rights cannot be underestimated. In Chapter 6 we identified four crucial functions of property. One way in which to think about property, although not the only way, is to see it as a coping mechanism that states use to adjust to internal and external stresses. Given the importance of the property mechanism to states, its territoriality is not surprising.

Our question, then, is: what basic arrangements would parties in the international original position choose for property? Obviously the stakes are high. The preceding discussion shows the importance of property's territoriality to the state. Our question really has two parts. Would those in the original position seek to make international arrangements for intellectual property? If so, which arrangements are they likely to prefer and which would they reject on the grounds that they were not consistent with the principles of international justice? The answer to both questions depends in large part upon the state of knowledge of the original participants. It is important to bear in mind that, at the stage where the participants come to conclude an arrangement for property, they have already chosen principles of justice that govern international legal relations. Following Rawls' idea of increasing the levels of knowledge in the original position as the parties move to greater levels of institutional particularity, we can say that in the context of the property discussion the relevant level of knowledge of the parties is the following. Parties would know that they represented states in a world in which human and physical resources were scattered unevenly amongst those states. They would know that states organized themselves in different ways, that states were in very different stages of economic development and that there were social and cultural differences between peoples. The parties would not know the specific societies they represented, although they would be broadly aware of the kind of society they were representing. This last condition is important. Even though the parties would have chosen the principle of justice by the time they came to discuss the arrangements for property, detailed identifying information might lead some representatives to try and fix property arrangements to suit their own situation or at least tilt those arrangements in their own favour. The assumption of rationality continues to apply to the representatives.

Under these conditions, would participants choose to make an international arrangement for property? The answer is probably yes. Property rights remain fundamental to trade and so states would be likely to choose some minimal level of protection that safeguarded any trade interest that their state might have at some point in such rights. For instance, a state that had an advantage in design work would be keen to see those designs protected, but at the same time would only want minimal obligations in areas of intellectual property where it was weak. Prudent, rational representatives would probably opt for an international framework for intellectual property protection that allowed the territoriality of property to remain. It would be a framework that imposed minimal rather than maximal obligations on states, a framework which did enough to reward invention and provide an incentive for individuals to invest in creativity and innovation.[54]

Would participants in the original position rule out some basic arrangements for intellectual property as inconsistent with their chosen conception of justice for peoples? One arrangement which they might exclude on justice grounds is a globalized protectionist scheme of intellectual property. Before considering why, we need to make clear what is meant by a globalized protectionist scheme for intellectual property. Intellectual property becomes globalized when it loses its territoriality. It loses its territoriality when the principles, standards and policies of intellectual property become determined by a supranational regulatory institution rather than states.[55] States, when it comes to intellectual property, become, as it were, law takers rather than law makers.[56]

We can say that an arrangement for intellectual property protection is protectionist if (1) it favours longer periods of protection rather than shorter; (2) it propertizes more areas of information rather than fewer; (3) it imposes substantive standards of intellectual property protection uniformly on all states; (4) it has few or no discretionary mechanisms that allow nation states to adjust substantive standards and the levels of protection to suit their level of economic development.[57] The converse of these propositions would characterize a non-protectionist scheme.

There are perhaps a number of different arrangements for intellectual property that parties at the justice conference might develop. A little earlier we suggested that they would consider some minimal scheme of international protection for intellectual property rights. The one arrangement they would reject, though, is a globalized protectionist scheme. Such a scheme would be rejected on the ground that it was inconsistent with the principles of justice for peoples. Parties in our international original position would not be prepared to assent to developing property rights in this way. They would be worried by the impact of such a scheme on the sovereignty of peoples and the balance of power in the world. As rational agents, they would not want to enter the world of dependency relationships (discussed in Chapter 7) concerning resources that such a scheme would entail. Why would the representatives of peoples agree to an arrangement which, for instance, allowed the ownership of the world's microbial processes and cultures to fall into the hands of a few collectors?

In order to appreciate why this negative outcome concerning the property rights of states is likely, we need to remind ourselves that, under the constructivist procedure for principles of justice (that is, the original position), information that is likely to produce bias and distortion on the part of the parties applying the principles of justice is denied to those parties. Clearly a globalized protectionist model would be favoured by an information-exporting country. Such a model would maximize that country's economic gains. If one were a net importer of information within the world economy and the regime of global property rights was highly protectionist then, on simple cost grounds, as a net importer one would not be in favour of such a regime. Why would one as a matter of trade agree to a system which raised the price of a non-rivalrous good like information? One might do so if one thought that at some future time one was going to be a net exporter. It might be rational to remain in a system in which one took some short-term losses in order to take profits in the long run.[58] But this is more a reason for rational agents to adopt some flexible international framework for regulating the intellectual property of *all* peoples than a reason for adopting a globalized protectionist scheme that advantaged only some. In any case these kinds of narrow economically self-interested calculations would not be open to parties in the original international position, because the information necessary to make the calculations would be denied to them.

Under the constraints of the constructivist view of justice, parties in the original position would have to think more broadly and less partially about the role of property and states. Any property arrangements would have to be consistent with the principles of justice already included in the law of peoples. And so property rules would have to be developed in a way that upheld the autonomy of peoples. Taking the autonomy of peoples seriously would almost certainly rule out of contention a global protectionist scheme for intellectual property. The reasons in part lie in the lessons of history. The existence of hegemonic powers in world history is a fact. Hegemonic powers must have control over raw materials, the sources of capital, markets and competitive advantages in the production of highly valued goods.[59] Once a global protectionist system of intellectual property rights was in place, those few countries which had a build-up of human capital might be tempted to use the system of global property in order to gain some kind of permanent ascendancy or hegemony over other states. Human capital, like physical resources, has always been unevenly distributed amongst states. A state with a high build-up of human capital has, all other things being equal, a greater capacity to produce the kind of scientific and technological knowledge that is important to economic growth than a state which has a low level of human capital. Whether or not a state captures the economic benefits of the knowledge it generates depends on a vast array of factors. These include the state's organizational capacity, its processes of commercialization, the prevailing business culture, its legal infrastructure and the presence of other capable competitors. While knowledge remains a public good, a state with high levels of human capital investment may in effect be producing an international public good for states with lower levels of human capital investment.[60] A global protectionist scheme that allows for the ownership of economically important abstract objects (and therefore economically important knowledge) presents any potential hegemon with a temptation of biblical proportions. The previous chapter argued that abstract objects are a foundational form of capital. It was argued that these objects are capital in themselves as well as being a gateway to other important kinds of capital resources. The temptation for any potential hegemon is to use a global protectionist system of intellectual property to institutionalize its control over vital capital resources. For hegemonic power based on abstract objects to be stable, many of those objects have to shift from being non-rivalrous, non-excludable objects to non-rivalrous, excludable objects.

There are two further aspects to a hegemonic power based on abstract objects that would shape the application of the law of peoples to international property arrangements. Briefly, they are these. Hegemonic power over abstract objects would not be power just over economically important objects but, potentially at least, over local cultural objects. The chapter on Hegel is suggestive of this: we argued in Chapter 4 that personality, through a global system of intellectual property, has the potential to reach into other social worlds and communities. This may well have negative outcomes. Local or territorially based cultural objects may be appropriated for use in global markets. Those with a comparative advantage in the generation, appropriation and delivery of abstract objects become colonizers of a different kind. Sacred objects become commercial objects.[61] Equally the meaning of these local objects for their communities may fade as communities find themselves swamped by a global trade in such objects, a trade that sates global market demands rather than meeting local community needs.

There is one last point to make. A global protectionist scheme of intellectual property might not only create opportunities for a hegemonic state. In Chapter 6, making use of Madison's argument about the property origins of factions, it was argued that intellectual property rights had a dangerous inner logic. The ownership of intellectual property rights allowed owners to shape the opportunity sets of others. This, we suggested, was a major incentive for the formation of intellectual property factions. If we are right about this, a global protectionist scheme for intellectual property would help to promote the formation of global factions. One danger of this is global rent seeking. The price of a global protectionist scheme for intellectual property would be that it would give opportunistic actors the chance to engage in directly unproductive, profit-seeking activities.[62] Multinational elites might be tempted to increase their profits through the simple stratagem of persuading a supranational body to ratchet up levels of protection for abstract objects already in existence. It is hard to see how the wealth transfers involved in such activities could be thought to be consistent with either Rawls' domestic principles of justice or those of the law of peoples. At the domestic level, the increase in private power a highly protectionist intellectual property scheme would cause would not be consistent with either of the two principles of justice. The wealth transfers that such a scheme would involve would not be consistent with the second principle. At the international level a protectionist global arrangement is hardly likely to be agreed to by parties in the original position. Such an arrangement offers too many opportunities for any hegemon to entrench its hegemony. The loss of control by states over the property mechanism has too many adverse consequences for it to be seen as consistent with the independence of peoples.

Conclusion

This chapter represents something of a preliminary venture into the justice of information and then a somewhat restricted one, in that it sails exclusively under a Rawlsian flag. The case for regarding information as a primary good of a political as well as an economic kind is very strong. Under conditions of Rawlsian procedural rationality for justice, the role of any property scheme in relation to information should be to minimize proprietorial control over information. This is true at both the domestic and global levels. It is not consistent with the principles of justice at either of these levels to use a protectionist scheme of intellectual property to create conditions of artificial scarcity for the primary good of information. This is a modest but important consequence of our argument. Theories of global justice often seek to impose duties of redistribution of some kind on well-resourced states.[63] Establishing such positive global duties within the context of

Rawls' theory is difficult. Our argument does not seek to establish such a positive duty when it comes to considering property arrangements for abstract objects. It does suggest that a protectionist intellectual property system achieves the opposite of what is sought to be achieved by positive distributive duties. It encourages a redistribution back to opportunistic actors.

Our argument has been a negative one. It concludes that protectionist arrangements for intellectual property should be excluded by contractarian principles of national and international justice. They are excluded because such arrangements constitute a deep interference in the distribution of information, a primary good which by its nature is not a scarce resource. Parties in the original position, our argument suggests, would never agree to an arrangement under which some high level of this primary good, a good that mattered to them both politically and economically, fell into the orbit of private power. This raises the question of what we ought to do when it comes to making arrangements for intellectual property protection. Nothing in our argument so far commits us to a blanket rejection of all intellectual property forms. A rough answer to our question is this. Under a contractarian, constructivist view of justice, property is not the basis for justice but an instrument of justice. By the time the original parties come to consider property rights, the principles of justice are already out in the open. This commits the original parties to thinking about property rights in an instrumental fashion. Thinking instrumentally about intellectual property is the subject of the next and last chapter.

A final comment before closing. One of the interesting consequences of looking at the justice of information is that it shows that the principle of some things being held in common may be defensible, not simply as a normatively desirable social goal, but because it may have some purchase in the system of production.[64] Liberal theories of distributive justice have been, it has been suggested, 'singularly equivocal' in their treatment of economic causality.[65] A possible explanation might be that these theories appear isolated from economic models of production because those economic models have been relatively unsophisticated in terms of understanding the dynamics of economic growth. After all, it was only with the work of Machlup that the beginnings of some genuine understanding of the role of information in the American economy began to develop. Concepts like human capital will, in the long run, probably prove to be more sensitive to human actors as intentional agents. When it comes to a consideration of the role of knowledge, theories of distributive justice and theories of economic growth may find a common meeting place. What we have said about information at least hints at this possibility.

Notes

1 J. Rawls, *A Theory of Justice* (London, Oxford, New York, 1972), 128.

2 See C. Brown, 'International Affairs' in B. Goodin and P. Pettit (eds.), *A Companion to Contemporary Political Philosophy* (Oxford, 1993), 515.

3 For an identification and analysis of the different approaches, see T. Campbell, *Justice* (London, 1988); P. Pettit, *Judging Justice* (London, 1980).

4 R. Nozick, *Anarchy, State, and Utopia* (Oxford, 1974).

5 See D. Cornell, M. Rosenfeld and D.G. Carlson (eds.), *Deconstruction and the Possibility of Justice* (New York, 1992); S.M. Okin, 'Justice and Gender', 16 *Philosophy and Public Affairs*, 42 (1987).

6 'A man's property is some object related to him. This relation is not natural, but moral, and founded on justice. 'Tis very preposterous, therefore, to imagine, that we can have any idea of property, without fully comprehending the nature of justice, and shewing its origin in the artifice and contrivance of men.' David Hume, *A Treatise of Human Nature* (1739; L.A. Selby-Bigge ed., 2nd ed. by P.H. Nidditch, Oxford, 1978), Book II, part 2, section II, 491.

7 See T. Campbell, *Justice* (London, 1988), 12.

8 J. Rawls, *A Theory of Justice* (London, Oxford, New York, 1972), 62.

9 Id., 440–446.

10 The original position is a hypothetical scenario in which rational individuals meet to choose principles of justice. They do so in ignorance of any information about how these principles will specifically benefit them as individuals. The purpose of this restriction is to make individuals think about principles of justice that might benefit them as members of a social group rather than as individuals directly.

11 Id., 93.

12 Rawls at 260 makes it clear that his theory of primary goods depends on psychological premises.

13 Id., 411.

14 For a sophisticated economic treatment of the consequences of imperfect information for social institutions and the theory of income distribution, see D. Starrett, 'Social Institutions, Imperfect Information, and the Distribution of Income', 90 *Quarterly Journal of Economics*, 261 (1976).

15 For an excellent survey of the various definitional approaches, see S. Braman, 'Defining Information', 13 *Telecommunications Policy*, 233 (1989).

16 J. Rawls, *A Theory of Justice* (London, Oxford, New York, 1972), 60 and 83.

17 See T. Campbell, 'Rationales for Freedom of Communication' in T. Campbell and W. Sadurski (eds.), *Freedom of Communication* (Aldershot, 1994), 17, 23–33.

18 In theory, however, trademark and trade secret protection can go on indefinitely.

19 For a discussion, see P. Drahos, 'Decentring Communication: The Dark Side of Intellectual Property' in T. Campbell and W. Sadurski (eds.), *Freedom of Communication* (Aldershot, 1994), 249.

20 In the *Commonwealth of Australia* v. *John Fairfax & Sons* (1980) 32 ALR 485, the Commonwealth government was able to restrain the publication of some official documents relating, amongst other things, to the East Timor crisis by relying on its copyright in those documents.

21 J. Rawls, *A Theory of Justice* (London, Oxford, New York, 1972), 275–277.

22 Id., 277.

23 The idea of information as a form of capital has been a steadily emerging theme to be found within the economics of information and organization. Machlup's work showed that a significant part of the US economy was involved in the production and dissemination of knowledge. Arrow's work on organization suggested

that ways of organizing for the reception, analysis and communication of information were fundamental to gaining economic advantages. For a survey of this literature, see D.M. Lamberton, 'The Economics of Information and Organization' in M.E. Williams (ed.), *Annual Review of Information Science and Technology* (American Society for Information Science and Technology, White Plains, NY, 1984), 3; K.J. Arrow, *The Limits of Organization* (New York, 1974); A.G. Ramos, *The New Science of Organizations* (Toronto, Buffalo, 1981).

24 J. Rawls, *A Theory of Justice* (London, Oxford, New York, 1972), 138.

25 See G.S. Becker, K.M. Murphy and R. Tamura, 'Human Capital, Fertility, and Economic Growth', 98 (5) pt. 2, *Journal of Political Economy*, S12, S15 (1990). For a useful discussion of human capital and its relation to development theory, see the articles in the special issue of vol. 98 (5) pt. 2, *Journal of Political Economy* (1990).

26 See G.S. Becker, 'Nobel Lecture: The Economic Way of Looking at Behaviour', 101 *Journal of Political Economy*, 385, 392–395 (1993). See also G.S. Becker, 'Investment in Human Capital: A Theoretical Analysis', 70 *Journal of Political Economy*, S9 (1962); G.S. Becker, *Human Capital* (New York, National Bureau of Economic Research, 1964). Other important early work in this area includes T.W. Schultz, 'Capital Formation by Education', 68 *Journal of Political Economy*, 571 (1960); J. Mincer, 'Investment in Human Capital and Personal Income Distribution', 66 *Journal of Political Economy*, 281 (1958); B.A. Weisbrod, 'The Valuation of Human Capital', 69 *Journal of Political Economy*, 425 (1961).

27 On the importance of human capital to the economic growth of the US up to 1956, see T.W. Schultz, 'Investment in Human Capital', 51 *American Economic Review*, 1 (1961).

28 C.R. Beitz, *Political Theory and International Relations* (Princeton, New Jersey, 1979), 149–151. For Rawls' reply to this kind of criticism, see J. Rawls, 'The Law of Peoples' in S. Shute and S. Hurley (eds.), *On Human Rights* (New York, 1993), 42, 66. Examples of other theorists who defend a global conception of justice are H. Shue, *Basic Rights* (Princeton, New Jersey, 1980) and T.W. Pogge, *Realizing Rawls* (Ithaca, N.Y., 1989). For a survey and discussion of the literature on global justice, see C. Brown, 'International Affairs' in B. Goodin and P. Pettit (eds.), *A Companion to Contemporary Political Philosophy* (Oxford, 1993), 515, 521–523.

29 J. Rawls, *A Theory of Justice* (London, Oxford, New York, 1972), 4.

30 C.R. Beitz, *Political Theory and International Relations* (Princeton, New Jersey, 1979), 145.

31 This point is also made by B. Barry, *The Liberal Theory of Justice* (Oxford, 1973), 129.

32 C.R. Beitz, *Political Theory and International Relations* (Princeton, New Jersey, 1979), 129–136, 143–153.

33 For a discussion, see P. Dicken, *Global Shift: The Internationalization of Economic Activity* (2nd ed., New York, 1992); OECD, *Regulatory Co-operation for an Interdependent World* (Paris, 1994); M. Waters, *Globalization* (London, New York, 1995).

34 See J.C. Turner and P.J. Oakes, 'Self-Categorization Theory and Social Influence', in P.B. Paulus (ed.), *Psychology of Group Influence* (2nd ed., Hillsdale, New Jersey, 1989), 233. See also J.C. Turner, *Rediscovering the Social Group* (Oxford, New York, 1987).

35 J. Rawls, *A Theory of Justice* (London, Oxford, New York, 1972), 19.

36 See C.R. Beitz, 'Cosmopolitan Ideals and National Sentiment', LXXX *The Journal of Philosophy*, 591, 595 (1983).

37 It is the existence of differences which forms the basis of feminist critiques of Rawls' theory. See S.M. Okin, 'Justice and Gender', 16 *Philosophy and Public Affairs*, 42 (1987).

38 Feasibility is a condition imposed by Beitz on international justice. See C.R.

Beitz, 'Cosmopolitan Ideals and National Sentiment', LXXX *The Journal of Philosophy*, 591, 595 (1983).

39 Some philosophers take the view that the dispute over transnational obligations has been settled: there are such obligations. See D. Jamieson, 'Global Environmental Justice' in R. Attfield and A. Belsey (eds.), *Philosophy and the Natural Environment* (Cambridge, 1994), 199, 200.

40 For a criticism of prioritizing domestic over international justice, see H. Shue, 'The Burdens of Justice', LXXX *The Journal of Philosophy*, 600, 603–604 (1983).

41 J. Rawls, 'The Law of Peoples' in S. Shute and S. Hurley (eds.), *On Human Rights* (New York, 1993), 42.

42 J. Rawls, *A Theory of Justice* (London, Oxford, New York, 1972), 377–382.

43 J. Rawls, 'The Law of Peoples' in S. Shute and S. Hurley (eds.), *On Human Rights* (New York, 1993), 42, 67.

44 Id., 55.

45 Id., 71.

46 Id., 76–77.

47 For an account of this four-stage sequence, see J. Rawls, *A Theory of Justice* (London, Oxford, New York, 1972), 195–201.

48 J. Rawls, 'The Law of Peoples' in S. Shute and S. Hurley (eds.), *On Human Rights* (New York, 1993), 42, 54.

49 This is a plausible way in which to interpret his theory after the publication of J. Rawls, 'Kantian Constructivism in Moral Theory', 77 *The Journal of Philosophy*, 515 (1980). For an examination of Rawls' theory in the light of his subsequent publications, see C. Kukathas and P. Pettit, *Rawls: A Theory of Justice and its Critics* (Cambridge, 1990), chapter 7.

50 J. Rawls, 'The Law of Peoples' in S. Shute and S. Hurley (eds.), *On Human Rights* (New York, 1993), 42, 55.

51 For a discussion, see *Island of Palmas Case (1928)*, vol. 2 *Reports of International Arbitral Awards*, 831, 838–840.

52 For an excellent discussion of Locke on territoriality, see G. Gale, 'John Locke on Territoriality: An Unnoticed Aspect of the *Second Treatise*', 1 *Political Theory*, 472 (1973).

53 John Locke, *Two Treatises of Government* (1690; P. Laslett ed., Cambridge, 1988), II, 120.

54 Much like the framework which did in fact emerge at the end of the 19th century in the form of the Paris and Berne Conventions. See note 57 below.

55 The World Trade Organization can be thought of as a prototype of such a supranational organization. For a more detailed discussion of the role of such organizations in the emerging supranational regulatory order, see P. Drahos and R.A. Joseph, 'Telecommunications and Investment in the Great Supranational Regulatory Game', 19 *Telecommunications Policy*, 619 (1995).

56 The Trade-Related Aspects of Intellectual Property Rights (TRIPS) agreement represents a significant shift towards the globalization of property. Any country wishing to enter the multilateral trading system has to implement the agreement. TRIPS is to be found in Annex 1C of the Final Act Embodying the Results of the Uruguay Round of Multilateral Trade Negotiations concluded at Marrakesh, 15 April 1994. For the implications of the change in intellectual property protection, see F.K. Beier and G. Schricker (eds.), *GATT or WIPO? New Ways in the International Protection of Intellectual Property* (Munich, 1989).

57 What we have in mind here are the kinds of adjustive mechanisms open to states under the Paris Convention for the Protection of Industrial Property 1883 as revised, and the Berne Convention for the Protection of Literary and Artistic Works 1886 as revised. For example, both these conventions recognize the principle of national treatment. This principle requires member states of the conventions to

extend the same rights to foreigners as they do to their own nationals. The principle of national treatment does not necessarily produce a uniform global scheme of intellectual property protection because the principle does not allow a country to insist upon a reciprocity of substantive standards of protection. The fact that country A creates extra rights for its nationals, for example, does not mean that it can require country B to recognize those rights as a condition of country A recognizing the rights of country B's nationals. See F.K. Beier, 'One Hundred Years of International Cooperation – The Role of the Paris Convention in the Past, Present and Future', 15 *International Review of Industrial Property and Copyright Law*, 1 (1984); H.P. Kunz-Hallstein, 'The United States Proposal for a GATT Agreement on Intellectual Property and the Paris Convention for the Protection of Industrial Property', 22 *Vanderbilt Journal of Transnational Law*, 265 (1989).

58 For a discussion of the possible benefits of intellectual property protection for developing countries, see C.A.P. Braga, 'The Economics of Intellectual Property Rights and the GATT: A View from the South', 22 *Vanderbilt Journal of Transnational Law*, 243 (1989).

59 R.O. Keohane, *After Hegemony* (Princeton, 1984), 32–33.

60 In the 1960s the US and the UK had high expenditures on R&D without corresponding high economic growth. Japan experienced high economic growth for a correspondingly small outlay on R&D. See B.R. Williams, *Technology, Investment and Growth* (London, 1967), chapter 1.

61 For examples of the way in which Australian Aboriginal art has been appropriated, see *Yumbulul* v. *Reserve Bank of Australia* (1991) 21 IPR 481; *Milpurrurru* v. *Indofurn Pty. Ltd.* (1995) 30 IPR 209.

62 The essence of such activity is that an agent makes a profit without providing corresponding goods or services that form part of a utility function. See J.N. Bhagwati, 'Directly Unproductive, Profit-seeking (DUP) Activities', 90 *Journal of Political Economy*, 988, 989 (1982).

63 See, for example, B. Barry, 'Humanity and Justice in Global Perspective', in J.R. Pennock and J.W. Chapman (eds.), *Ethics, Economics and the Law* (New York, London, 1982), 219.

64 For the pessimistic view that common ownership has no relevance to production, see J. Dunn, 'Property, Justice and Common Good after Socialism' in J.A. Hall and I.C. Jarvie (eds.), *Transition to Modernity* (Cambridge, 1992), 281.

65 Id., 283.

9 Intellectual Property: For Instrumentalism, Against Proprietarianism

Attitudes influence approaches. This last chapter argues that in approaching issues and theories related to the justification, formation, extension and enforcement of intellectual property rights we should have an instrumental attitude rather than a proprietarian one.

No attempt is made to propose a general theory of intellectual property. Such a theory would belong to a number of disciplines because intellectual property deals with information, rights, economic growth and power, not to mention the many subplots which are part of the whole story of intellectual property. This makes it a natural target for theorizing within ethics, political philosophy, economics, sociology and legal theory. Elaborating a satisfactorily integrated multidimensional theory of intellectual property is a big job. And, in any case, the goal of attempting to theorize a super-theory of intellectual property might be questioned. Post-modernists might see in such a theory a futile attempt to deliver the undeliverable about property – objective truths and relations. Property, they might say, is like an institutional shell which is used to cover a set of relations that are historically and culturally contingent and which over time are being continually reconfigured. The truth, they might say, is that there is no essentialist truth about property.

This kind of scepticism does threaten gloom for those in the business of normative theory and policy development, as well as for those who would like to end a book on a positive note about the way in which theory development in intellectual property should be taken. Bearing in mind this post-modernist scepticism, we shall suggest some directions in which theory building in intellectual property should be taken. We begin by stating a negative case. One way in which the theory of intellectual property should not be developed is to underpin it with proprietarianism. The dangers of this approach are heightened when it is combined with a system of law that operates in a mode of formal rationality. The positive case begins by arguing that an instrumental attitude should to be taken towards intellectual property. Roughly the idea is that talk about rights in intellectual property should be replaced by talk about privilege. Intellectual property privileges, it will be argued, are necessarily accompanied by duties that circumscribe the exercise of the privilege.

The Proprietarian Creed

Proprietarianism is sometimes used to refer to those theories of justice which make natural rights their centrepiece.[1] Locke, we saw in Chapter 3, is one older exemplar of this tradition and in recent times Nozick is another. There are two striking features of theories that claim naturalness for rights. First, these rights are said to have a pre-societal and pre-institutional existence. Precise detail over their ontological status varies, depending on whether the accompanying metaphysic is, for example, theological or non-theological. A second critical feature is that these rights function in Nozick's words as constraints on decision making. This means that such rights set permanent limits on what is morally permissible. On this view rights are like fixtures. They cannot be moved because some better result might be obtained by doing so. So, to take a standard example, the liberty of an innocent individual cannot be infringed simply because this would make a populace happier.

This natural rights-based proprietarianism is not the target of analysis in this chapter. Proprietarianism for us has a broader meaning. Its chief characteristic is that it assigns to property rights a fundamental and entrenched status. Property rights are given a priority ranking over other kinds of rights and interests. The arguments that are used to justify this fundamental and entrenched status for property rights vary. In rights-based versions of proprietarianism, appeals are made to natural rights or some notion of property being a fundamental background right.[2] But equally proprietarianism can be supported within a consequentialist framework. Proprietarianism is a view that can be upheld within the context of very different moral theories. Bentham's views on property provide a useful illustration of this analytical point. Like any consistent utilitarian, he rejects the idea of natural rights and so therefore the idea of natural property rights. And yet he believes that 'a state cannot grow rich except by an inviolable respect for property'.[3]

Bentham has good reasons for assigning a fundamental respect to property rights within his utilitarian framework. He sees clearly that those who are guided by the principle of utility might think that it is justifiable to invade property rights of wealthy individuals for distributional purposes if this results in an overall increase in happiness. The purpose behind the invasion of property rights need not even be a noble one. Looting probably creates a great deal of temporary happiness if a majority of a population engage in it. Clearly a normative theory which legitimates this kind of behaviour could hardly be expected to be taken seriously. The way in which Bentham seeks to avoid destabilizing property rights is to argue that the ideal legislator should elevate the goals of subsistence and security above those of abundance and equality. Security for Bentham means that, for the most part, expectations which individuals have about the conduct of others in normal social interaction will be met. His discussion of security and law sees the law being assigned a dual role: first, expectations are created through the law and, second, law stabilizes these expectations and protects them. Property is exclusively the work of law for Bentham: 'Property and law are born together, and die together.'[4] The expectations it establishes and institutionalizes are vital for the happiness of society because these expectations provide individuals with reasons to labour. Like Locke, Bentham thinks that individuals have to be driven to labour: property rights are needed to vanquish 'the natural aversion to labour'.[5] With property rights people have an incentive to labour and industry will prosper. Without property rights there will be a 'deadening of industry'.[6] Hence his conclusion that property deserves an inviolable respect. Linking property rights and inviolability is a move any proprietarian would be happy with. It is an entrenching move that ensures that property rights are ranked higher than other rights or interests.

Proprietarianism in the way that we have described it is not really a theory of property. Rather it is a creed and an attitude which inclines its holders towards a property fundamentalism. The consequence within normative theory is that property interests are continuously given a moral primacy. Its impact in intellectual property law is the subject of the next section, but first we need to mention two other features of our brand of proprietarianism. Proprietarianism also advocates in some form or another a first connection thesis about property rights. A general formulation of the first connection thesis is this. A person who is first connected to an object that has economic value or with an activity that produces economic value is entitled to a property right in that object or activity. The property right can be thought of as an extraction right. It is a right to extract or appropriate economic value. The nature of this first connection must take the form of some personal act of demarcation. There must be in terms of Locke's metaphor some individual act of mixing one's labour that establishes the first connection to the object of the property right. Borrowing from Hegel, one might say that the first connection thesis is the requirement that personality in some fashion first imprints itself upon the object of proprietorial desire. Less metaphorically, the first connection thesis requires some act of control. The most usual way in which this occurs is through an act of first possession. The trapping of animals, the spearing of whales, finding a plant variety, the mining of the sea-bed, discovering land or resources in it, placing a satellite in orbit, synthesizing derivatives of penicillin, locating a gene and using the electromagnetic spectrum are all examples of acts of control that may give rise to property rights under first possession rules.

The last defining feature of proprietarianism is a belief in negative community. Drawing on our discussion from Locke, we can stipulate that this means that the proprietarian takes the stance that things at first instance exist in a state of negative commons. They are not owned, but their ownership is open to any one individual. We can sum up our conceptualization of proprietarianism as follows. Proprietarianism consists of three core beliefs: a belief in the moral priority of property rights over other rights and interests, a belief in the first connection thesis and the existence of a negative commons. A proprietarian is one who believes that activities that first give rise to economic value also necessarily create property rights and that there is no limit to the things in the world at which such activities may be aimed. Proprietarianism is a creed which says that the possessor should take all, that ownership privileges should trump community interests and that the world and its contents are open to ownership. This is proprietarianism in its strongest sense. It is not tied to any specific moral theory, at least within liberalism. We have suggested that it can be accommodated within consequentialist and non-consequentialist frameworks. Probably, although we shall not pursue the matter here, it has strong links with individualism.

At the philosophical level it is hard to find proponents of the kind of strong proprietarianism we have just described. Whether Locke is an example depends on the interpretation of his work. Tully's claim (discussed in Chapter 3) that Locke was a supporter of the positive commons disqualifies Locke from membership of the strong proprietarian creed. But Locke clearly was a supporter of the first connection thesis and so a proprietarian in some weaker sense of the concept. In any case our purpose is not to filter various historical figures through our definition of proprietarianism. Our claim is that proprietarianism has infiltrated the development and direction of intellectual property law and policy. This charge of infiltration calls for some illustrations and it is this call that the next section attempts to answer.

A last point which concerns the link between proprietarianism and the ideology of capitalism needs to be made. The claim that proprietarianism is becoming the main influence upon intellectual property gives rise to some other questions. Why is proprietarianism in the ascendancy? Whose interests does it serve? These are important questions, but they are outside the scope of the present inquiry. The answer they require is of a causal and explanatory kind. One style of answer is to make use of ideology theory, but this is in an unsatisfactory state.[7] This chapter does not offer causal explanations for the rise of proprietarianism. That is an issue that clearly requires a separate treatment. The question we address here is the normative one. Should we defend proprietarianism in intellectual property or should we replace it with something else? Our suggested replacement, we shall see, is instrumentalism. But first we need to provide some examples of proprietarianism in action.

Proprietarianism in Action

Showing that proprietarianism is the dominant normative influence on intellectual property law and policy in the world is an empirical claim and rather a large one. To confirm the claim would involve a massive comparative law exercise. This is not going to be done here. This section simply offers some examples of proprietarianism in action in the law of intellectual property. These examples are not intended to be a substitute for the broader comparative work which would have to be done in order to verify the proposition being put.

There is another qualification to make. Proprietarianism is a creed on the move. This means that it does not yet hold sway in all parts of intellectual property. It is, however, in the process of gaining a juristic and ideological ascendancy within thinking about the production of intellectual property. By focusing on the idea of a core of distinctive normative beliefs which we have labelled proprietarianism, it is possible to see a pattern in the various changes in the different parts of intellectual property. The beliefs we have identified as characterizing proprietarianism are deeply involved in a complex causal process that results in a pattern of increasing individual ownership of abstract objects. This pattern is not complete and in places is fuzzy. Proprietarian beliefs do not explain all current decision making within intellectual property. We will see a little later that some judges have come out against proprietarianism. It is hardly surprising that some individuals should resist endorsing it. Intellectual fashions, like other fashions, are not chosen by everybody. But the fact that there are fashion resisters has not stopped the proprietarian tide. Nor should we expect it to. Proprietarianism has deeper roots in the nature of international capitalism, the evolution of that capitalism under conditions of competition, the uncertainty that such competition promotes and finally the desire for hegemonic status by some nation states.

Trademark law, patents and copyright all provide examples of proprietarian beliefs in action. Within trademark law proprietarian beliefs manifest themselves in an expanded view of what may be used as a trademark. More things in the negative commons are now capable of serving the trademark proprietor. Under old trademark legislation, only visible marks of some kind were eligible for registration.[8] Modern trademark law admits colour, sounds, smells and tastes to the category of trademark signs.[9] Harley Davidson can now seek registration for the sound of their motor bikes and BP for their colour green.

Trademark proprietarianism surfaces in other ways. It does so in a clear way in the debates over the function of trademarks.[10] Advocates of proprietarianism tend to couch their arguments in terms of making trademark law relevant to the needs of the market. Their legitimating themes are those of modernization and the needs of commerce. The consequence of accepting these arguments is that trademarks become tradeable entities in their own right that serve the interests of their owners. The importance of consumer and public interests in trademark law, which was recognized in early trademark thinking, quietly slips from view.

Telling this story would require much more space than we have here, but we can add a little more detail. In 19th-century English law the essence of a trademark was thought to be that it served to distinguish the goods of one trader from those of another: 'The right which a manufacturer has in his trade mark is the exclusive right to use it for the purpose of indicating where, or by whom, or at what manufactory the article to which it is affixed was manufactured.'[11] Trademarks were symbols that indicated to persons understanding the symbol the trade origins of the particular goods (later this came to include services).[12] Trademarks were in a sense highly derivative forms of intellectual property. The exclusive use of the mark related only to its use in connection with articles to which it had been applied. A trademark, judges made clear, could not be protected as an entity in its own right.

Information about origin was not then and is not now the only function of a trademark. Consumers have a primary interest in knowing something about the quality of the goods rather than simply where they hail from. Once consumers have experience with a particular trademarked good, the meaning of the trademark expands to convey information about quality of the good or other types of goods made by the manufacturer. The trademark comes to mediate the reputation of those making the goods.

The origin, quality and goodwill functions of trademarks can be aggregated into a general communication function. Trademarks might be said to have the broad function of communicating the origin and properties of goods. Clearly there are some advantages that flow from this kind of communication. Consumers can rely on a trademark as a form of shorthand for information that would otherwise be time consuming and costly to ascertain. In economic terms, trademarks lower the search costs of consumers.[13] Traders gain in that they know that the trademarks they use will become in the consumer market the faithful transmitters of information about the products they make. This provides traders with one kind of incentive to maintain or raise standards.

The early judicial development of trademark law in England took seriously the idea that trademarks served consumer and public interests.[14] Distinctiveness, perhaps the foundational concept of trademark law, was explicated in terms of the probability that others would want to make a legitimate use of those same symbols.[15] There was 'no absolute right to register any trade mark'.[16] Trademark registration was a privilege, not a right. Practices which may have been customary in the relevant trade, like letting other traders make use of the mark, were not the basis upon which judgements of validity concerning the mark were made. The crucial factor was whether the practice in question deceived the public.[17] This emphasis of the common law upon the public nature of trademarks is readily understandable. A trademark only comes into existence on a commercial plane when consumers in the market invest the mark with meaning and recognition. Trademarks begin their commercial life through an iterated series of acts of recognition by members of the consuming public. At the same time as this happens the trader acquires an abstract object that can, at least potentially, be exploited independently of the goods and services to which the mark relates. Roughly speaking, the common law and the legislature took the view that any independent exploitation of the mark had to be consistent with those acts of recognition by the consuming public which had first breathed commercial life into the mark. Marks that had become valuable through the grant of a statutory privilege and public use could not simply be turned over to their individual proprietors for their unrestricted use. Trademark legislation placed restrictions on what trademark owners could do with their trademarks by way of licensing and assignment.[18] Much of the spirit of this approach is captured in the following passage from *Bowden Wire Ld.* v. *Bowden Brake Co Ld.*[19]

> The object of the law is to preserve for a trader the reputation he has made for himself, not to help him in disposing of that reputation as of itself a marketable commodity, independent of his goodwill, to some

> other trader. If that were allowed, the public would be misled, because they might buy something in the belief that it was the make of a man whose reputation they knew, whereas it was the make of someone else.

The expansion of the meaning of sign to include sounds, scents, colours, shapes, the relaxing of the restrictions on trafficking in trademarks and allowing trademarks to be used to divide territorially markets when there is no consumer benefit in doing so point to a trademark law that is increasingly shifting towards proprietarianism.[20] Under the influence of proprietarianism the dominant purpose of trademark law comes to be the protection of the interests of traders. The description of trademarks in terms of privilege and monopoly falls into disuse. This language is replaced by the more generic and therefore ambiguous language of property. The effect is that the development of trademark law is more and more dictated by the needs of trademark owners with consumer interests now relegated to some other part of the law. Structurally speaking, this relegation is dangerous. For, so long as the protection of consumer interests remained a dominant purpose of trademark law, the privates uses of a publicly granted monopoly privilege had to remain consistent with that purpose. This placed a constraint on the development of trademark law to resist the purposes of opportunistic actors. Once the linkage between trademark law and the interests of the consumer market is severed then, somewhat predictably, there follows an expansion of the narrow statutory privilege granted to traders.[21] Traders no longer have to show a convergence of their interests and the interests of consumers. The statutory privilege now comes to serve private interests and private use. Trademark law, like other areas of intellectual property law, slowly shifts to accommodate the desires of rent seekers.

A spectacular example of proprietarian thinking in action is to be found in the history of US copyright law in the form of the 'sweat of the brow' doctrine. The case of *Jeweler's Circular Pub. Co.* v. *Keystone Pub. Co.* provides an illustration.[22] The plaintiff had compiled a directory of trademarks related to the jewellery trade. The defendant had brought out a similar directory, which was double the length of the plaintiff's, but which the plaintiff claimed was based on its directory. The defendant lost. In an important passage the court hoisted the proprietarian flag:

> The right to copyright a book upon which one has expended labor in its preparation does not depend upon whether the materials which he has collected consist or not of matters which are publici juris, or whether such materials show literary skill or originality, either in thought or in

> language, or anything more than industrious collection. The man who goes through the streets of a town and puts down the names of each of the inhabitants, with their occupations and their street number, acquires material of which he is the author.[23]

In *Jeweler's*, as in the English directory cases upon which the decision was based, the fundamental premise upon which the court based its reasoning is that no one has, in the context of market relations, the right to appropriate the results of the labour of another. The court was careful not to omit the connection between copyright and the existence of a public domain. It pointed out that nothing prevents other individuals from going to original sources in order to create their own compilation.[24] This means that subsequent compilers 'must count the milestones' for themselves and, in the case of maps, 'go through the whole process of triangulation'.[25]

The *Jeweler's* case and others like it conceive of the public domain somewhat narrowly. The public domain is assumed to consist of pre-existing facts, but actually the public domain consists of reports of facts. Reports of facts which make up the public domain of facts are always reports in some language or another of events and objects in the world. Most of the time most people rely on reported facts rather than facts that they have directly verified themselves. Copyright proprietarianism in the form of the 'sweat of the brow' doctrine potentially transfers these public domain reports into private hands. The result of this is that the proliferation of reported knowledge or facts, reports which serve as access points to verifiable public domain knowledge, comes to depend upon the licensing activities of copyright owners.

Showing this in detail would involve, amongst other things, an extended discussion of the requirement of originality in copyright law. But we can provide a short version of the argument. Generally speaking, before an author can acquire copyright in a work he or she must satisfy the requirement of originality. This does not mean that the work must be original in some ultimate sense of 'never ever having been written about before', but something less than that. The problem has been in deciding on how much less than that ultimate standard is sufficient to qualify a work for copyright protection. Predictably, problems have arisen where authors have assembled, selected, ordered, arranged and so on pre-existing facts and material and claimed to have produced a work in which copyright subsists.[26] Courts have sometimes set the standard of originality quite low, allowing, for example, football betting coupons to get over the copyright line.[27]

The purpose of the originality requirement in copyright is clear enough. It obliges the author to engage in some independent creative effort before he or she can claim the benefits of copyright protection. This creative effort eventually finds its way into the intellectual commons, because copyright is limited in duration. One way in which to understand the originality requirement is to say that it helps to constitute the intellectual commons. It helps to keep certain information out of the reach of copyright ownership. And drawing upon our discussion of Locke in Chapter 3, we might say that copyright helps in this way to constitute a condition of positive community when it comes to facts. Facts (which are always reports) are not, as they would be in negative community, open to copyright ownership.

When the originality requirement is set very low or dispensed with altogether, facts and information of all kinds can be recycled as copyright works. Copyright now helps to constitute negative community. In this negative community many more information exchanges which involve facts become the object of copyright surveillance and enforcement. Copyright comes to function as a private tax on basic information exchanges.

The story of the 'sweat of the brow' doctrine in US copyright law has a sad ending from the proprietarian perspective. In *Feist Publications, Inc* v. *Rural Telephone Service Co Inc*, a case in which copyright is denied to a white pages directory, the US Supreme Court does its best to eliminate the doctrine from copyright law.[28] It proceeds by refocusing attention on the constitutionally stated goal of copyright law which is 'to promote the Progress of Science and useful Arts'.[29] Copyright aids this goal by helping to create a public domain with respect to facts, a domain in which all individuals have user rights. While the decision has been criticized, primarily it seems because of its supposed effects on the data base industry, the decision remains fundamentally correct.[30] One final observation before we leave this example: the demise of the 'sweat of the brow' doctrine does not mean that proprietarianism's march towards the ownership of facts has been defeated. Many of the initiatives taking place to provide special protection for data bases and their contents are arguably a reinvention of the 'sweat of the brow' doctrine in *sui generis* form.[31]

The third and final example of proprietarianism in action comes from patent law. One important distinction in patent law is between discovery and invention. Traditionally, the position has been that discoveries *per se* are not patentable.[32] Inventions, provided they satisfy various statutory criteria, are patentable. The distinction between discovery and invention in English law lies in the idea that discovery involves an act in which something of the world is revealed. It is, as it were, 'a lifting of the veil'.[33] Invention is a process in which the act of discovery is taken and joined to some process or object which itself can act upon the world. In an oft-quoted passage, Lindley LJ in *Lane Fox* v. *Kensington and Knightsbridge Electric Lighting*

Co gives an example of discovery: 'When *Volta* discovered the effect of an electric current from his battery on a frog's leg he made a great discovery but no patentable invention.'[34]

The common law's insistence upon the distinction between discovery and invention is readily understandable in light of the purpose of the patent system. We saw in Chapter 2 that this purpose was to encourage the build-up in England of skills relating to the industrial arts or trade. The patent system was intended to help expand and improve skills in existing trades or help form new trades. Clearly this practical objective could not be met through the mere discovery of knowledge. Those working in trades had to have tools, machines and processes to work with. The abstract object had in other words to take on a corporeal application before it could be the subject of a patent privilege. Importantly the distinction between discovery and invention ensured that certain abstract objects remained in the intellectual commons for all to use. Like the originality requirement in copyright law, the discovery/invention distinction helped to constitute the intellectual commons under the condition of positive community.

The Australian High Court in an influential decision suggested that the distinction between discovery and invention was not precise enough to be of much use.[35] What concerned the High Court was the fact that all inventions have an ideas component.[36] A strict parsing of inventions, particularly process inventions, into the categories of discovery and invention would see many patent claims defeated on the grounds that the idea amounted to a discovery and that there was no inventive merit in the implementation of that idea.

Judicial reservations about the clarity of the discovery/invention distinction stem from the worry that, applied badly, the distinction might defeat the traditional goal of the patent system. Proprietarianism attacks the discovery/invention distinction for different reasons. Under proprietarianism nothing of legal significance should hang on this distinction because discoveries, just like inventions, can be costly, labour-intensive and economically valuable.[37] The first connection thesis, negative community and the fundamental nature of property rights all combine to produce the conclusion that abstract information, whether in the form of a discovery or of an invention, should be the subject of a patent right. Nothing is said about the impact of this on community and creativity (see Chapter 3), on power relations (see Chapter 7), the distribution and access to important knowledge (see Chapter 8) or even the costs of the opportunistic behaviour (see Chapter 6) that such a development will bring with it.

The longer-term effect of proprietarianism in patent law will be that all kinds of abstract information previously in the public domain will fall into private ownership. While the patent system has always allowed for the temporary private ownership of ideas, these ideas have had to be expressed in an inventive form, a form that had utility in the industrial arts. One objection to the proprietarian demolition of the discovery/invention distinction is that useful abstract information will fall into private hands without there necessarily being in existence some corresponding useful industrial application of that idea. A danger of proprietarianism lies, in other words, in switching the patent system to protect useful ideas rather than ideas that exist in the form of useful effects.[38]

Some of the best examples of patent proprietarianism in action are to be found in the area of property rights in plant, animal and human genes and microbiological organisms. When in 1980 the US Supreme Court in *Diamond* v *Chakrabarty* approved the view that Congress intended patentable subject matter to '"include anything under the sun that is made by man"' it was in many respects a ringing endorsement of negative community – a world in which patents could single out anything at all for appropriation.[39] Moreover even at that time 'made' in reality included 'found', for there was already a body of US cases that had allowed patents on purified versions of naturally occurring substances.[40] If invention merely involves 'cleaning up' a substance one may well ask whither the discovery/invention distinction? Since *Chakrabarty* and even before it patent law has evolved in a way consistent with the influence of proprietarianism. While the rhetoric of the discovery/invention distinction remains there is a growing convergence around the view that biological materials (including genes) which are found in nature are patentable.[41] In related areas of law such as plant breeders' rights the distinction has vanished. Multinationals in the plant-breeding business may claim property rights in plant varieties that they have discovered as well as those that they may have bred.[42] The claims which accompany patent applications in the biotechnology area are characterized by the broadness of their reach over the intellectual commons.[43] Apart from its descent into molecular biology, the patent system has begun to ascend the evolutionary ladder in terms of its subject-matter. Animal patents, despite the ethical concerns of many, have been granted in the US and other jurisdictions.[44]

Against Proprietarianism

In Chapter 7 we argued that property rights in abstract objects give rise to dangerous levels of threat power. In passing we suggested that this would be of concern to those political traditions that value and defend negative liberty. The previous section gave some examples of the way in which the influence of proprietarian thinking in intellectual property is increasing the scope of private ownership of abstract objects. Proprietarian sentiments lie behind the expansion of intellectual property rights.[45] This expansion threatens the core value of negative liberty. The remainder of this section develops this idea.

A list of rights defended by classical liberals like Locke include at least the rights of life, liberty and property. These rights we can think of as negative rights.[46] They imply that others owe the right bearer an obligation not to interfere by killing him, depriving him of his freedom or taking his property. Negative liberty in its classical form involves the idea that there are actions of individuals that should not be obstructed. Hobbes, for example, states the idea in this way: "Liberty, or Freedome, signifieth ... the absence of Opposition ...A free man, is he, that ... is not hindered to doe what he has a will to.'[47] In Hohfeld's jural scheme these classical rights are claim rights – they have, as their correlatives, duties. Property rights are one form of negative right. A right of property that relates to land is a right amongst other things to prevent others from entering that land, selling it or interfering in some other way that is inconsistent with the property right. A right of copyright in a book is the right to prevent others from copying, translating or publishing the book.[48] Whether the right of property relates to a book, an invention, land or a car, the right is a right to stop others from interfering in a way determined by the content of the right.

While intellectual property rights are, like other kinds of property rights, negative rights, there are also important differences which flow from the connection between intellectual property rights and abstract objects. Abstract objects by their nature are capable of universal accessibility. In theory at least every person on the planet could simultaneously use the same algorithm. That could not be said of a block of land or a car. One consequence of this is that the pattern of interference that intellectual property rights set up in the lives of others is far greater than in the case of other kinds of rights. Rights of all kinds create patterns of interference. The fact that all individuals within a group have rights necessarily means that the action of any one individual is limited by the presence of other individuals with rights. Rights create zones of freedom by establishing a social basis on which to prevent freedom-threatening action by others. Preventing others from acting can be seen as a form of interference in the freedom of others. X's ownership of a block of land prevents others from owning it (assuming X does not want to sell it). But the limitations that negative rights place on freedom is a price that X and others are willing to pay for roughly the kinds of reasons that Hobbes identifies. The alternative to a stable rule-governed association is, at least on Hobbes' account, one in which all have privileges to do what they like. The price for this anarchy of privilege is that its exercise is contingent upon the desires and powers of others. And, as Hobbes argues, no one wants to pay this price. The Leviathan is a preferable alternative. Individuals, we might say, are prepared to tolerate the existence of negative rights for others because those rights operate in a reciprocal way to make coexistence possible.

Intellectual property rights create large patterns of interference in the freedom of others because abstract objects are a crucial kind of resource. We saw in Chapter 7 that they are a form of capital and a gateway to other kinds of capital. Abstract objects are vital to all kinds of social, cultural and economic projects. Property in such objects creates person-dependency relationships. Intellectual property rights differ in the reach of the pattern of interference they set up. The analogy between intellectual property rights and other kinds of property rights is only superficial. It is true that they both remain negative rights and so can be said to confer a right to prevent other persons from doing things, but this analysis of intellectual property rights remains incomplete because it does not take into account the systemic effects that occur because of the nature of the object to which the rights relate. Property rights in abstract objects have a dual character. They are negative rights, but they are also rights to interfere in the activities of others. The claim we are making can best be illustrated by an analogy between abstract objects and the ownership of all the land of a state by one individual. English feudalism is probably the best example of a situation where, through the system of tenures, one individual, the king, was the ultimate owner of all the land. One might say of such a situation that the king enjoyed a right of property, a right not to be interfered with. But clearly such a characterization would hardly capture the extent to which the king could, on the basis of his ownership of the land and the complex social structure that such ownership supported, interfere in the lives of all those who were connected with the system of land tenure. Drawing an analogy between the ownership of the abstract object and a king's feudal holdings is appropriate because in both cases the owner has control over a form of capital on which many others inescapably depend. In the case of the abstract object, that dependence may be global rather than just territorial.

This added quality of intellectual property rights that sets them apart from other negative rights can best be described as a capability-inhibiting quality. Intellectual property rights regulate access to knowledge and other kinds of capital which are foundational to the development of the capabilities of individuals. One important way in which individuals improve their capability is through investment in their stock of human capital. We suggested in Chapter 8 that intellectual property can adversely affect the use and build-up of human capital. It is precisely because of the fact that owners of abstract objects can, by virtue of that ownership, make decisions about whether or not other people will be allowed to conduct themselves in certain ways that intellectual property rights were historically thought of, and described, as privileges. The privilege that lies at the heart of all intellectual property is a state-based, rule-governed privilege to interfere in the negative liberties of others. We might call intellectual property rights liberty-inhibiting privileges, but there are also other kinds. Some privileges are created through the grant of an *exemption* from a common disadvantage. Tax exemptions are an example of this type. A third kind of privilege is based on the grant of a status *beyond* the common advantage of others. So, while all citizens may enjoy the freedom of communication, those with the status of parliamentarians are usually given an additional (often absolute) privilege when it comes to freedom of communication.

Intellectual property rights are a distinctive form of privilege that rely on the *creation* of a common disadvantage. The brief historical discussion of patents in Chapter 2 illustrated this. The history of monopolies, particularly in the first part of the 17th century, reveals clearly that these prerogative-based privileges had the feature of creating a common disadvantage so that the holder of the privilege could benefit.[49] It was because these privileges constituted such a profound interference in the negative liberties of the king's subjects, particularly economic liberties, that they incurred such deep opposition. Eventually their creation came to be a matter of public regulation.[50]

One of the reasons why intellectual property rights are no longer thought of in this way is that they are continually referred to by the aggregated term of rights. Through that process of reference they have become deeply entrenched in the discourse of private property rights. Their relocation in the language of private property has obscured their origins in public privilege.

Towards Instrumentalism

Our attention now turns to arguing for an instrumental attitude to intellectual property rights. Instrumentalism is a term that has different meanings. Within the philosophy of science it is the view that theories are a practical means of organizing observation statements in order to derive predictions and conclusions.[51] Theories are procedurally useful, but not true or false. Instrumentalism is also sometimes used to refer to the philosophy of pragmatism.[52] When used in connection with law, instrumentalism refers to the idea that law is a tool.[53] The instrumentalist attitude, which we argue should form the basis of an approach to property, is distinct from the specialized meanings of instrumentalism we have just mentioned.

Perhaps the first thing to say about an instrumentalism of property is that its primary focus is more on the behavioural aspects of property than on the metaphysical, ethical and epistemological issues that have characterized philosophical investigations of property. An instrumentalism of property does not aspire to reveal the deep structures of property or its essential nature. Its push to uncover the nature of property stops at the point at which property is seen as an institutional mechanism, a mechanism which in Chapter 7 we said can have sovereignty effects. Having arrived at that point, instrumentalism begins to investigate the contingent connections and processes that exist between property and individual behaviour and choice, between property and the formation of groups and factions, between property and power, between property and patterns of economic growth and development, and between property and the social patterns and organizations it gives rise to as well as the way in which property comes to be patterned and shaped by social organizations. Here there is already much good work to draw upon. The old and new institutionalism in economics is an example, as is the work being done on institutional theory and design.[54]

The instrumental attitude to property also draws on economic approaches to law. It endorses an approach that calculates the social costs of intellectual property protection. Economic approaches also have the merit that they make the distributive consequences of changes in property arrangements more transparent. But the instrumentalism we have in mind amounts to more than just a cost–benefit analysis, or asking the economic efficiency question or a simple means-to-an-end approach. Cost–benefit analyses have technical problems.[55] They should also be driven and limited by moral feeling rather than driving out moral values.[56] Similarly the view that property is simply a means to some predetermined end assumes that means and ends can be easily divided. But as Lon Fuller has argued, the relationship between means and ends is far from simple.[57] Institutions rarely serve one end. Our own discussion of the different functions of property makes this clear. Ends are conditioned by means and the other way around.

The property instrumentalism that we have in mind must serve moral values. There is a single and obvious qualification to this. Property cannot, in an instrumentalist theory of property, operate as a fundamental value or right, for this would be to push the theory in proprietarian directions. Property, the instrumentalist attitude says, serves moral values, but is not the basis of moral value. A natural question to ask is, which values? This we suggest is fundamentally a matter of choice. An instrumentalism of property does not commit its holder to any specific moral theory or values. It only rules out of contention the idea of property as a natural right, but not the idea of natural rights. It also might be said to have a humanist orientation. This means that explanations, analyses and justifications for property have in some way to contribute to an understanding or improvement of human experience. Clearly humanism articulated in this way permits property instrumentalism to be tied to very different moral theories.[58] Perhaps if we had to describe an instrumentalism of property in terms of labels we might say that it is a humanistic and naturalistic form of empiricism about property.

The requirement that an instrumentalism of property be humanist is a minimal one, but it does push theory development in intellectual property away from the narrow and technical into the wider and evaluative. An example of what we mean can be drawn from our discussion of human capital and the justice of information. That discussion suggested that intellectual property rules might adversely affect the formation of human capital and therefore have implications for economic growth. Under our property instrumentalism, economists would need to take an interest in distributive theories, for these theories are relevant to just those institutions which the economic model implicates as crucial in economic growth. Once, for example, we are persuaded by a model of endogenous economic growth that human capital is more crucial than physical capital, a question arises about the institutional design response to that finding. This inevitably leads the economist into just those institutions which the distributive theorist has to consider. In the case of human capital it is fundamental institutions like the family and education that are relevant to the economist and the theorist of justice alike. The principles of equality of opportunity and access to education, which may be prescribed by a theory of justice, may also matter to a long-run economic growth theory. It may be that such principles maximize the build-up of human capital because all parents will have an incentive to invest in their children's education. Equally theorists of justice need to think (at least at the level of non-ideal theory) about the link between economic growth and the major social institutions which operate distributively within a society, for it is the arrangement of those institutions which will have an impact on economic growth and thus place limits on what is distributively feasible. An instrumentalism of property would require this cross-pollination between economic theories of growth and distributive theories because property is a foundational institution in both and because the humanist principle in such an instrumentalism would require theory development to have, as its minimal goal, the improvement of human conditions and experience. Of course what would count as an improvement would itself be determined by moral theory. And, as we have seen, an instrumentalism of property is not committed to any specific moral theory.

The property instrumentalism we are developing proposes a limited negative metaphysical thesis: there are no natural rights of property. This thesis has a corollary. Property instrumentalism embraces a radical scepticism about the nature of property.[59] In particular it is sceptical about any theory of property that is based on the idea that property is a subjective right. The radical scepticism we have in mind can best be illustrated by making use of some of Kelsen's observations about property. As it happens, a radical instrumentalism about property rights is one of the consequences of Kelsen's pure positivism.[60]

Kelsen's radical instrumentalism about property rights stems from his rejection of the dualism that had characterized 19th-century positivism.[61] The legacy of natural law had found its way into this positivism through the dichotomies that had been created between objective and subjective law or right, and public and private law. Subjective right in this kind of positivism involved the idea that there were independently existing rights that objective law served in some way. Property, argues Kelsen, is 'the prototype of the subjective right'.[62] Subjective right has, for Kelsen, a clear ideological function. This function stems from the realization that with a positivistic conception of law the state is free to chart its own destiny. The content of its legal order is to be determined only by the legal order, that is to say, the state. Within democratic societies particularly, the content of law acquires a previously undreamt of contingency. If they so choose, legal orders can remake themselves in fundamental ways. Monarchies can become republics. Against this backdrop of a positivism limited only by will, the notion of private property (subjective right) becomes a means to setting limits on what the legal order may do to property interests. Kelsen, describing the ideological function of subjective right, puts it thus: 'subjective right, which really means private property, is a category transcending the objective law, it is an institution putting unavoidable constraints on the shaping of the content of the legal system'.[63] This claim of Kelsen's is an important part of his larger mission, which is to deliver a positivist theory of law that is an ideological theory of law in the sense that it remains a normative theory, but is anti-ideological in the sense that special interests and pleadings do not form part of the normative character of law. The Pure Theory of Law proposed by Kelsen eliminates subjective right. Subjective right and objective law become one.

One immediate reaction to the proposal to reduce all manifestations of subjective right to objective law is to say this has serious and negative implications for individual liberty. Subjective right, it might be said, is the last philosophical bulwark against a liberty-robbing state. This kind of response, however, does not take seriously the radical scepticism and instrumentalism we are advocating for a treatment of property. First, under instrumentalism the question of the effects of subjective right on patterns of liberty is not a question that could be settled exclusively through *a priori* philosophical techniques any more than one could come to a serious conclusion about the pattern of liberty in a country by reading its constitution: the Soviet constitution, for example, read well. Patterns of liberty depend ultimately on the way given concrete rights evolve and operate in the context of social systems that have particular distributions of wealth, resources and institutional structures. There is, in other words, a much higher synthetic component in the debates over property and liberty than is commonly realized.

A radical scepticism about property would remain open to the possibility that property, as subjective right, might, somewhat counterintuitively, have under certain circumstances an adverse impact on the liberty of citizens. We can sketch such a possibility. The essence of Kelsen's analysis of property is that the functional role of subjective property rights is to place a restraint on a potentially hostile objective legal order. In those social systems where there are significant inequalities in the distribution of wealth and power the capacity of some to utilize the ideological function of property as subjective right will be much greater than that of others. Subjective property becomes a subtle tool which the well resourced may use for resisting the changes the objective legal order may wish to make to the norms of property. The dangers of aligning subjective property with intellectual property are high. Intellectual property, we have argued, takes the form of liberty-inhibiting privileges. Also, for the reasons we gave in Chapter 7, it creates private forms of sovereignty within a society. Those that possess such privileges are inclined, for the reasons we outlined in Chapter 6, to seek their extension. The notion of subjective right when linked to intellectual property offers privilege seekers opportunities to extend and create privileges that endanger the liberties of others. When the notion of subjective right is linked to intellectual property it functions to entrench the special interests of privilege holders. Privilege holders, for reasons of rational self-interest, campaign for greater privileges. Their outlook does not take account of the social cost of such privileges, their possible injustice or the threat that the power of such privileges poses to fundamental democratic institutions. Under the guise of subjective right intellectual property rights are treated like any other form of property. Their distinct character and the threats they pose are clouded by a rhetoric of private property in which a universal subjective will is mobilized to defend the special interests of privilege seekers. The developmental costs of this to others is steadfastly ignored.

One worry about adopting a sceptical instrumentalism of property might be this: such an instrumentalism locates the genesis of property rights in positive law; it might be argued that individual property rights are an essential part of what is needed to make individual liberty secure and the notion of subjective right in turn makes property rights secure. On an instrumental approach to property, property rights are seemingly at the mercy of the state. Such rights become too fragile. Another reason for not endorsing an instrumentalism of property is the adverse effect that such an instrumentalism might have on the fundamental values that cluster around the notion of property as a subjective right. Here the idea is that property is inseparably linked with freedom, with the protection of individual personality and privacy. The problem with sceptical instrumentalism, it might be argued, is that in the final analysis it amounts to a procedure that costs such rights according to some narrow economic metric. As it happens, because of the overtly economic character of most intellectual property rights (such as copyright in sound recordings and published editions, or plant variety rights), employing an economic metric to judge such rights is appropriate. Nevertheless there are some kinds of rights to be found in intellectual property that institutionalize values which individuals as a social group hold to be important and meaningful in a way that transcends any conclusion that might be reached about their usefulness on the basis of cost. They are, as it were, cost-transcending rights. By running such rights through a sceptical instrumentalist mill, the cultural or symbolic value these rights derive from their link with fundamental values would be missed. The right of an author to be acknowledged as the author of the work or the right of an author to prevent the destruction of his work might be examples of such rights. Such rights might not be economically efficient because they inhibit trade in artistic goods. Even if this were the case, the rights could be defended on other grounds. The existence of works of art might be thought to be intrinsically valuable.[64] Rights which promoted or preserved artistic works could be justified on the ground that they helped to promote an intrinsic good. This is still an instrumental style of justification, but one which is no longer influenced by some procedure of costing the right.

These two misgivings about a sceptical instrumentalism are misplaced. The first suggested that property rights were too important to individual liberty to risk breaking the linkage between subjective right and property. This does not amount to an objection against our sceptical instrumentalism. It does show that a sceptical instrumentalism of property needs to be entrenched in a broader account of what constitutes individual freedom. Under an instrumentalism of property it is crucial that this account be developed independently of the property relation. It is a mistake, in other words, to identify the nature of individual freedom with a treatment of the property relation in such a way that that treatment becomes the inductive basis upon which conclusions about individual freedom in the broad are reached. So, by way of example, for liberals a sceptical instrumentalism about property means asking about the effects of property norms on negative liberty rather than using property rights as the paradigmatic instance of negative liberty. By not asking the instrumentalist question about property, liberals open themselves up to the possibility that they will in the case of intellectual property endorse a liberty-inhibiting system of privilege.

The second misgiving about instrumentalism invoked the idea of cost-transcending rights. This kind of misgiving is not well founded. First we need to be clear that the real-world costs of property rights matter morally. The presence of costs means that resources are being used that could have been used otherwise. This matters morally as well as economically. The fact that resources within a given society are being transferred to meet the cost of a given system has implications for the developmental capacities of individuals within a given society. Rwanda has a patent system which, like all patent systems, generates costs. Should a country like Rwanda use precious resources in creating, maintaining and enforcing a patent system? A sceptical instrumentalism about property encourages this kind of question. And it is a question which is perfectly consistent with a defence of fundamental values like autonomy and self-determination. An attempt to trump an instrumentalism of property through some form of moral fundamentalism ignores the fact that the defence of one fundamental value often occurs at the expense of others.

Under a sceptical instrumentalism it does not follow that no property rights will survive. What follows is that the generic term 'right' will be disaggregated into its constituent parts. The shape of this disaggregation will be determined by the relevant deontic logic that is chosen to do the job. Some species of property rights will end up being classified as claim rights. Others, like intellectual property, will end up having the status of privileges. Depending on the moral theory used to accommodate the sceptical instrumentalism, some property rights in certain kinds of objects may end up being plausibly defended as important claim rights.[65] In short, a sceptical instrumentalism would seek to avoid the tendency, which Bentham observed, for individuals to describe every benefit or advantage conferred upon them by law as their property.[66]

This completes our outline of a sceptical instrumentalism of property. Before concluding there is one short task that needs to be done. This is to show that an instrumentalist theory of intellectual property is also committed to instrumentalist duties.

The Duties of Privilege

There are two questions that this section endeavours to answer. How are instrumental duties to be derived from privileges? What kind of duties can be derived? Some examples drawn from cases are used to illustrate the answer to the second question. A word of caution is needed here. An instrumentalist theory of intellectual property would be a normative theory. It could serve in the role of legal exegesis and casuistry. The practical import of the theory would be that the interpretation of intellectual property law would be driven in a systematic fashion by the purpose of that law rather than more diffuse moral notions about the need to protect pre-legal expectations based on the exercise of labour and the creation of value. It would, in other words, be a counter to proprietarianism. The examples which we discuss are intended to illustrate the kinds of duties that can be derived from instrumentalist axioms. We are not claiming that the courts in these instances were in fact working with an instrumentalist theory of the kind we outlined in the previous section.

Intellectual property rights are liberty-inhibiting privileges. Our claim is that instrumentally based privileges are accompanied by duties that fall on the holder of the privilege. If the purpose in creating the privilege is to fulfil some approved goal then it should also follow that the privilege holder is subject to duties not to exercise the privilege in a way that defeats the purpose for which the privilege was granted in the first place. The idea of linking a set of duties to promote the end for which the privilege was designed has some analogies with the conception of government put forward by earlier philosophies of democratic radicalism. Locke, in developing a model of government, made constant use of the concept of a trust in order to establish that the powers of government were circumscribed in various ways by the obligations it had to the people. Referring to the legislature as a 'Fiduciary Power' Locke goes on to say: 'For all *Power given with trust* for the attaining an *end*, being limited by that end, whenever that *end* is manifestly neglected, or opposed, the *trust* must necessarily be *forfeited*'.[67]

The intuitive idea is that the holder of power has that power limited in ways that are consistent with the object for which that power was given. In the case of property privileges we want to argue that the limitation on the scope of the privilege takes the form of duties. This leads to the question with which we began this section. How are instrumental duties to be derived from the privileges? The answer is that the derivation of such duties is, like the creation of the initial privilege, instrumentally based. More formally, we can say that holders of intellectual property privileges are subject to those duties that maximize the probability that the purpose for which the privilege was first created is achieved. The duties exist as a means to promote the satisfaction of the goal that is the target of the privilege. Without the existence of such duties the grant of the privilege would be self-defeating and the failure to create them would be irrational.

There might also be a non-instrumental way of establishing the existence of the duties we are considering here. Showing this would be harder than the instrumental method we have employed. Briefly the non-instrumental route would involve linking duties to the existence of power. Intellectual property is a sovereignty mechanism. The holder of intellectual property occupies a station of power. Connected to this station are a set of duties that dictate that the power be exercised in a responsible way.[68] This way of proceeding is different from the instrumentalist derivation we have just discussed. The instrumentalist derivation is based on a means–ends rationality which, amongst other things, counsels us not to act in self-defeating ways. The instrumentalist derivation selects duties on the basis of their goal-promoting utility. The non-instrumental justification we are venturing here proceeds on the assumption that necessarily tied to stations of power are duties. These duties exist irrespective of whether they are needed to satisfy the goal that is the object of the privilege. That may be a consequence of the duties, but not the reason for their existence. These duties may in fact qualify as intrinsic duties. These are duties that do not exhibit a correlative dependency upon the rights of others, but instead exist independently of rights. An example, one which Raz develops, is the duty that the first friend has to the second friend to compensate her for harm done to her even where the actions of the first friend that caused the harm were not blameworthy in any sense.[69] The source of the duty lies in what is entailed by the nature of friendship. The core argument is that certain actions are the subject of intrinsic duties because of a shared conception of what is fundamentally valuable. A respect for the love of children might be an example of another source of intrinsic duties.

By combining the idea that certain duties follow stations of power with the concept of intrinsic duties, it may be possible to prove the existence of duties of privilege in a non-instrumental way. Such a line of argument may have advantages over the instrumentalist justification. There may be occasions where one is concerned not just with the narrower question of how the goal of the privilege is best implemented but rather with the responsible exercise of the power that the privilege confers. For example, intellectual property owners can enforce their privileges through litigation. While there is no question about the existence of this right to enforce, one might also want to argue that there are duties on the holder of the privilege to exercise the right of enforcement in responsible ways. The common law recognized, for example, that a person relying on an *invalid* patent could nevertheless make threats of litigation that were calculated to destroy the business of others:

> Many persons would immediately cease selling an alleged patented article rather than run the risk of being drawn into a litigation which might be of a very formidable character. And the utmost danger might be occasioned to the public if a man were to take out a patent for a thing notoriously of great antiquity, and by issuing circulars to monopolise a very large trade and destroy the trade of others.[70]

In those cases where the threats were without basis, the English law gave the person who was threatened a remedy.[71] The basis of the duty on intellectual property owners not to threaten litigation in certain circumstances might be grounded not, as a matter of normative theory, in the rights of other traders (for that would lead back to instrumentalism) but rather in a shared conception about the nature of the power of privilege in a democratic and just society. Showing that the duties of privilege can in the case of the privileges of intellectual property be derived non-instrumentally is, as we said earlier, going to be difficult. We have not inspected this possibility in any detail, but have merely shown how it might be made plausible.

It only remains to make some general comments about the kinds of instrumental duties one might derive from intellectual property privileges. Clearly, because the duties would have the instrumental purpose of helping to bring about the goal that the privilege itself was designed to serve, the relevant duties would have to be strongly connected to that goal. The kind of instrumental duties that would exist would depend on the way the goal of the relevant privilege was characterized, as well as the behavioural effects it was thought that the privilege would have. So, for example, if the goal of the patent system was stipulated to be simply the production of wealth *and* it was thought that the more of a reward the patent privilege constituted the more wealth would be produced, the instrumental duties needed to support the achievement of the goal might turn out to be few in number, the reason being that it might be argued that, the fewer the restrictions placed on the patentee, the greater the reward the privilege would turn out to be. This argument would only be defensible under an instrumental approach to intellectual property if it turned out to be empirically the case that patent privileges did play a significant role in wealth creation and that minimal duties on the privilege holder had a significant incentive effect.

Other characterizations of the goal of the patent system would produce a different or expanded set of duties. The history of the patent system is instructive in this regard. One historically important goal of the English patent system, as we have seen, was to help create certain trades or industries thought to be vital to the needs of the country. So one finds early on in the evolution of patent law the view that patentees had a duty to work the patent in the realm so that relevant industrial expertise was made accessible to all. Various English patent statutes contained provisions prohibiting the abuse of patent rights. A reading of these provisions shows that their purpose was to facilitate the transfer or circulation of the patented knowledge in the United Kingdom.[72] The English courts in fact went a long way towards imposing instrumental duties on the patentee in order to ensure that this particular goal of the patent system was met. One case laid down that patentees had to attempt to create a demand.[73] Compulsory licensing in part can be seen as the remedy for the failure by the patentee to abide by the instrumental duty of diffusing knowledge.[74] Another example of what we would term 'instrumental duties' is to be found in US court discussions of the existence of the misuse of copyright defence and the misuse of patent defence. The misuse defence bars a plaintiff from succeeding in an action for the infringement of a copyright or patent in those cases where the plaintiff uses the privilege in a way which is inconsistent with the public policy that lies behind the grant of the privilege.[75] The misuse doctrine is itself an example of a privilege-related duty that might be naturally deduced under instrumentalist axioms about intellectual property. In passing we might observe that, under an instrumentalist theory, the duty not to misuse intellectual property would be a duty that existed independently of the effect of the defendant's conduct on the plaintiff.

Conclusion

The overall direction in which the instrumentalist attitude would take intellectual property should now be evident. It would aspire to be a replacement for proprietarianism. Instrumentalism would require a strongly articulated conception of the public purpose and role of intellectual property. The juristic development of intellectual property law would have to adhere rigidly to that purpose. Instrumentalism would require an old-fashioned way of talking: the language of property rights would be replaced by the language of monopoly privileges. The grant of these monopolies would be tied to the idea of duty. Duty-bearing privileges would form the heart of an instrumentalism of intellectual property. Under instrumentalism intellectual property would be located in the context of some broader moral theory and set of values. Property rights would be morality's servants and not its drivers. Finally, an instrumentalist theory of intellectual property would rest upon a naturalistic empiricism. Legislative experiments with these rights would be driven by information about their real-world costs and abuses.

Notes

1 P. Pettit, *Judging Justice* (London, 1980), 75.

2 On the distinction between background rights and institutional rights, see R. Dworkin, *Taking Rights Seriously* (London, 4th impression, 1984), 93.

3 J. Bentham, 'The Theory of Legislation' in C.B. Macpherson (ed.), *Property* (Toronto, 1978), 41–48, 55.

4 Id., 52.

5 Id., 53.

6 Id., 55.

7 See J. Elster, *Making Sense of Marx* (Cambridge, 1985), chapter 8.

8 See, for instance, *Trade Mark Act, 1905* (UK), section 3. Mark is there defined to include 'device, brand, heading, label, ticket, name, signature, word, letter, numeral, or any combination thereof'.

9 At an international level the scope of sign has been progressively expanded. The First Council Directive of 21 December 1988 to Approximate the Laws of the Member States relating to Trademarks (OJ L 040 11.02.89 p.1 in article 2) states that a trademark may consist of any sign capable of being represented graphically. See also Article 15 of the Agreement on Trade-Related Aspects of Intellectual Property Rights (TRIPS). For an example of the domestic implementation of the TRIPS definition, see the definition of sign in section 6 of the *Trade Marks Act 1995* (Australia).

10 See F.I. Schechter, 'The Rational Basis of Trademark Protection', 40 *Harvard Law Review*, 813 (1927); R.S. Brown, Jr., 'Advertising and the Public Interest: Legal Protection of Trade Symbols', 57 *Yale Law Journal*, 1165 (1948); L.N. Klar, 'An Argument for the Restructuring of the Law of Trade Marks', 12 *Osgoode Hall Law Journal*, 223 (1974); T. Martino and W. Ullah, 'The Quality Guarantee Function of Trade Marks: An Economic Viewpoint' [1989] 8 *European Intellectual Property Review*, 267; S.L. Carter, 'The Trouble with Trademarks', 99 *Yale Law Journal*, 759 (1990).

11 *The Leather Cloth Company* v. *The American Leather Cloth Company* (1865) 11 H.L.C. 523, 533–534. See also James, LJ in *Massam* v. *Thorley's Cattle Food Co.* (1880) 14 Ch.D. 748, 755; Rigby, LJ in *In re* Magnolia Metal Company's Trademarks [1897] 2 Ch., 371, 390. This position was carried over into the 20th century. See *Aristoc Ltd.* v. *Rysta Ltd.* [1945] A.C. 68, 96.

12 See S. Ricketson, *The Law of Intellectual Property* (Sydney, 1984), 603; W.R. Cornish, *Intellectual Property* (2nd ed., London, 1989), 399.

13 For discussions of the economics of trademarks, see W.R. Cornish and J. Phillips, 'The Economic Function of Trade Marks: An Analysis with Special Reference to Developing Countries', 13 *International Review of Industrial Property and Copyright Law*, 41 (1982); W.M. Landes and R.A. Posner, 'Trademark Law: An Economic Perspective', 30 *The Journal of Law and Economics*, 265 (1987).

14 Judges still see that a fundamental purpose of trademark law is to protect consumers from deception. See the judgement of McHugh J in *New South Wales Dairy Corporation* v. *Murray Goulburn Co-operative Co. Ltd.* (1991) 171 CLR 363, 414. For a brief discussion of the common law of trademarks and the accommodation that was worked out by the courts between the interests of traders and consumers, see Lord Diplock in *GE Trade Mark* [1973] R.P.C. 297, 325–327.

15 See Lord Parker, *Registrar of Trade Marks* v. *W. & G. Du Cros, Ltd.* [1913] A.C. 624, 635.

16 *In re Applications of W. & G. Du Cros, Ltd.* [1912] 1 Ch. 644, 660.

17 For a case which is emblematic of this approach, see *Wood* v. *Butler* (1886) 3 R.P.C. 81.

18 So, for example, trademark statutes typically prohibited the practice of trademark trafficking. See *Re 12 Applications by American Greetings Corporation to Register the Trade Mark 'Holly Hobbie'* (1984) 1 IPR 486. The common law took the view that trademarks were assignable but only if the business goodwill was also transferred. See *GE Trade Mark* [1973] R.P.C., 297, 326.

19 (1914) 31 R.P.C. 385, 392. The Bowden decision has become increasingly less relevant to modern trademark law. For a discussion, see W.R. Cornish, *Intellectual Property* (2nd ed., London, 1989), 470–471.

20 The use of trademarks to divide markets territorially is a complex matter about which it is hard to generalize. For an excellent discussion of the law, see W.A. Rothnie, *Parallel Imports* (London, 1993), chapter 2. For a discussion of attempts to segment markets in the European context using trademarks, see W.R. Cornish, *Intellectual Property* (2nd ed., London, 1989), 481–489.

21 Another example of the change that proprietarianism brings can be seen in the way in which the requirement for the public use of the trademark has changed. Under the common law, title to a trademark was established on the basis of public use. Compare this with articles 15 and 19 of the TRIPS Agreement which do not require use either as a condition of registrability or for the maintenance of registration.

22 281 F 83 (CA2 1922).

23 281 F 83, 88 (CA2 1922).

24 281 F 83, 91 (CA2 1922).

25 *Kelly* v. *Morris* (1866) L.R. 1 Eq. 697, 701–702 and approved by *Jeweler's* at 281 F 83, 91.

26 This area of copyright law has attracted considerable academic discussion. See, for example, R.A. Gorman, 'Copyright Protection for the Collection and Representation of Facts', 76 *Harvard Law Review*, 1569 (1963); L.R. Patterson and C. Joyce, 'Monopolising the Law: The Scope of Copyright Protection for Law Reports and Statutory Compilations', 36 *UCLA Law Review*, 719 (1989); J.C. Ginsburg, 'Creation and Commercial Value: Copyright Protection of Works of Information', 90 *Columbia Law Review*, 1865 (1990); S. Ricketson, 'The Concept of Originality in Anglo-Australian Copyright Law', 39 *The Journal of the Copyright Society of the USA*, 265 (1992); T. Dreier and G.W.G. Karnell, 'Originality of the Copyrighted Work: A European Perspective', 39 *The Journal of the Copyright Society of the USA*, 289 (1992).

27 *Ladbroke (Football), Ltd.* v. *William Hill (Football), Ltd.* [1964] 1 All E.R., 465.

28 111 S. Ct. 1282 (1991).

29 US Constitution, article I, § 8, cl. 8.

30 See, for example, J.C. Ginsberg, 'No "Sweat"? Copyright and Other Protection of Works of Information After *Feist* v. *Rural Telephone*', 92 *Columbia Law Review*, 338 (1992); A.C. Yen, 'The Legacy of *Feist*: Consequences of the Weak Connection Between Copyright and the Economics of Public Goods', 52 *Ohio State Law Journal*, 1343 (1991).

31 See European Commission, *Amended proposal for a Council Directive on the legal protection of databases*, OJ 1993 C308/1, 15 November 1993; see also J. Morton, 'Draft EC Directive on the Protection of Electronic Databases: Comfort after *Feist*', 8(2) *Computer Law and Practice*, 38 (1992).

32 See *Harwood* v. *Great Northern Railway Co.* (1865) 11 H.L. C. 654; Lindley LJ in *Lane Fox* v. *Kensington and Knightsbridge Electric Lighting Co.* [1892] 3 Ch. 424, 428; Buckley J in *Case* v. *Cressy* (1900) 17 R.P.C. 255, 261.

33 See Buckley J in *Reynolds* v. *Herbert Smith & Co.* (1903) 20 R.P.C., 123 at 126. Approved in the High Court of Australia by Isaacs J in *Neilson* v. *The Minister of Public Works for New South Wales* (1914) 18 C.L.R. 423 at 429–430. See also *Moore and Hesketh* v. *Phillips* (1907) 4 CLR 1411 at 1425–6. In the United Kingdom, section 1(2)(a) of the *Patents Act 1977* expressly excludes discoveries from invention. In the United States the case of *Funk Brothers Seed Co.* v. *Kalo Inoculant Co.* 333 U.S. 127 (1948) is one important case that makes it clear that products of nature are not patentable.

34 [1892] 3 Ch. 424, 428.

35 *National Research Development Corp.* v. *Commissioner of Patents* (1959) 102 C.L.R. 252.

36 Patent specifications in fact disclose an idea. See Dixon J in *Radiation Ltd.* v. *Galliers & Klaerr Pty Ltd.* (1938) 60 C.L.R. 36, 51.

37 For an example of where this was argued unsuccessfully in relation to a well-organized research programme that resulted in the discovery of a naturally-occurring biological substance, see *Genentech Inc.* v. *Wellcome Foundation Ltd.* [1989] R.P.C. 147.

38 The High Court in *National Research Development Corp.* v. *Commissioner of Patents* (1959) 102 C.L.R. 252 thought that the patent system had as its main purpose the production of economically useful effects.

39 447 US 303, 309 (1980).

40 See R.S. Eisenberg, 'Patenting the Human Genome', 39 *Emory Law Journal*, 721, 727–729 (1990).

41 C. Correa, 'Biological Resources and Intellectual Property Rights' [1992], 5 *European Intellectual Property Review*, 154, 155. For a discussion of the European and US positions concerning gene patents, see B. Looney, 'Should Genes Be Patented? The Gene Patenting Controversy: Legal, Ethical, and Policy Foundations of an International Agreement', 26 *Law and Policy in International Business*, 231 (1994).

42 See the definition of 'breeder' in article 1 of the *International Convention for the Protection of New Varieties of Plants* of 2 December 1961, as revised at Geneva on 10 November 1972, on 23 October 1978, and on 19 March 1991. For an example of the domestic implementation of that obligation, see *Plant Breeder's Rights Act 1994* (Aus.) section 5.

43 See T. Roberts, 'Broad Claims for Biotechnological Inventions' [1994], 9 *European Intellectual Property Review*, 373; R.S. Crespi, 'Biotechnology, Broad Claims and the EPC' [1995], 6 *European Intellectual Property Review*, 267.

44 D. Manspeizer, 'The Cheshire Cat, the March Hare, and the Harvard Mouse: Animal Patents Open Up a New, Genetically-Engineered Wonderland', 43 *Rutgers Law Review*, 417 (1991); L. Maher, 'The Patent Environment: Domestic and European Community Frameworks for Biotechnology', 33 *Jurimetrics Journal*, 67 (1992).

45 For a discussion of the way in which new rights are created, see W.R. Cornish, 'The International Relations of Intellectual Property', 52 *Cambridge Law Journal*, 46, 54–63 (1993).

46 Positive liberty centres around the desire of individuals to be in control, to be self-directed rather than just unobstructed. See I. Berlin, *Four Essays on Liberty* (London, 1969), 123; T. Campbell, *The Left and Rights* (London, 1983), 29–30; Q. Skinner, 'The Idea of Negative Liberty: Philosophical and Historical Perspectives' in R. Rorty, J.B. Schneewind and Q. Skinner (eds.), *Philosophy in History* (Cambridge, 1984), 193.

47 T. Hobbes, *Leviathan* (1651; C.B. Macpherson ed., Harmondsworth, 1968), 261–262.

48 Hence the description in *Corelli* v. *Grey* (1913) 29 T.L. R. 570 of copyright as a negative right.

49 On the history of monopolies, see E.F. Churchill, 'Monopolies', 41 *The Law*

Quarterly Review, 275 (1925); W.H. Price, *The English Patents of Monopoly* (Cambridge, Mass., 1913).

50 *Statute of Monopolies of 1623.*

51 See E. Nagel, *The Structure of Science* (London, 1961), 129.

52 John Dewey uses the term to refer to pragmatism. See J. Dewey, *Philosophy and Civilization* (New York, 1931), 26. For an excellent discussion of the philosophy of pragmatism and its history, see H.S. Thayer, *Meaning and Action* (Indianapolis, New York, 1968). See also M.G. White, *The Origin of Dewey's Instrumentalism* (New York: Morningside Heights, 1943).

53 For a discussion of instrumentalism in law and its links to pragmatism and American Legal Realism, see R.S. Summers, *Instrumentalism and American Legal Theory* (Ithaca and London, 1982).

54 For an overview of this literature, see R.E. Goodin, 'Institutions and Their Design' in R.E. Goodin (ed.), *The Theory of Institutional Design* (Cambridge, 1996), 1.

55 For a discussion, see A.K. Dasgupta and D.W. Pearce, *Cost Benefit Analysis: Theory and Practice* (London, 1972).

56 See S. Hampshire, 'Morality and Pessimism' in S. Hampshire (ed.), *Morality and Conflict* (Oxford, 1983), 82.

57 L.L. Fuller, 'Means and Ends' in K.I. Winston (ed.), *The Principles of Social Order: Selected Essays of Lon L. Fuller* (Durham, N.C. 1981), 48.

58 On the relationship between moral theory and the principle of humanism, see J. Raz, *The Morality of Freedom* (Oxford, 1986), 194.

59 Examples of good sceptical approaches to intellectual property are A. Plant, 'The Economic Theory Concerning Patents for Inventions', 1 *Economica* (new series), 30 (1934); A. Plant, 'The Economic Aspects of Copyright in Books', 1 *Economica* (new series), 167 (1934); S. Breyer, 'The Uneasy Case for Copyright: A Study of Copyright in Books, Photocopies, and Computer Programs', 84 *Harvard Law Review*, 281 (1970).

60 I am indebted to Stanley Paulson for bringing Kelsen on property to my attention.

61 Places in which Kelsen discusses this include H. Kelsen, *Introduction to the Problems of Legal Theory* (1934; B. Paulson and S.L. Paulson (trs.), Oxford, 1992), chapter 4; H. Kelsen, 'The Pure Theory of Law and Analytical Jurisprudence', 55 *Harvard Law Review*, 44 (1941); H. Kelsen, 'Law, State and Justice in the Pure Theory of Law', 57 *Yale Law Journal*, 377 (1948); H. Kelsen, 'Foundations of Democracy', LXV *Ethics*, 68 (1955).

62 H. Kelsen, *Introduction to the Problems of Legal Theory* (1934; B. Paulson and S.L. Paulson (trs), Oxford, 1992), 38.

63 Id., 40–41.

64 J. Raz, *The Morality of Freedom* (Oxford, 1986), 201.

65 It would seem that this is even possible under consequentialism, albeit of a modified kind. An example of such an approach is to be found in the goal rights system proposed by Sen. See A. Sen, 'Rights and Agency', 11 *Philosophy and Public Affairs*, 3 (1982). See also P. Pettit, 'The Consequentialist Can Recognise Rights', 38 *The Philosophical Quarterly*, 42 (1988). These approaches deal with the following problem of rights. Deontological views of rights do not allow one to solve complex interdependency problems by having regard to the consequences of those rights. Consequentialist approaches of the welfarist kind are good at dealing with interdependencies in that they link individuals by counting all relevant individual preferences in a given situation. But they miss out on the fact that there are aspects of social and moral life that are not amenable to resolution simply through a calculation based on utility information. The advantages of a hybrid approach like Sen's is that it allows the radical instrumentalist about property to evaluate rights (such as moral rights in copyright) consequentially, while recognizing that the

consequences that matter lie well beyond those that welfare consequentialism recognizes.

66 J. Bentham, *An Introduction to the Principles of Morals and Legislation* (1780; J.H. Burns and H.L.A. Hart, London, 1970), 211.

67 John Locke, *Two Treatises of Government* (1690; P. Laslett ed., Cambridge, 1988), Book II, para 149.

68 The language of station and duties comes from the essay, 'My Station and Its Duties' by F.H. Bradley in *Ethical Studies* (2nd ed., Oxford, 1927), 160.

69 For a general discussion of intrinsic duties, see J. Raz, *The Morality of Freedom* (Oxford, 1986), 210–213.

70 *Axmann* v. *Lund* (1874) L.R. 18 Eq. 330, 336.

71 Section 32 of the *Patents, Designs, and Trade-Marks Act*, 1883 dealt with the problem of unfounded threats of patent litigation. See *Driffield and East Riding Pure Linseed Cake Company* v. *Waterloo Mills Cake and Warehousing Company* (1886) 31 Ch.D. 638 for an instance of its application. Prior to the 1883 Act courts had recognized that a person was liable to an action if he made threats of litigation on the basis of a patent he knew to be invalid. See *Halsey* v. *Brotherhood* (1880) 15 Ch.D. 514, 518. The equitable principle, that groundless threats of litigation could not be used to harm the trade interests of others, was also recognized in the US. See *Emack* v. *Kane* 34 Fed. R. 46 (1888).

72 See, for instance, section 27 of the *Patents and Designs Act, 1907* (allowing for the revocation of patents that were mainly or exclusively worked outside the UK).

73 See *Boult's Patent* (1909) 26 R.P.C. 383, 387. See also *Kent's Patent* (1909), 26 R.P.C. 666; *In the Matter of Johnson's Patent* (1908), 25 R.P.C. 709, 727.

74 For an elaboration of the motives for compulsory licensing in the United Kingdom, see W.R. Cornish, *Intellectual Property* (2nd ed., London, 1989), 206–208.

75 For a formulation of the defence as a principle of equity, see *Morton Salt Co* v. *G.S. Suppiger* 314 US 488 (1942). For an application of the defence in copyright law, see *Lasercomb America, Inc* v. *Job Reynolds* 911 F.2d 970 (4th Cir. 1990). The defendants had bought some software from the plaintiff, made some infringing copies and then released a version of the software that turned out to be almost identical to that of the plaintiff's. Despite their conduct the defendants were able to plead successfully the misuse of copyright defence. The plaintiffs had inserted provisions in their licensing agreement that obliged any licensee not to develop software similar to the plaintiff's. The purpose of the plaintiffs was clear. They were trying to use copyright to monopolize the idea of computer-assisted die manufacture. The attempt to use copyright to gain control of an idea amounted to a misuse of copyright (see 911 F.2d at 979).

References

Ackerman, B.A. (ed.), *Economic Foundations of Property Law* (Boston, 1975).

Alchian, A.A. and Allen, W.R., *Exchange and Production* (3rd ed., Belmont, California, 1983).

Alford, W.P., 'Don't Stop Thinking About ... Yesterday: Why There was No Indigenous Counterpart to Intellectual Property Law in Imperial China', 7 *Journal of Chinese Law*, 3 (1993).

Arber, E. (ed.), *A Transcript of the Registers of the Company of Stationers of London 1554–1640 A.D.* (London, 1875–94, privately printed, 5 volumes).

Aristotle, *Nicomachean Ethics*.

Arnold, E.V., *Roman Stoicism* (London, 1911, reissued 1958).

Arrow, K.J., 'Economic Welfare and the Allocation of Resources for Invention' in *The Rate and Direction of Inventive Activity: Economic and Social Factors* (A Report of the National Bureau of Economic Research, Princeton, 1962), 609.

Arrow, K.J., *The Limits of Organization* (New York, 1974).

Arup, C., *Innovation, Policy, and Law* (Cambridge, 1993).

Austin, J., *Lectures on Jurisprudence* (5th ed., London, 1885).

Australian Law Reform Commission, *Designs* (DP 58, Australia, 1994).

Avineri, S., *Hegel's Theory of the Modern State* (Cambridge at the University Press, 1972).

Bain, J.S., *Barriers to New Competition* (Cambridge, Mass., 1956).

Baldwin, D.A., *Paradoxes of Power* (New York and Oxford, 1989).

Barnett, S.R., 'At a Crossroads: The Right of Publicity in the United States', 160 *Revue Internationale du Droit d'Auteur*, 5 (1994).

Barry, B., *The Liberal Theory of Justice* (Oxford, 1973).

Barry, B., 'Humanity and Justice in Global Perspective', in J.R. Pennock and J.W. Chapman (eds.), *Ethics, Economics and the Law* (New York, London, 1982), 219.

Basic Framework of GATT Provisions on Intellectual Property, Statement of Views of the European, Japanese and United States Business Communities, June 1988, The Intellectual Property Committee, Keidanren, UNICE.

Becker, G.S., 'Investment in Human Capital: A Theoretical Analysis', 70 *Journal of Political Economy*, S9 (1962).
Becker, G.S., *Human Capital* (New York, National Bureau of Economic Research, 1964).
Becker, G.S., 'Nobel Lecture: The Economic Way of Looking at Behaviour', 101 *Journal of Political Economy*, 385 (1993).
Becker, G.S., Murphy, K.M. and Tamura, R., 'Human Capital, Fertility, and Economic Growth', 98 (5) pt. 2, *Journal of Political Economy*, S12, S15 (1990).
Becker, L.C., *Property Rights – Philosophic Foundations* (London, Boston, 1977).
Becker, L.C., 'Too Much Property', 21 *Philosophy and Public Affairs*, 196 (1992).
Beier, F.K., 'One Hundred Years of International Cooperation – The Role of the Paris Convention in the Past, Present and Future', 15 *International Review of Industrial Property and Copyright Law*, 1 (1984).
Beier, F.K. and Schricker, G. (eds.), *GATT or WIPO? New Ways in the International Protection of Intellectual Property* (Munich, 1989).
Beitz, C.R., *Political Theory and International Relations* (Princeton, New Jersey, 1979).
Beitz, C.R., 'Cosmopolitan Ideals and National Sentiment', LXXX *The Journal of Philosophy*, 591 (1983).
Bell, A.P., *Modern Law of Personal Property in England and Ireland* (London, Edinburgh, 1989).
Bentham, J., *An Introduction to the Principles of Morals and Legislation* (1780; J.H. Burns and H.L.A. Hart (eds.), London, 1970).
Berlin, I., *Four Essays on Liberty* (London, 1969).
Bhagwati, J.N., 'Directly Unproductive, Profit-seeking (DUP) Activities', 90 *Journal of Political Economy*, 988 (1982).
Blackstone, W., *Commentaries on the Laws of England* (1765; 1783 ed. reprinted by Garland Publishing, New York, London, 1978).
Blagden, C., *The Stationers' Company: A History, 1403–1959* (Cambridge, 1960).
Boehm, K., *The British Patent System, I: Administration* (Cambridge at the University Press, 1967).
Bogart, J.H., 'Lockean Provisos and State of Nature Theories', 95 *Ethics*, 828 (1985).
Bogsch, A., *Brief History of the First 25 Years of the World Intellectual Property Organization* (Geneva, 1992).
Bonyhady, T., *The Law of the Countryside: The Rights of the Public* (Milton Park Estate, Abingdon, 1987).
Boss, H., *Theories of Surplus and Transfer* (Boston, 1990).
Boulding, K.E., *Three Faces of Power* (Newbury Park, London, New Delhi, 1989).
Boyle, J., 'A Theory of Law and Information: Copyright, Spleens,

Blackmail, and Insider Trading', 80 *California Law Review*, 1413 (1992).

Bradley, F.H., *Ethical Studies* (2nd ed., Oxford, 1927).

Braga, C.A.P., 'The Economics of Intellectual Property Rights and the GATT: A View from the South', 22 *Vanderbilt Journal of Transnational Law*, 243 (1989).

Braithwaite, J. and Pettit, P., *Not Just Deserts* (Oxford, 1990).

Braman, S., 'Defining Information', 13 *Telecommunications Policy*, 233 (1989).

Brennan, A., *Conditions of Identity* (Oxford, 1988).

Brennan, G. and Buchanan, J.M., *The Reason of Rules: Constitutional Political Economy* (Cambridge, 1985).

Breyer, S., 'The Uneasy Case for Copyright: A Study of Copyright in Books, Photocopies, and Computer Programs', 84 *Harvard Law Review* 281 (1970).

Brodhurst, S., 'Is Copyright a Chose in Action?', 11 *Law Quarterly Review*, 64 (1895).

Brown, C., 'International Affairs' in B. Goodin and P. Pettit (eds.), *A Companion to Contemporary Political Philosophy* (Oxford, 1993), 515.

Brown, Jr., R.S., 'Advertising and the Public Interest: Legal Protection of Trade Symbols', 57 *Yale Law Journal*, 1165 (1948).

Brunt, M., '"Market Definition" Issues in Australian and New Zealand Trade Practices Litigation', 18 *Australian Business Law Review*, 86 (1990).

Buckland, W.W., *The Main Institutions of Roman Private Law* (Cambridge at the University Press, 1931).

Buckland, W.W., *A Text-Book of Roman Law from Augustus to Justinian* (3rd ed., revised by Peter Stein, Cambridge, 1963).

Buckle, S., *Natural Law and the Theory of Property* (Oxford, 1991).

Bugbee, B.W., *Genesis of American Patent and Copyright Law* (Washington, D.C., 1967).

Butler, M.A., 'Early Liberal Roots of Feminism: John Locke and the Attack on Patriarchy', in R. Ashcraft (ed.), *John Locke* (London, New York, 1991) vol. 3, 639.

Cain, M. and Hunt, A., *Marx and Engels on Law* (London, New York, San Francisco, 1979).

Calabresi, G. and Melamed, A.D., 'Property Rules, Liability Rules, and Inalienability: One View of the Cathedral', 85 *Harvard Law Review*, 1089 (1972).

Campbell, T., *The Left and Rights* (London, 1983).

Campbell, T., *Justice* (London, 1988).

Campbell, T., 'Rationales for Freedom of Communication', in T. Campbell and W. Sadurski (eds.), *Freedom of Communication* (Aldershot, 1994).

Carter, J.W., Lane, P., Tolhurst, G.J. and Peden, E.M., *Helmore Com-*

mercial Law and Personal Property in New South Wales (10th ed., Sydney, 1992).
Carter, S.L., 'The Trouble with Trademarks', 99 *Yale Law Journal*, 759 (1990).
Churchill, E.F., 'Monopolies', 41 *Law Quarterly Review* 275 (1925).
Coase, R.H., 'The Problem of Social Cost', 3 *Journal of Law and Economics*, 1, (1960).
Cohen, G.A., *Karl Marx's Theory of History* (Oxford, Princeton, 1978).
Cohen, G.A., 'Base and Superstructure: A Reply to Hugh Collins', 9 *Oxford Journal of Legal Studies*, 95 (1989).
Cohen, M.R., 'Property and Sovereignty', 13 *Cornell Law Quarterly*, 8 (1927).
Coleman, J.L., *Markets, Morals and the Law* (Cambridge, New York, 1988).
Collins, H., *Marxism and Law* (Oxford, 1982).
Colquhoun, P., *A Summary of the Roman Civil Law* (London, author's preface, 1851).
Commons, J.R., *Institutional Economics* (New York, 1934).
Copyright Law Review Committee, *The Importation Provisions of the Copyright Act 1968* (Canberra, 1988).
Cornell, D., Rosenfeld, M. and Carlson D.G. (eds.), *Hegel and Legal Theory* (New York, London, 1991).
Cornell, D., Rosenfeld, M. and Carlson, D.G. (eds.), *Deconstruction and the Possibility of Justice* (New York, 1992).
Cornes, R. and Sandler, T., *The Theory of Externalities, Public Goods, and Club Goods* (Cambridge, New York, 1986).
Cornish, W.R., *Intellectual Property* (2nd ed., London, 1989).
Cornish, W.R., 'The International Relations of Intellectual Property', 52 *Cambridge Law Journal*, 46 (1993).
Cornish, W.R. and Phillips, J., 'The Economic Function of Trade Marks: An Analysis with Special Reference to Developing Countries', 13 *International Review of Industrial Property and Copyright Law*, 41 (1982).
Correa, C., 'Biological Resources and Intellectual Property Rights', 5 *European Intellectual Property Review*, 154 (1992).
Costello, P.M., 'The Tetracycline Conspiracy: Structure, Conduct and Performance in the Drug Industry', 1 *Antitrust Law and Economics Review*, 13 (1968).
Cotterrell, R.B.M., *The Sociology of Law* (London, 1984).
Council of Europe, *International Legal Protection of Cultural Property* (Strasbourg, 1984).
Crespi, R.S., 'Biotechnology, Broad Claims and the EPC', 6 *European Intellectual Property Review*, 267 (1995).
Damich, E.J., 'The Right of Personality: A Common-Law Basis for the Protection of the Moral Rights of Authors', 23 *Georgia Law Review*, 1 (1988).

Dasgupta, A.K. and Pearce, D.W., *Cost Benefit Analysis: Theory and Practice* (London, 1972).
Davison, M.J., 'The Market for Books: Open or Closed?', 18 *Australian Business Law Review*, 179 (1990).
De Jasay, A., *Social Contract, Free Ride: A Study of the Public Goods Problem* (Oxford, New York, 1989).
De Jouvenel, B., 'Authority: The Efficient Imperative', in C.J. Friedrich (ed.), *Authority* (Cambridge, Mass., 1958), 159.
Demsetz, H., 'Toward a Theory of Property Rights', 57 *American Economic Review*, 347 (1967).
De Roover, R., 'Monopoly Theory Prior to Adam Smith: A Revision', 65 *Quarterly Journal of Economics*, 492 (1951).
Dewey, J., *Philosophy and Civilization* (New York, 1931).
Dicken, P., *Global Shift: The Internationalization of Economic Activity* (2nd ed., New York, 1992).
Dowding, K.M., *Rational Choice and Political Power* (Aldershot, 1991).
Dragun, A.K., 'Externalities, Property Rights, and Power, XVII *Journal of Economic Issues*, 667 (1983).
Drahos, P., 'Intellectual Property Law and Basic Science: Extinguishing Prometheus?', 10 *Law in Context*, 56 (1992).
Drahos, P., 'Decentring Communication: The Dark Side of Intellectual Property', in T. Campbell and W. Sadurski (eds.), *Freedom of Communication* (Aldershot, 1994), 249.
Drahos, P., 'Global Property Rights in Information: The Story of TRIPS at the GATT', 13 *Prometheus*, 6 (1995).
Drahos, P. and Joseph, R.A., 'Telecommunications and Investment in the Great Supranational Regulatory Game', 19 *Telecommunications Policy*, 619 (1995).
Dreier, T. and Karnell, G.W.G., 'Originality of the Copyrighted Work: A European Perspective', 39 *The Journal of the Copyright Society of the USA*, 289 (1992).
Drucker, P.F., *Post-Capitalist Society* (New York, 1993).
Dunn, J., *Locke* (Oxford, 1984).
Dunn, J., 'Property, Justice and Common Good after Socialism', in J.A. Hall and I.C. Jarvie (eds.), *Transition to Modernity* (Cambridge, 1992), 281.
Dury, S.B., 'Locke and Nozick on Property', in Richard Ashcraft (ed.), *John Locke: Critical Assessments*, (London and New York, 1991), vol. 3, 495.
Dutton, D. and Krausz, M. (eds.), *The Concept of Creativity in Science and Art* (The Hague, Boston, London, 1981).
Dworkin, R., *Taking Rights Seriously* (London, 4th impression, 1984).
Easterbrook, F.H., 'Insider Trading, Secret Agents, Evidentiary Privileges, and the Production of Information', *The Supreme Court Review*, 309 (1981).

Easterbrook, F.H., 'Intellectual Property Is Still Property', 13 *Harvard Journal of Law and Public Policy*, 108 (1990).
Edelman, B., *Ownership of the Image* (E. Kingdom tr., London, Boston, Henley, 1979).
Eisenberg, R.S., 'Patenting the Human Genome', 39 *Emory Law Journal*, 721, 727–729 (1990).
Eisenberg, R.S., 'A Technology Policy Perspective on the NIH Gene Patenting Controversy', 55 *University of Pittsburgh Law Review*, 633 (1994).
Elphinstone, H.W., 'What is a Chose in Action?', 9 *Law Quarterly Review*, 311 (1893).
Elster, J., *Making Sense of Marx* (Cambridge, 1985).
Elster, J., *Nuts and Bolts for the Social Sciences* (Cambridge, 1989).
Engels, F., 'Socialism: Utopian and Scientific' (1880), in Karl Marx and Frederick Engels, *Selected Works* (Moscow, 1970), vol. 3, 95.
Epstein, R.A., 'On the Optimal Mix of Private and Common Property', 11 *Social Philosophy and Policy*, 17 (1994).
Farber, D.A. and Frickey, P.P., *Law and Public Choice: A Critical Introduction* (Chicago, 1991).
Fels, A. and Walker, J., 'The Market for Books and the Importation Provisions of the Copyright Act 1968', 17 *Melbourne University Law Review*, 566 (1990).
Field, H.H., *Science Without Numbers* (Oxford, 1980).
Foster, M.B., *The Political Philosophies of Plato and Hegel* (Oxford at the Clarendon Press, 1935, reprinted 1968).
Foucault, M., *Power/Knowledge* (C. Gordon ed., Brighton, Sussex, 1980).
Foucault, M., *The History of Sexuality* (R. Hurley tr., New York, 1980), vol. 1.
Friedman, A.E., 'The Economics of the Common Pool: Property Rights in Exhaustible Resources', 18 *UCLA Law Review*, 855 (1971).
Friedman, D., 'A Positive Account of Property Rights', 11 *Social Philosophy and Policy*, 1 (1994).
Friedman, M., *Capitalism and Freedom* (Chicago and London, 1962), 127.
Fuller, L.L., 'Means and Ends' in K.I. Winston (ed.), *The Principles of Social Order: Selected Essays of Lon L. Fuller* (Durham, N.C., 1981), 48.
Gadsden, G.D., *The Law of Commons* (London, 1988).
Galbraith, J.K., *The New Industrial State* (Harmondsworth, 1967).
Gale, G., 'John Locke on Territoriality: An Unnoticed Aspect of the *Second Treatise*', 1 *Political Theory*, 472 (1973).
Gaus, G.F., 'Property, Rights, and Freedom', 11 *Social Philosophy and Politics*, 209 (1994).
Gerber, D.J., 'Prometheus Born: The High Middle Ages and the Relationship Between Law and Economic Conduct', 38 *Saint Louis University Law Journal*, 673, 720–725 (1994).

Ginsburg, J.C., 'Creation and Commercial Value: Copyright Protection of Works of Information', 90 *Columbia Law Review*, 1865 (1990).
Ginsberg, J.C., 'No "Sweat"? Copyright and Other Protection of Works of Information After *Feist v. Rural Telephone*', 92 *Columbia Law Review*, 338 (1992).
Goldberg, S., *Understanding Relativity: Origin and Impact of a Scientific Revolution* (Oxford, 1984).
Goodin, R.E., 'Institutions and Their Design' in R.E. Goodin (ed.), *The Theory of Institutional Design* (Cambridge, 1996), 1.
Gordon, H.S., 'The Economic Theory of a Common Property Resource: The Fishery', 62 *Journal of Political Economy*, 124 (1954).
Gorman, R.A., 'Copyright Protection for the Collection and Representation of Facts', 76 *Harvard Law Review*, 1569 (1963).
Gray, K., 'Property in Thin Air', 50 *Cambridge Law Journal*, 252 (1991).
Grotius, H., *Mare Liberum* (1608; R. Van Deman Magoffin tr., New York, 1916).
Grotius, H., *De Jure Belli Ac Pacis Libri Tres* (1625; F.W. Kelsey tr., New York, London, 1964).
Grunebaum, J.O., *Private Ownership* (London, New York, 1987).
Haddock, D.D., 'First Possession Versus Optimal Timing: Limiting the Dissipation of Economic Value', 64 *Washington University Law Quarterly*, 775 (1968).
Hahm, D.E., *The Origins of Stoic Cosmology* (Columbus, Ohio, 1977).
Hale, B., *Abstract Objects* (Oxford, 1987).
Hale, R.L., 'Coercion and Distribution in a Supposedly Non-Coercive State', 38 *Political Science Quarterly*, 470 (1923).
Hale, R.L., 'Bargaining, Duress, and Economic Liberty', 43 *Columbia Law Review*, 603 (1943).
Hampshire, S., 'Morality and Pessimism', in S. Hampshire, *Morality and Conflict* (Oxford, 1983), 82.
Harsanyi, J.C., 'A New General Solutions Concept for Both Cooperative and Non-cooperative Games', in J.C. Harsanyi, *Papers in Game Theory* (Dordrecht, Holland, 1982), 211.
Hauser, A., *The Social History of Art* (S. Godman tr., London, 1951).
Hayek, F.A., *The Road to Serfdom* (London, 1944).
Hegel, G.W.F., *Philosophy of Right* (1821; T.M. Knox tr., Oxford at the Clarendon Press, 1952, 1st ed., 1967 reprint).
Hegel, G.W.F., 'The Scientific Ways of Treating Natural Law, Its Place in Moral Philosophy, and Its Relation to the Positive Sciences of Law' (1802, 1803; T.M. Knox tr., Philadelphia, 1975).
Hegel's Political Writings (T.M. Knox tr., Oxford at the Clarendon Press, 1964).
Henry, M., 'Mortgages of Intellectual Property in the United Kingdom', 5 *European Intellectual Property Review*, 158 [1992].

Hettinger, E.C., 'Justifying Intellectual Property', 18 *Philosophy and Public Affairs*, 31 (1989).
Hindess, B., *Politics and Class Analysis* (Oxford, 1987).
Hobbes, T., *Leviathan* (1651; C.B. Macpherson ed., Harmondsworth, 1968).
Hohfeld, W.N., *Fundamental Legal Conceptions* (W.W. Cook ed., Westport, Connecticut, 1919, reprinted 1978).
Holdsworth, W.S., 'The History of the Treatment of Choses in Action by the Common Law', 33 *Harvard Law Review*, 997 (1920).
Holdsworth, W.S., 'The Commons Debates 1621', 52 *Law Quarterly Review*, 481 (1936).
Holdsworth, W.S., *A History of English Law* (2nd ed., London, 1937), vol. 6.
Honoré, A.M., 'Ownership', in A.G. Guest (ed.), *Oxford Essays in Jurisprudence* (Oxford, 1961).
Hoppe, H., *The Economics and Ethics of Private Property* (Boston, 1993).
Howard, M.C. and King, J.E., *The Political Economy of Marx* (2nd ed., London, New York, 1985).
Hughes, J., 'The Philosophy of Intellectual Property', 77 *Georgetown Law Journal*, 287 (1988).
Hulme, E.W., 'The History of the Patent System Under the Prerogative and at Common Law', 12 *Law Quarterly Review*, 141 (1896).
Hume, D., *A Treatise of Human Nature* (1739; L.A. Selby-Bigge ed., 2nd ed. by P.H. Nidditch, Oxford, 1978).
Industrial Property Statistics (WIPO, Geneva, 1992).
Industry Commission, *Report on Vehicle and Recreational Marine Craft Repair and Insurance Industries* (Australia, 1994).
The Institutes of Gaius (F. De Zulueta ed. and tr., Oxford at the Clarendon Press, 1946).
Irvine, A.D. (ed.), *Physicalism in Mathematics* (Dordrecht, Boston, London, 1990).
Jamieson, D., 'Global Environmental Justice', in R. Attfield and A. Belsey (eds.), *Philosophy and the Natural Environment* (Cambridge, 1994), 199.
Jenks, E., *A Short History of English Law* (6th ed., London, 1949).
Jolowicz, H.F. and Nicholas, B., *Historical Introduction to the Study of Roman Law* (3rd ed., Cambridge, 1972).
Joyner, C.C., 'Legal Implications of the Concept of the Common Heritage of Mankind', 35 *International and Comparative Law Quarterly*, 190 (1986).
Junankar, P.N., *Marx's Economics* (Oxford, 1982).
Justinian's Institutes (translated with an Introduction by Peter Birks and Grant McLeod, Ithaca, New York, 1987).
Kamenka, E. (ed.), *The Portable Karl Marx* (Harmondsworth, 1983).
Kant, I., *The Metaphysics of Morals* (M.J. Gregor tr., Cambridge, 1991).

Kaplan, B., *An Unhurried View of Copyright* (New York and London, 1967).
Kaplow, L., 'The Patent-Antitrust Intersection: A Reappraisal', 97 *Harvard Law Review*, 1815 (1984).
Katz, A.S., 'The Doctrine of Moral Right and American Copyright Law – A Proposal', 24 *Southern California Law Review*, 1 (1951).
Kelsen, H., 'The Pure Theory of Law and Analytical Jurisprudence', 55 *Harvard Law Review*, 44 (1941).
Kelsen, H., 'Law, State and Justice in the Pure Theory of Law', 57 *Yale Law Journal*, 377 (1948).
Kelsen, H., 'Foundations of Democracy', LXV *Ethics*, 68 (1955).
Kelsen, H., *Introduction to the Problems of Legal Theory* (1934; B. Paulson and S.L. Paulson trs., Oxford, 1992).
Keohane, R.O., *After Hegemony* (Princeton, 1984).
Keynes, J.M., 'The General Theory of Employment', 51 *The Quarterly Journal of Economics*, 209 (1937).
Kingston, W., *The Political Economy of Innovation* (The Hague, Boston, Lancaster, 1984).
Klar, L.N., 'An Argument for the Restructuring of the Law of Trade Marks', 12 *Osgoode Hall Law Journal*, 223 (1974).
Kling, R. (ed.), *Computerization and Controversy: Value Conflicts and Social Choices* (2nd ed., San Diego, forthcoming).
Koestler, A., *The Act of Creation* (London, 1964).
Koestler, A., 'The Three Domains of Creativity', in D. Dutton and M. Krausz (eds.), *The Concept of Creativity in Science and Art* (The Hague, Boston, London, 1981), 1.
Kristeller, P.O., 'Creativity and Tradition', XLIV *Journal of the History of Ideas*, 105 (1983).
Kuhn, T.S., *The Structure of Scientific Revolutions* (2nd ed., Chicago, 1970).
Kukathas, C. and Pettit, P., *Rawls: A Theory of Justice and its Critics* (Cambridge, 1990).
Künne, W.K., 'Criteria of Abstractness', in B. Smith (ed.), *Parts and Moments* (Munchen, Wien, 1982).
Kunz-Hallstein, H.P., 'The United States Proposal for a GATT Agreement on Intellectual Property and the Paris Convention for the Protection of Industrial Property', 22 *Vanderbilt Journal of Transnational Law*, 265 (1989).
LaCapra, D. and Kaplan, S. (eds.), *Modern European Intellectual History: Reappraisals and New Perspectives* (Ithaca, N.Y., 1982).
Lahore, J., *Copyright Law* (*Service*; Sydney, 1988).
Lall, S., 'The Patent System and the Transfer of Technology to Less-Developed Countries', 10 *Journal of World Trade Law*, 1 (1976).
Lamberton, D.M. (ed.), *The Economics of Information* (Harmondsworth, 1971).

Lamberton, D.M., 'The Economics of Information and Organization', in M.E. Williams (ed.), *Annual Review of Information Science and Technology* (American Society for Information Science and Technology, White Plains, NY, 1984), 3.
Lamberton, D.M., 'Innovation and Intellectual Property', in M. Dodgson and R. Rothwell (eds.), *The Handbook of Industrial Innovation* (Cheltenham, UK, 1994), 301.
Lamberton, D.M. (ed.), *The Economics of Communication and Information* (Cheltenham, UK, 1996).
Landes, W.M. and Posner, R.A., 'Market Power in Antitrust Cases', 94 *Harvard Law Review*, 937 (1981).
Landes, W.M. and Posner, R.A., 'Trademark Law: An Economic Perspective', 30 *Journal of Law and Economics*, 265 (1987).
Landes, W.M. and Posner, R.A., 'An Economic Analysis of Copyright Law', 18 *Journal of Legal Studies*, 325 (1989).
Larkin, P., *Property in the Eighteenth Century* (Dublin, Cork, 1930).
Larschan, B. and Brennan, B.C., 'The Common Heritage of Mankind Principle in International Law', 21 *Columbia Journal of Transnational Law*, 305 (1983).
Lasswell, H.D. and Kaplan, A., *Power and Society* (New Haven, 1950).
Lehmann, M., 'Property and Intellectual Property – Property Rights as Restrictions on Competition in Furtherance of Competition', 20 *International Review of Industrial Property and Copyright Law*, 1 (1989).
Lindahl, L., *Position and Change* (Dordrecht, Boston, 1977).
Locke, J., *Two Treatises of Government* (1690; P. Laslett, ed., Cambridge, 1988).
Looney, B., 'Should Genes Be Patented? The Gene Patenting Controversy: Legal, Ethical, and Policy Foundations of an International Agreement', 26 *Law and Policy in International Business*, 231 (1994).
Lowie, R.H., *Primitive Society* (New York, 1920).
Luce, R.D. and Raiffa, H., *Games and Decisions* (New York, 1958).
Luhmann, N., *A Sociological Theory of Law* (M. Albrow ed., E. King and M. Albrow trs., London, 1985).
Lukes, S., *Power: A Radical View* (London, Basingstoke, 1974).
Lyons, D., 'Logic and Coercion in Bentham's Theory of Law', 57 *Cornell Law Review*, 335 (1972).
MacCormick, N., *Legal Right and Social Democracy* (Oxford, 1982).
Machlup, F., *An Economic Review of the Patent System* (Study No. 15 of the Subcommittee on Patents, Trademarks, and Copyrights of the Committee on the Judiciary, U.S. Senate, 85th Congress, Washington, D.C., 1958).
Machlup, F. and Penrose, E., 'The Patent Controversy', X *The Journal of Economic History*, 1 (1950).
Mackie, J.L., *Ethics* (Harmondsworth, 1977).
Macpherson, C.B. (ed.), *Property* (Toronto, 1978).

Macpherson, C.B., *The Political Theory of Possessive Individualism* (Oxford, 1979).
Madow, M., 'Private Ownership of Public Image: Popular Culture and Publicity Rights', 81 *California Law Review*, 127 (1993).
Maher, L., 'The Patent Environment: Domestic and European Community Frameworks for Biotechnology', 33 *Jurimetrics Journal*, 67 (1992).
Maitland, F.W., 'The Mystery of Seisin', in *Select Essays in Anglo-American History* (edited by a committee of the Association of American Law Schools, Cambridge at the University Press, 1909).
Mandeville, T., Lamberton, D. and Bishop, J., 'The Use of Patent Information: Economics of Disclosure', in *The Economic Implications of Patents in Australia* (Canberra, 1981), 271.
Manspeizer, D., 'The Cheshire Cat, the March Hare, and the Harvard Mouse: Animal Patents Open Up a New, Genetically-Engineered Wonderland', 43 *Rutgers Law Review*, 417 (1991).
Marshall, O.R., *The Assignment of Choses in Action* (London, 1950).
Martino, T. and Ullah, W., 'The Quality Guarantee Function of Trade Marks: An Economic Viewpoint', 8 *European Intellectual Property Review*, 267 (1989).
Marx, K., *Capital* I (1867; Moscow, 1959).
Marx, K., *Grundrisse* (1857–58; M. Nicolaus tr., London, 1973),
Marx, K. and Engels, F., *Selected Works* (Moscow, 1969, 1970), vols. 1 and 3.
Marx, K. and Engels, F., *Collected Works* (London, 1975, 1976), vols. 3, 5 and 6.
McCarthy, J.T., 'Intellectual Property and Trade Practices Policy: Co-existence or Conflict? The American Experience', 13 *Australian Business Law Review*, 198 (1985).
McLean, I., *Public Choice: An Introduction* (Oxford, 1991).
McMillan, J., 'The Free-rider Problem: A Survey', 55 *Economic Record*, 95 (1979).
Merton, R.K., *The Sociology of Science* (Chicago, 1973).
Mincer, J., 'Investment in Human Capital and Personal Income Distribution', 66 *Journal of Political Economy*, 281 (1958).
Mokyr, J., *The Lever of Riches* (New York, 1990).
Monson, C.H., 'Locke and his Interpreters', in R. Ashcraft (ed.), *John Locke* (London, New York, 1991), vol. 3, 13.
Morris-Suzuki, T., *Beyond Computopia* (London, New York, 1988).
Morton, J., 'Draft EC Directive on the Protection of Electronic Databases: Comfort after *Feist*', 8(2) *Computer Law and Practice*, 38 (1992).
Moufgang, R., 'Patenting of Human Genes, Cells and Parts of the Body? – The Ethical Dimensions of Patent Law', 25 *International Review of Industrial Property and Copyright Law*, 487 (1994).

Mowery, D.C. and Rosenberg, N., *Technology and the Pursuit of Economic Growth* (Cambridge, 1989).
Munzer, S.R., *A Theory of Property* (Cambridge, 1990).
Murumba, S.K., *Commercial Exploitation of Personality* (Sydney, 1986).
Nagel, E., *The Structure of Science* (London, 1961).
Neale, A.D. and Goyder, D.G., *The Antitrust Laws of the USA* (3rd ed., Cambridge, 1980).
Needham, J., *Science and Civilization in China* (Cambridge at the University Press, 1954, vols. 1–.
Needham, J., *The Grand Titration* (London, 1969).
Nelson, J.A. and Ferber, M.A. (eds.), *Beyond Economic Man: Feminist Theory and Economics* (Chicago, 1993).
Nelson, R.R., 'The Simple Economics of Basic Scientific Research', 67 *Journal of Political Economy*, 297 (1959).
Nicholas, B., *An Introduction to Roman Law* (Oxford University Press, 1962).
Noonan, H. (ed.), *Identity* (Aldershot, 1993).
Nordhaus, W.D., 'The Optimum Life of a Patent: Reply', 62 *American Economic Review*, 428 (1972).
North, D.C., *Structure and Change in Economic History* (New York, 1981).
North, D.C., *Institutions, Institutional Change and Economic Performance* (Cambridge, New York, 1990).
North, D.C. and Thomas, R.P., *The Rise of the Western World: A New Economic History* (Cambridge, 1973).
Nozick, R., *Anarchy, State, and Utopia* (Oxford, 1974).
Nozick, R., 'Coercion' in S. Morgenbesser, P. Suppes and M. White (eds.), *Philosophy, Science, and Method* (New York, 1969), 440.
Oakley, A., *Marx's Critique of Political Economy* (London, 1985), vol. 2.
Oddi, A.S., 'The International Patent System and Third World Development: Reality or Myth?', *Duke Law Journal*, 831 (1987).
OECD, *Competition Policy and Intellectual Property Rights* (Paris, 1989).
OECD, *Regulatory Co-operation for an Interdependent World* (Paris, 1994).
Office of Regulation Review, *An Economic Analysis of Copyright Reform* (Commonwealth of Australia, 1995).
Okin, S.M., 'Justice and Gender', 16 *Philosophy and Public Affairs*, 42 (1987).
Olivecrona, K., 'Legal Language and Reality', in R.A. Newman (ed.), *Essays in Jurisprudence in Honor of Roscoe Pound* (Indianapolis, New York, 1962), 151.
Olivecrona, K., *Law as Fact* (2nd ed., London, 1971).
Olivecrona, K., 'Locke's Theory of Appropriation', in R. Ashcraft (ed.), *John Locke* (London, New York, 1991) vol. 3, 327.
Olson, M., *The Logic of Collective Action* (Cambridge, Mass., 1965).

Parkes, S. (ed.), *The English Book Trade 1660–1853*, (New York and London, 1974), 42 vols.

Parsons, T., 'An Outline of the Social System', in T. Parsons and E.A. Shils (eds.), *Theories of Society* (New York, 1965).

Parsons, T., 'Law as an Intellectual Stepchild', in H.M. Johnson (ed.), *Social System and Legal Process* (San Francisco, London, 1978), 11.

Parsons, T. and Shils, E.A. (eds.), *Toward a General Theory of Action* (New York, 1951).

Pashukanis, E.B., *Law and Marxism: A General Theory* (C. Arthur ed., B. Einhorn tr., London, 1978).

Patents, Innovation and Competition in Australia (Industrial Property Advisory Committee, Australia, 1984).

Patterson, L.R., *Copyright in Historical Perspective* (Nashville, 1968).

Patterson L.R., and Joyce, C., 'Monopolising the Law: The Scope of Copyright Protection for Law Reports and Statutory Compilations', 36 *UCLA Law Review*, 719 (1989).

Patterson, L.R. and Lindberg, S.W., *The Nature of Copyright* (Athens, London, 1991).

Pelczynski, Z.A. (ed.), *Hegel's Political Philosophy: Problems and Perspectives* (London, Cambridge, 1971), 230.

Penrose, E.T., *The Economics of the International Patent System* (Baltimore, 1951).

Penrose, E.T., 'International Patenting and the Less-Developed Countries', 83 *Economic Journal*, 766 (1973).

Pettit, P., *Judging Justice* (London, 1980).

Pettit, P., 'The Consequentialist Can Recognise Rights', 38 *The Philosophical Quarterly*, 42 (1988).

Pettit, P., *The Common Mind* (New York, Oxford, 1993).

Plamenatz, J., *Ideology* (London, 1970).

Plamenatz, J., 'History as the Realization of Freedom', in Z.A. Pelczynski (ed.), *Hegel's Political Philosophy: Problems and Perspectives* (Cambridge, London, 1971).

Plant, A., 'The Economic Aspects of Copyright in Books', 1 *Economica* (new series), 167 (1934).

Plant, A., 'The Economic Theory Concerning Patents for Inventions', 1 *Economica* (new series), 30 (1934).

Pogge, T.W., *Realizing Rawls* (Ithaca, N.Y., 1989).

Pollard, S.M., 'Aspects of Lenders' Security Over Computer Software', 6 *Australian Intellectual Property Journal*, 80 (1995).

Pollock, F., 'What is a Thing?', 10 *Law Quarterly Review*, 318 (1894).

Pollock, F. and Maitland, F.W., *The History of English Law* (2nd ed., Cambridge at the University Press, 1898, reissued 1968).

Popper, K.R., *Objective Knowledge* (Oxford, 1972).

Posner, R.A., 'The Social Costs of Monopoly and Regulation', 83 *Journal of Political Economy*, 807 (1975).

Posner, R.A., *Economic Analysis of Law* (4th ed., Boston, 1992).
Price, W.H., *The English Patents of Monopoly* (Cambridge, Mass., 1913).
Prices Surveillance Authority, *Inquiry Into Book Prices: Final Report* (Canberra, December 1989).
Prices Surveillance Authority, *Inquiry Into the Prices of Sound Recordings* (Canberra, December 1990).
Prices Surveillance Authority, *Inquiry Into Prices of Computer Software: Final Report* (Canberra, December 1992).
Pufendorf, S., *De Jure Naturae et Gentium Libri Octo* (1672; translation of 1688 ed. by C.H. and W.A. Oldfather, New York, London, 1964).
Putnam, G., *Books and Their Makers During the Middle Ages 1476–1600* (New York, 1962).
Radin, M.J., 'Property and Personhood', 34 *Stanford Law Review*, 957 (1982).
Ramos, A.G., *The New Science of Organizations* (Toronto, Buffalo, 1981).
Ransom, H., *The First Copyright Statute* (Austin, 1956).
Rawls, J., *A Theory of Justice* (London, Oxford, New York, 1972).
Rawls, J., 'Kantian Constructivism in Moral Theory', 77 *The Journal of Philosophy*, 515 (1980).
Rawls, J., 'The Law of Peoples', in S. Shute and S. Hurley (eds.), *On Human Rights* (New York, 1993), 42.
Raz, J., *The Morality of Freedom* (Oxford, 1986).
Reeve, A., *Property* (London, 1986).
Reeve, A., 'Property' in R.E. Goodin and P. Pettit (eds.), *A Companion to Contemporary Political Philosophy* (Oxford, 1993).
Reid, T., *Practical Ethics* (K. Haakonssen ed., Princeton, New Jersey, 1990).
Reidel, M., *Between Tradition and Revolution* (W. Right tr., Cambridge, 1984).
Renner, K., *The Institutions of Private Law* (O. Kahn-Freund ed., A. Schwarzchild tr., London, 1949).
Ricketson, S., *The Law of Intellectual Property* (Sydney, 1984).
Ricketson, S., *The Berne Convention for the Protection of Literary and Artistic Works: 1886–1986* (London, 1987).
Ricketson, S., 'The Concept of Originality in Anglo-Australian Copyright Law', 39 *The Journal of the Copyright Society of the USA*, 265 (1992).
Rist, J.M., *Stoic Philosophy* (Cambridge, 1969).
Roberts, T., 'Broad Claims for Biotechnological Inventions', 9 *European Intellectual Property Review*, 373 (1994).
Roemer, J.E., *A General Theory of Exploitation* (Cambridge, Mass., 1982).
Roemer, J. (ed.), *Analytical Marxism* (Cambridge, 1986).
Romer, P.M., 'Increasing Returns and Long-Run Growth', 94 *Journal of Political Economy*, 1002 (1986).
Rorty, R. (ed.), *The Linguistic Turn* (Chicago and London, 1967).

Rose, G., *Hegel Contra Sociology* (London, 1981).
Rose, V. (ed.), Bellamy and Child, *Common Market Law of Competition* (4th ed., London, 1993).
Rosenberg, N., *Technology and American Economic Growth* (New York, 1972).
Rosenberg, N. and Birdzell Jr., L.E., *How the West Grew Rich* (New York, 1986).
Rothnie, W.A., *Parallel Imports* (London, 1993).
Russell, B., *Power: A New Social Analysis* (London, 1938).
Ryan, A., *Property and Political Theory* (Oxford, New York, 1984).
Salter, M., 'Justifying Private Property Rights: A Message from Hegel's Jurisprudential Writings', 7 *Legal Studies*, 245 (1987).
Samuels, W.J. (ed.), *The Economy as a System of Power* (New Brunswick, New Jersey, 1979).
Samuelson, P.A., 'The Pure Theory of Public Expenditure', 36 *The Review of Economics and Statistics*, 387 (1954).
Samuelson, P.A., 'Diagrammatic Exposition of a Theory of Public Expenditure', 37 *The Review of Economics and Statistics*, 350 (1955).
Samuelson, P.A., 'Aspects of Public Expenditure Theories', 40 *The Review of Economics and Statistics*, 332 (1958).
Sandbach, F.H., *The Stoics* (London, 1975).
Schachter, O., *International Law in Theory and Practice* (Dordrecht, Boston, London, 1991).
Schechter, F.I., 'The Rational Basis of Trademark Protection', 40 *Harvard Law Review*, 813 (1927).
Scherer, F.M., *Industrial Market Structure and Economic Performance* (2nd ed., Chicago, 1980).
Scherer, F.M., 'Nordhaus' Theory of Optimal Patent Life: A Geometric Reinterpretation', 62 *American Economic Review*, 422 (1972).
Schmidtz, D., 'The Institution of Property', 11 *Social Philosophy and Policy*, 42 (1994).
Schmookler, J., *Invention and Economic Growth* (Cambridge, Mass., 1966).
Schmookler, J., *Patents, Invention, and Economic Change* (Z. Griliches and L. Hurwicz eds., Cambridge, Mass., 1972).
Schulz, F., *History of Roman Science* (Oxford at the Clarendon Press, 1946).
Schulz, F., *Classical Roman Law* (Oxford at the Clarendon Press, 1951).
Schultz, T.W., 'Capital Formation by Education', 68 *Journal of Political Economy*, 571 (1960).
Schultz, T.W., 'Investment in Human Capital', 51 *The American Economic Review*, 1 (1961).
Schumpeter, J.A., *The Theory of Economic Development* (Cambridge, Mass., 1949).

Schumpeter, J., *Capitalism, Socialism and Democracy* (5th ed., London, 1976).
Sedley, D., 'The Stoic Theory of Universals', in R.H. Epp (ed.) *Recovering the Stoics* XXIII, Supplement, *Southern Journal of Philosophy*, 87, (1985).
Seliger, M., *The Marxist Conception of Ideology: A Critical Essay* (Cambridge, 1977).
Sen, A.K., 'Rational Fools: A Critique of the Behavioral Foundations of Economic Theory', 6 *Philosophy and Public Affairs*, 317 (1977).
Sen, A., 'Rights and Agency', 11 *Philosophy and Public Affairs*, 3 (1982).
Sextus Empiricus (R.G. Bury tr., London, Cambridge, Mass., 1935).
Sharkey, W.W., *The Theory of Natural Monopoly* (Cambridge, 1982).
Shue, H., *Basic Rights* (Princeton, N.J., 1980).
Shue, H., 'The Burdens of Justice' LXXX *The Journal of Philosophy*, 600 (1983).
Simons, P., 'What is Abstraction and What is it Good For?', in A.D. Irvine (ed.), *Physicalism in Mathematics* (Dordrecht, Boston, London, 1990).
Skinner, Q., 'The Idea of Negative Liberty: Philosophical and Historical Perspectives', in R. Rorty, J.B. Schneewind and Q. Skinner (eds.), *Philosophy in History* (Cambridge, 1984), 193.
Smart, C., *Feminism and the Power of Law* (London, New York, 1989).
Smith, A., *An Inquiry into the Nature and Causes of the Wealth of Nations* (1776; Glasgow ed., Indianapolis, 1981).
Spector, H.M., 'An Outline of a Theory Justifying Intellectual and Industrial Property Rights', 8 *European Intellectual Property Review*, 270 [1989].
Starrett, D., 'Social Institutions, Imperfect Information, and the Distribution of Income', 90 *Quarterly Journal of Economics*, 261 (1976).
Steinberg, T., 'God's Terminus: Boundaries, Nature, and Property on the Michigan Shore', XXXVII *The American Journal of Legal History*, 65 (1993).
Stern, R.H., 'Some Reflections on Parallel Importation of Copyrighted Products into the United States and the Relation of the Exhaustion Doctrine to the Doctrine of Implied Licence', 4 *European Intellectual Property Review*, 119 [1989].
Stigler, G.J., 'Perfect Competition, Historically Contemplated', LXV *Journal of Political Economy*, 1 (1957).
Stone, A., 'The Place of Law in the Marxian Structure-Superstructure Archetype', 19 *Law and Society Review*, 39 (1985).
Stoneman, P. and Diederen, P., 'Technology Diffusion and Public Policy', 104 *The Economic Journal*, 918 (1994).
Strömholm, S., 'Droit Moral – The International and Comparative Scene from a Scandinavian Viewpoint', 14 *International Review of Industrial Property and Copyright Law*, 1 (1983).

Summers, R.S., *Instrumentalism and American Legal Theory* (Ithaca, London, 1982).
Sweet, C., 'Choses in Action', 10 *Law Quarterly Review*, 303 (1894).
Sweet, C., 'Choses in Action', 11 *Law Quarterly Review*, 238 (1895).
Tawney, R.H., *Religion and the Rise of Capitalism* (West Drayton, Middlesex, 1938 ed.).
Taylor, C., *Hegel and Modern Society* (Cambridge, 1979).
Taylor, C.T. and Silbertson, Z.A., *The Economic Impact of the Patent System* (Cambridge, 1973).
Telser, L.G., *A Theory of Efficient Cooperation and Competition* (Cambridge, New York, 1987).
Tennant, N., *Anti-Realism and Logic* (Oxford, 1987).
Thayer, H.S., *Meaning and Action* (Indianapolis, New York, 1968).
The Federalist Papers (1788; I. Kramnick ed., Harmondsworth, 1987).
Thompson, E., 'International Protection of Performers' Rights: Some Current Problems', 107 *International Labour Review*, 303 (1973).
Thomson, J.J., *The Realm of Rights* (Cambridge, Mass., 1990).
Tisdell, C.A., *Microeconomics of Markets* (Brisbane, 1982).
Tool, M.R. and Samuels, W.J. (eds.), *State, Society and Corporate Power* (2nd ed., New Brunswick, Oxford, 1989).
Trade Practices Commission, *Application of the Trade Practices Act to Intellectual Property* (Commonwealth of Australia, July 1991).
Tuck, R., *Natural Rights Theories* (Cambridge, 1979).
Tully, J., *A Discourse on Property* (Cambridge, 1980).
Tully, J., (ed.), *Meaning and Context: Quentin Skinner and his Critics* (Cambridge, 1988).
Turner, C., 'Copyright and Parallel Importation: The Australian Experience and Recent Initiatives', 7 *Intellectual Property Journal*, 149 (1992).
Turner, J.C., *Rediscovering the Social Group* (Oxford, New York, 1987).
Turner, J.C. and Oakes, P.J., 'Self-Categorization Theory and Social Influence', in P.B. Paulus (ed.), *Psychology of Group Influence* (2nd ed., Hillsdale, New Jersey, 1989), 233.
Tushnet, M., 'An Essay on Rights', 62 *Texas Law Review*, 1363 (1984).
Vaitos, C.V., *Intercountry Income Distribution and Transnational Enterprises* (Oxford, 1974).
Van Caenegem, W.A., 'Inventions in Russia: From Public Good to Private Property', 4 *Australian Journal of Intellectual Property*, 232 (1993).
Varga, C. (ed.), *Marxian Legal Theory* (Aldershot, 1993).
Veblen, T., *Absentee Ownership* (London, 1924).
Veblen, T., *The Theory of Business Enterprise* (1904, reprinted New York, 1965).
Verberke, G., *The Presence of Stoicism in Medieval Thought* (Washington, D.C., 1983).

Vojacek, J., *A Survey of the Principal National Patent Systems* (London, 1936).
Von Neumann, J. and Morgenstern, O., *Theory of Games and Economic Behaviour* (3rd ed., Princeton, 1953).
Waldron, J., 'Enough and As Good Left for Others', 29 *Philosophical Quarterly*, 319 (1979).
Waldron, J., *The Right to Private Property* (Oxford, 1988).
Waller, S.W. and Byrne, N.J., 'Changing View of Intellectual Property and Competition Law in the European Community and the United States of America', XX *Brooklyn Journal of International Law*, 1 (1993).
Warmelo, P., 'The Institutes of Justinian as Students' Manual', in P.G. Stein and A.D.E. Lewis (eds.), *Studies in Justinian's Institutes in Memory of J.A.C. Thomas* (London, 1983), 164.
Waters, M., *Globalization* (London, New York, 1995).
Watson, A., 'Justinian's Institutes and Some English Counterparts', in P.G. Stein and A.D.E. Lewis (eds.), *Studies in Justinian's Institutes in Memory of J.A.C. Thomas* (London, 1983), 181.
Watson, G., *The Stoic Theory of Knowledge* (Belfast, 1966).
Weisbrod, B.A., 'The Valuation of Human Capital', 69 *Journal of Political Economy*, 425 (1961).
Wertheimer, A., *Coercion* (Princeton, New Jersey, 1987).
Weyl, H., *Philosophy of Mathematics and Natural Science* (Princeton, 1949).
White, A.R., *Rights* (Oxford, 1984).
White, M., *Philosophy, the Federalist, and the Constitution* (New York, Oxford, 1987).
White, M.G., *The Origin of Dewey's Instrumentalism* (New York, Morningside Heights, 1943).
Wicklund, R.A., 'The Appropriation of Ideas', in P.B. Paulus (ed.), *Psychology of Group Influence* (2nd ed., Hillsdale, NJ, Hove, London, 1989).
Williamson, O.E., *The Economic Institutions of Capitalism* (New York, London, 1985).
Williams, B.R., *Technology, Investment and Growth* (London, 1967).
Williams, T.C., 'Property, Things in Action, and Copyright', 11 *Law Quarterly Review*, 223 (1895).
Winter, G., 'Patent Law Policy in Biotechnology', 4 *Journal of Environmental Law*, 167 (1992).
Wolf Jr., C., 'Market and Non-Market Failures: Comparison and Assessment', 7 *Journal of Public Policy*, 43 (1987).
Wrong, D.H., *Power* (Chicago, 1988).
Wyatt, G., *The Economics of Invention* (Brighton, 1986).
Yen, A.C., 'The Legacy of *Feist*: Consequences of the Weak Connection Between Copyright and the Economics of Public Goods', 52 *Ohio State Law Journal*, 1343 (1991).

Zimmermann, R., *The Law of Obligations* (Cape Town, Wetton, Johannesburg, 1990).

International Conventions, Treaties and Other Instruments

Agreement on Trade-Related Aspects of Intellectual Property Rights contained in Annex 1C of the Final Act Embodying the Results of the Uruguay Round of Multilateral Trade Negotiations, Marrakesh, 15 April 1994.
Berne Convention for the Protection of Literary and Artistic Works 1886, as revised.
Convention Establishing the World Intellectual Property Organization, signed at Stockholm on 14 July 1967.
Declaration of Principles Governing the Sea-bed and the Ocean Floor, and the Subsoil Thereof, beyond the Limits of National Jurisdiction, UNGA Res. 2749 (XXV), 17 December 1970.
International Convention for the Protection of New Varieties of Plants of 2 December 1961, as revised at Geneva on 10 November 1972, on 23 October 1978, and on 19 March 1991.
Paris Convention for the Protection of Industrial Property 1883, as revised.
Treaty Establishing The European Economic Community, 1957 (renamed the European Community Treaty in 1992).
Treaty on Intellectual Property in Respect of Integrated Circuits (Washington, 1989).
The UNESCO Convention for the Protection of the World Cultural and Natural Heritage (1972).

Cases

Aristoc Ltd. v. *Rysta Ltd.* [1945] A.C. 68.
Austin v. *Columbia Gramophone Co. Ltd.* (1923) Macg.C.C. (1917–1923) 398.
Axmann v. *Lund* (1874) L.R. 18 Eq. 330.
BMG Music v. *Perez,* 952 F.2d 318 (9th Cir.), *cert denied,* 112 S. Ct. 2997 (1992).
Boult's Patent (1909) 26 R.P.C. 383.
Bowden Wire Ld. v. *Bowden Brake Co. Ld.* (1914) 31 R.P.C. 385.
British Leyland Motor Corporation Ltd v. *Armstrong Patents Company Ltd* [1986] 1 All E.R. 850.
Case v. *Cressy* (1900) 17 R.P.C. 255.
Clark v. *Adie* (1875) L.R. 10 Ch. App. 667.
Commonwealth of Australia v. *John Fairfax & Sons* (1980) 32 ALR 485.

Computer Associates International, Inc v. *Altai, Inc* 982 F.2d 693 (2d Cir. 1992).
Corelli v. *Grey* (1913) 29 T.L.R. 570.
D'Almaine v. *Boosey* (1835) 1 Y. & C. EX. 288; 160 E.R. 117.
Darcy v. *Allen* (1602) Moore K.B. 671, 72 E.R. 830.
Darcy v. *Allin* (1602) Noy 173, 74 E.R., 1131.
Davis v. *The Commonwealth* (1988) 166 C.L.R. 79.
Diamond v. *Chakrabarty* 447 US 303(1980).
Donaldson v. *Beckett* (1974) 4 Burr. 2408; 98 E.R. 257.
Driffield And East Riding Pure Linseed Cake Company v. *Waterloo Mills Cake And Warehousing Company* (1886) 31 Ch.D. 638.
Edwards & Co. v. *Picard* [1909] 2 K.B. 903.
Emack v. *Kane* 34 Fed. R. 46 (1888).
Feist Publications, Inc v. *Rural Telephone Service Co Inc* 111 S. Ct. 1282 (1991).
Francis Day & Hunter Ltd v. *Bron* [1963] Ch. 587.
Frank M Winstone (Merchants) Ltd v. *Plix Products Ltd* (1985) 5 IPR 156.
Franz Hanfstaengl v. *H R Baines & Co. Ltd.* [1895] A.C. 20.
Funk Brothers Seed Co. v. *Kalo Inoculant Co.* 333 U.S. 127 (1948).
Genentech Inc v. *Wellcome Foundation Ltd* [1989] R.P.C. 147.
GE Trade Mark [1973] R.P.C. 297.
Halsey v. *Brotherhood* (1880) 15 Ch.D. 514.
Hartford-Empire Co. v. *United States* 323 U.S., 386 (1944).
Harwood v. *Great Northern Railway Co.* (1865) 11 H.L.C. 654.
In re Applications of W. & G. Du Cros, Ltd. [1912] 1 Ch. 644.
In re Heath's Patent [1912] W.N. 137.
In re Magnolia Metal Company's Trademarks [1897] 2 Ch., 371.
In the Matter of Johnson's Patent (1908), 25 R.P.C. 709.
Island of Palmas Case (1928), vol. 2 *Reports of International Arbitral Awards*, 831.
Jefferys v. Boosey (1854) 4 H.L.C. 815; 10 E.R. 681.
Jeweler's Circular Pub. Co. v. *Keystone Pub. Co.* 281 F 83 (CA2 1922).
Kelly v. *Morris* (1866) L.R. 1 Eq. 697.
Kent's Patent (1909), 26 R.P.C. 666.
Ladbroke (Football), Ltd. v. *William Hill (Football), Ltd.* [1964] 1 All E.R., 465.
Lampet's Case (1612) 10 Co. Rep. 46b, 77 E.R. 994.
Lane Fox v. *Kensington and Knightsbridge Electric Lighting Co.* [1892] 3 Ch. 424.
Lasercomb America, Inc v. *Job Reynolds* 911 F.2d 970 (4th Cir. 1990).
Massam v. *Thorley's Cattle Food Co.* (1880) 14 Ch.D. 748.
Millar v. Taylor (1769) 4 Burr. 2303; 98 E.R. 201.
Milpurrurru v. *Indofurn Pty. Ltd.* (1995) 30 IPR 209.
Minnesota Mining & Manufacturing Co and 3M Australia Pty Ltd v. *Beiersdorf (Aust.) Ltd* (1980) 29 ALR 29.

Moore and Hesketh v. *Phillips* (1907) 4 C.L.R. 1411.
Morton Salt Co. v. *G. S. Suppiger* 314 US 488 (1942).
National Research Development Corp. v. *Commissioner of Patents* (1959) 102 C.L.R. 252.
Neilson v. *The Minister of Public Works for New South Wales* (1914) 18 C.L.R. 423.
New South Wales Dairy Corporation v. *Murray Goulburn Co-operative Co Ltd* (1991) 171 C.L.R. 363.
Nordenfelt v. *Maxim Nordenfelt Guns and Ammunition Company* [1894] A.C. 535.
Norris v. *Staps* (1616) 11 Co. Rep. 53a; 80 E.R. 357.
Pacific Film Laboratories Pty. Ltd. v. *Federal Commissioner of Taxation* (1970) 121 C.L.R. 154.
Parkdale Custom Built Furniture Pty. Ltd. v. *Puxu Pty. Ltd.* (1981–82) 149 C.L.R. 191.
Queensland Wire Industries Pty. Ltd. v. *BHP Ltd.* (1988–89) 167 C.L.R., 177.
Radiation Ltd v. *Galliers & Klaerr Pty. Ltd.* (1938) 60 C.L.R. 36.
Re 12 Applications by American Greetings Corporation to Register the Trade Mark 'Holly Hobbie' (1984) 1 IPR 486.
Registrar of Trade Marks v. *W. & G. Du Cros, Ltd.* [1913] A.C. 624.
Reynolds v. *Herbert Smith & Co.* (1903) 20 R.P.C., 123.
The Case of Monopolies (1602) 11 Co. Rep. 84b; 77 E.R. 1260.
The Case of the Tailors, &c. of Ipswich (1614) 11 Co. Rep. 53a; 77 E.R. 1218.
The Clothworkers of Ipswich Case (1615) Godbolt, 252; 78 E.R. 147.
The Leather Cloth Company v. *The American Leather Cloth Company* (1865) 11 H.L.C. 523.
Trego v. *Hunt* [1896] A.C. 7.
United States v. *Krasnov* 143 F. Supp 184 (E.D. Pa. 1956), *aff'd per curiam*, 355 U.S. 5 (1957).
Wheaton v. *Peters* 33 U.S. (8 Peters) 591 (1834).
Whelan Associates, Inc. v. *Jaslow Dental Laboratory Inc.*, 797 F. 2d 1222 (3rd Cir. 1986).
Williams Electronics, Inc., v. *Artic Intern., Inc.*, 685 F.2d 870 (3d Cir. 1982).
Wood v. *Butler* (1886) 3 R.P.C. 81.
Yumbulul v. *Reserve Bank of Australia* (1991) 21 IPR 481.

Legislation

Act of Anne 8 Anne, c. 19 (1709)
Australian Bicentennial Authority Act 1980 (Aus.)
Clayton Act (1914) (US)

Copyright Act 1905 (Aus.)
Copyright Act 1968 (Aus.)
European Commission, First Council Directive of 21 December 1988 to Approximate the Laws of the Member States relating to Trade-marks, OJ L 040 11.02.89
European Commission, Amended Proposal for a Council Directive on the Legal Protection of Databases, OJ 1993 C308/1 15 November 1993
Patent Act of 1793 (US)
Patents Act 1977 (UK)
Patents Act 1990 (Aus.)
Patents and Designs Act, 1907 (UK)
Patents, Designs, and Trade-Marks Act, 1883 (UK)
Plant Breeder's Rights Act 1994 (Aus.)
Semiconductor Chip Protection Act 1984 (US)
Sherman Act 1890 (US)
Statute of Monopolies 21 Jac 1 c. 3 (1623)
Trade Mark Act, 1905 (UK)
Trade Marks Act 1995 (Aus.)
Trade Practices Act 1974 (Aus.)

Index

For Product Safety Concerns and Information please contact our EU
representative GPSR@taylorandfrancis.com
Taylor & Francis Verlag GmbH, Kaufingerstraße 24, 80331 München, Germany

www.ingramcontent.com/pod-product-compliance
Ingram Content Group UK Ltd.
Pitfield, Milton Keynes, MK11 3LW, UK
UKHW020012200926
475702UK00014B/1835
9781138254701